ONE WEEK LOAN

THE STRUCTURES OF THE CRIMINAL LAW

The Structures of the Criminal Law

Edited by
RA DUFF
LINDSAY FARMER
SE MARSHALL
MASSIMO RENZO
VICTOR TADROS

OXFORD
UNIVERSITY PRESS

OXFORD
UNIVERSITY PRESS

Great Clarendon Street, Oxford OX2 6DP

Oxford University Press is a department of the University of Oxford.
It furthers the University's objective of excellence in research, scholarship,
and education by publishing worldwide in

Oxford New York

Auckland Cape Town Dar es Salaam Hong Kong Karachi
Kuala Lumpur Madrid Melbourne Mexico City Nairobi
New Delhi Shanghai Taipei Toronto

With offices in

Argentina Austria Brazil Chile Czech Republic France Greece
Guatemala Hungary Italy Japan Poland Portugal Singapore
South Korea Switzerland Thailand Turkey Ukraine Vietnam

Oxford is a registered trade mark of Oxford University Press
in the UK and in certain other countries

Published in the United States
by Oxford University Press Inc., New York

© The several contributors 2011

The moral rights of the authors have been asserted
Database right Oxford University Press (maker)

Crown copyright material is reproduced under Class Licence
Number C01P0000148 with the permission of OPSI
and the Queen's Printer for Scotland

First published 2011

British Library Cataloguing in Publication Data

Data available

Library of Congress Cataloging in Publication Data

Library of Congress Control Number: 2011939849

Typeset by SPI Publisher Services, Pondicherry, India
Printed in Great Britain
on acid-free paper by
CPI Group (UK) Ltd, Croydon, CR0 4YY

ISBN 978–0–19–964431–5

1 3 5 7 9 10 8 6 4 2

Acknowledgements

This is the second volume to emerge from a research project on Criminalization, funded by a grant from the Arts and Humanities Research Council (Grant No 128737). We are grateful to the Arts and Humanities Research Council for the grant that made this project possible, and to our own universities for the further material and administrative support that they provided—the University of Stirling and the Stirling Department of Philosophy, the University of Glasgow and the School of Law, and the University of Warwick and the School of Law.

We are in particular grateful to the authors who have contributed to this volume, and to all of the participants at the workshops and meetings from which this volume emerged. These meetings and workshops once again confirmed how productive the community of criminal lawyers and philosophers can be in advancing our understanding. In particular, we are grateful to those who commented on earlier drafts of the papers: Vera Bergelson, Peter Duff, Antony Hatzistavrou, Claes Lernestedt, and Stuart Macdonald. We are also especially grateful to Christine Kelly for producing the index.

Antony Duff, Lindsay Farmer, Sandra Marshall,
Massimo Renzo, Victor Tadros

Contents

Contributors

Marcia Baron is Rudy Professor of Philosophy at Indiana University.

Andrew Cornford is a PhD Candidate in Law at the University of Warwick.

Sharon Cowan is Senior Lecturer in Law at the University of Edinburgh.

RA Duff is Professor in the Department of Philosophy, University of Stirling, and in the Law School, University of Minnesota.

Lindsay Farmer is Professor of Law at the University of Glasgow.

Adil Ahmad Haque is Associate Professor of Law at Rutgers University.

SE Marshall is a Professor in the Department of Philosophy, University of Stirling.

MR McGuire is Senior Lecturer in Criminology at London Metropolitan University.

Alan Norrie is Professor of Law at the University of Warwick.

Peter Ramsay is a Lecturer in Law at the London School of Economics.

Massimo Renzo is Lecturer in the Law School at the University of York.

Paul H Robinson is the Colin S. Diver Professor of Law at the University of Pennsylvania.

Victor Tadros is a Professor in the School of Law, University of Warwick.

Malcolm Thorburn is Associate Professor of Law and Canada Research Chair in Crime, Security and Constitutionalism in the Faculty of Law at Queen's University, Canada.

1

Introduction

The Structures of the Criminal Law

RA Duff, Lindsay Farmer, SE Marshall, Massimo Renzo, and Victor Tadros

The essays in this volume are drawn from two workshops that were held in the course of 2010 as part of the Arts and Humanities Research Council-funded project on Criminalization.[1] The authors were given the brief of writing on the theme 'Structures of Criminal Law' and, as will quickly become apparent, took up this theme in a variety of different ways, in places going far beyond our original understanding of the relevance of structures. We will shortly go on to say something about how we see the different papers in the collection relating to this theme of 'structures', but before doing so we should first say something about our own choice of this term and how we see it as relating to issues of criminalization—for at first glance it might appear that the issues of structures (to the extent that they are relevant at all) have little to add to the consideration of issues of criminalization.

The bulk of the existing literature on criminalization is concerned with the substance and content of the criminal law. The huge literature on the harm principle, for example, is mainly concerned with questions of content: whether or not the criminalization of certain forms of conduct can be justified in terms of the harm caused or threatened by that conduct. Equally, debates over law reform or policy are dominated by questions of the aims of a particular reform, or whether or not the proposed change is likely to alter conduct and bring about that aim in a particular area of social life. What is often missing from such analyses is an investigation of the constraints that might accompany the use of criminal law, as opposed to law in general. This question can be formulated in a slightly different way from the issue raised in

---

[1] The aims of and background to the overall project are described in the Introduction to the first volume of papers that it produced: *Boundaries of the Criminal Law* (Oxford: OUP, 2010).

the first collection of essays from the Criminalization project, which was concerned with the question of boundaries.[2] If the question raised in that volume was primarily a matter of substance, of when it was appropriate to use criminal law, as opposed to other types of legal regulation (or none at all), the question here can initially be posed in this form: once it has been decided to use the criminal law, are there any particular constraints that accompany this? This is thus to ask whether the use of the criminal law, with its particular distinctions between general and special part, offence and defence, *actus reus* and *mens rea*, and its special procedures and burdens of proof, might impose constraints on the manner and extent of criminalization. This then goes to the question of whether there are certain structural features of criminal law which contribute to or limit our understanding of what it is proper to criminalize.[3]

This type of issue has been central to one recent important contribution to the debate on criminalization. In his book *Overcriminalization*, Husak has argued that the use of the criminal law operates (or should operate) to impose forms of internal constraint on the content of the criminal law, an argument that he mobilizes against what he sees as trends towards over-criminalization in contemporary law. He identifies four forms of internal constraint that he sees arising from the structure of the criminal law.[4] These are what he calls the 'wrongfulness constraint', the non-trivial harm or evil constraint, the desert constraint, and the burden of proof constraint. The 'wrongfulness' constraint (that 'criminal liability may not be imposed unless the defendant's conduct is (in some sense) wrongful'[5]), for example, is derived from the distinction between offence and defence, and in particular the distinction between justification and excuse, and is used to argue against the imposition of strict liability where, in Husak's view, the conduct criminalized is not properly wrongful. And the desert constraint (that punishment can only be justified where it is imposed on an offender for wrongful conduct—and that it is therefore unjustifiable to punish non-wrongful conduct) is directly linked to the structural feature of criminal law that it imposes punishment rather than any other sort of remedy. This argument is not uncontroversial, relying as it does on certain assumptions about the nature of criminal law, but its

---

[2] *Boundaries of the Criminal Law* (n 1 above).

[3] See eg A. J. Ashworth, *Principles of Criminal Law* 6th edn (Oxford: OUP, 2009) ch 3. At least some of the principles identified by Ashworth can be attributed to a kind of 'inner morality' of criminal law, and can be understood in terms of structural features of criminal law eg the principle of *mens rea*. See Lon L. Fuller, *The Morality of Law* 2nd edn (Yale: Yale University Press, 1969) ch 2 on the 'inner morality' of law.

[4] D. Husak, *Overcriminalization: The Limits of the Criminal Law* (Oxford: OUP, 2007) ch 2.

[5] *Op cit* p 66.

importance for us here lies in the fact that it suggests at least one important new avenue for exploring theoretical issues of criminalization.

The question of burden of proof and its relation to legal structure has also been controversial in relation to two other recent developments in the criminal law, notably the increasingly widespread use of reverse burdens of proof and the use of preventive orders.[6] The first of these concerns the practice of defining crime in a way which places the burden on the accused person to disprove one or more elements of the crime, or the availability of a defence.[7] One of the main criticisms of this development—that such crimes subvert the criminal law which typically places the burden of proof on the state[8]—can be understood in terms of the structure of the criminal law. The concern here is that the criminal law has developed in such a way as to impose certain structural constraints on the use of state power, and that the systematic reversal of such burdens by the state rides roughshod over these important protections.

This also gives rise to questions about the relationship between the structure of crimes and procedural and evidential requirements. Should the burden of proof be placed on the prosecution to prove not only that the defendant committed an offence, but also that he or she was not entitled to a defence? Should the standard of proof be the same in each case? And if not, what implications does this have for the way in which the distinction between offences and defences is to be understood? That there is some normative foundation to the distinction between offences and defences is difficult to deny,[9] but the basis of the distinction is contested. We might refer to the way in which offences and defences guide the conduct of citizens,[10] the role of the distinction at trial,[11] or the role of offences in condemning offenders,[12] or perhaps to more than one of these. The issue, however, which needs to be

---

[6] For discussion see A. J. Ashworth and L. Zedner, 'Defending the Criminal Law: Reflections on the Changing Character of Crime, Procedure and Sanctions' (2008) 2 *Criminal Law & Philosophy* 21–51; A. J. Ashworth, 'Social Control and "Anti-Social Behaviour": The Subversion of Human Rights?' (2004) 120 *Law Quarterly Review* 263–91.

[7] These have been mapped most systematically in A. Ashworth and M. Blake, 'The Presumption of Innocence in English Criminal Law' (1996) *Criminal Law Review* 306.

[8] The term is used by Duff, 'Subverting the Criminal Law' in Duff et al, *Boundaries* (n 1 above).

[9] Though it has been denied. See, G. Williams, 'Offences and Defences' (1982) 2 *Legal Studies* 233.

[10] See K. Campbell, 'Offences and Defences' in I. Dennis, *Criminal Law and Criminal Justice* (London: Sweet and Maxwell, 1987) and J. Gardner, 'Justifications and Reasons' in A. P. Simester and A. T. H. Smith, *Harm and Culpability* (Oxford: OUP, 1996).

[11] See R. A. Duff, *Answering for Crime* (Oxford: Hart, 2007) ch 9.

[12] See V. Tadros, *Criminal Responsibility* (Oxford: OUP, 2005) ch 4.

explored further, is that of the ways in which the distinction shapes criminalization.

The second development, of which the British Anti-Social Behaviour Order (or ASBO) is best known, typically takes the form of a civil order, the breach of which will lead to punishment. Such orders are controversial for a number of reasons: that they criminalize behaviour which would not amount to offences under criminal law; that they deliberately seek to circumvent procedural protections relating to the burden of proof and evidential standards by characterizing the initial proceedings as civil; and that the 'two-step' form of the order limits any requirement to investigate the mental state of the offender at the time of the carrying out of the initial course of conduct.[13] However, once again it can readily be seen that at least some of these criticisms rely on claims about the structure of criminal law and the constraints that it places on the state both in terms of the definition of criminal conduct and the proof of that conduct against any individual as a condition of punishment. The two-step structure is criticized for breaking the necessary link between *actus reus* and *mens rea*, and the structuring of the offence in terms of closely connected civil and criminal elements for ignoring what should be a distinct boundary between the two areas.

What these examples suggest is that, even if it is not always referred to explicitly in these terms, the idea that the criminal law has an underlying structure and that consideration of this structure is at least relevant to thinking about criminalization is one that has some currency and importance—and one of the aims of this volume is accordingly to begin to draw out what this might mean for thinking about criminalization. This will not, of course, be a straightforward process, for even if there is agreement on this basic claim, there remains wide scope for disagreement over the type of structure and its implications for the law, such that this claim can at best be regarded as a starting point. However, from this starting point, it quickly became apparent that the issue of structure raises a wider range of issues than we had originally conceived, as the contributors, and the discussion at the workshops, took this initial idea in a number of different directions. The book is accordingly concerned with a range of much broader senses of the importance of structures, of which it is worth singling out three central themes.

---

[13] For a full discussion of such criticisms see A. P. Simester and A. von Hirsch, *Crimes, Harms, and Wrongs* (Oxford: Hart, 2011) chs 11–12.

I. The Structure of the Criminal Law

The first sense concerns the internal structure of the criminal law itself. One kind of issue here is raised by the familiar distinctions in terms of which offences are traditionally analyzed: the distinctions between, for instance, offence and defence, between *actus reus* and *mens rea*, between action and outcome, between evidential rules and rules of substantive law. Are these distinctions that it is (still) useful to draw—or do they obfuscate and distort as much as they illuminate? Do these distinctions have any real normative significance; or are they, at best, 'helpful expository device[s]',[14] which might assist 'convenient exposition' of the law by legislators, judges, and textbook writers,[15] and which should be dropped when they lose that pragmatic utility? Would our understanding of the logic of the criminal law be improved by drawing more, or different, or fewer such distinctions? In this context, for example, Andrew Cornford examines the tension between resultant harm (often portrayed as a matter of moral luck) and agent culpability in the criminal law: in particular, he argues that different general considerations will typically apply to offences of attacking and of endangering.

Other issues arise in relation to the classification of crimes. Crimes were traditionally classified by reference to the type of wrong or harm (the 'mischief') involved, but recent expansions of the criminal law, involving the creation of new 'objects of criminalization' (new kinds of interest to be protected, against new kinds of mischief) put that schema under increasing pressure. As Mike McGuire suggests in his essay, we might even see persons and their attributes as the objects of the criminal law rather than, or alongside, their actions. In the growing range of crimes of preparation, possession, and association, and of *mala prohibita*, offences are often defined far more broadly than the mischief at which they are supposedly aimed requires, capturing conduct that is ever more remote from that mischief—which can make it harder even to identify a mischief at which the offence could plausibly be aimed, and to sustain the orthodox classificatory schema. Furthermore, the orthodox conception of crimes as wrongful or harmful actions that must be proved against a defendant is also undermined by the legislative tendency to weaken fault requirements and to relieve the prosecution of some of its traditional burden of proof (whilst laying heavier probative burdens on the defendant); the presumption of innocence, once portrayed as the 'golden

---

[14] A. P. Simester and G. R. Sullivan, *Criminal Law: Theory and Doctrine* (Oxford: Hart, 2003) 71.

[15] D. Ormerod, *Smith and Hogan: Criminal Law* 11th edn (Oxford: OUP, 2005) 35.

thread' running 'throughout the web of English Criminal Law',[16] now seems to have been, if not broken, seriously frayed. As Peter Ramsay in his essay indicates, this is especially pertinent in the area of terrorism law, where the scope of the law has been stretched well beyond that found in any other area, and where the relationship between criminal offences and those values which many see as providing the core concern of the criminal law has been stretched to breaking point.

Consideration of the structures of criminal law in this first sense also raises further fundamental questions about the proper standards to apply to criminalization decisions—the question of whether criminal responsibility should be defined in 'subjective' or in partly 'objective' terms, for instance. It also raises a question addressed by Marcia Baron about the role that a conception of the 'reasonable person' should play in setting the standards against which defendants' actions are to be judged. It might seem that serious doubt must be cast on the way such a standard is characterized once we reflect upon the way in which, as Sharon Cowan brings out, different conceptions of self and identity, particularly the sexual self, are beginning to impinge on the criminal law.

An important task for philosophers of criminal law is to ask whether, and how, we should reshape traditional ideas and conceptions of and within the criminal law in the light of such recent developments. Should we criticize such developments as being inconsistent with the principles by which an acceptable system of criminal law must be structured? Or should we instead recognize that a changing world requires a more adaptable criminal law, whose basic structures and doctrines may need to be rethought or recast to meet the new challenges and dangers that we face? This question is addressed by Alan Norrie, who argues that the basic forms of the criminal law need to be rendered more flexible by incorporating a more complex range of moral factors into procedural decisions to prevent the more rigid forms of the law from leading to injustice in practice.

II. The Structure of Law

A second sense of structure has to do with the place of the criminal law within the larger structure of law. One set of questions here concerns the distinguishing marks of criminal law and its relationships with other aspects of law, including both private law and public law (topics that figure in different ways

---

[16] *Woolmington v DPP* [1935] AC 462, 481 (Viscount Sankey).

in the papers by Haque and Thorburn). What are the distinctive features of criminal law as a particular type of regulation? What makes it appropriate to use the criminal law, rather than some other mode of legal regulation: is this just a question of which mechanism is most likely to be a cost-effective means to our social or political ends? What sense can be made of the traditional slogan that the criminal law should be used only as a 'last resort'? Thorburn argues that these questions require us to reflect on criminal law as part of a whole—as just one part of a legal system which is to be understood as having the crucial moral task of making it possible for individuals living together in a polity to secure their claims of individual moral freedom.

Other questions in this context have to do with how the criminal law is made, and by whom. How should a legislature go about deciding what to criminalize; what principles should guide such decisions? (This question clearly overlaps with those falling under the first sense of 'structure' discussed above.) What other people or bodies should have a role in making and developing the law: what kind of discretion should be allowed to, for instance, the police, prosecutors, judges, and juries—and how should it be exercised? This reminds us that achieving justice in the criminal law requires us to evaluate the substantive criminal law not only in the terms in which it is articulated in legislation and in case law, but also in the course of its application. One aspect of these questions concerns the relationship between the 'law in the books' and the 'law in action'—in action on the streets, in police stations, in prosecutorial offices, in the courts: how far is the law made, how far should it be made, in action rather than in a legislature; what principles should guide such law-making, and how can it be made accountable? As Norrie suggests, there may be difficult moral problems whose solution cannot be found in the forms of the substantive law itself, but must be sought elsewhere.

Such questions as these also draw attention to the relationship between substantive criminal law and other dimensions of criminal justice, both pre- and post-trial. What is the proper role of police or prosecutorial discretion in applying, or in making, the law? What considerations should bear on decisions about whether to take a case to trial, or to divert it from the criminal process (thus, in a sense, decriminalizing it)? What kinds of issue should be decided during a public trial rather than, for instance, in a prosecutor's office or at the sentencing stage? What role should juries, or other lay participants, have in the criminal process? Such questions also remind us of the complexity of the idea of criminalization: the processes involved in criminalizing (or indeed in decriminalizing) a type of conduct are not captured by the formal legislative process of statutory enactment.

III. Social and Political Structures

A third sense of structure concerns the relationships between legal structures and social and political structures. The criminal law is both a social and a political institution, and central to the issue of criminalization is the question of how the law is, or ought to be, related to social and political beliefs, values, and institutions. Those relationships can be analyzed in a number of ways.

The relationship between criminal law and broader political structures has a number of dimensions. The first, and perhaps most obvious, is the relationship between criminal law and the political processes through which it is made—for instance the way in which governments seem increasingly to resort to criminal law as a political response to social problems, through the creation of new crimes,[17] or through the escalation of punishments attached to existing crimes,[18] or of ever broader ancillary crimes. More broadly, however, as Haque urges, we should give attention to the wider context of international law both in the way in which context itself figures in the characterization of offences, and with a view to seeing what domestic law might learn from the evolving concepts of international law.

There are also questions about how certain political beliefs or ideologies shape the development of the criminal law. As Peter Ramsay suggests in his essay, the process of criminalization will depend not only on moral disagreements that people have about what the state should prohibit, but also on people's feelings of vulnerability in the face of crime. And as Paul Robinson argues in his contribution, conflicts between the moral judgements of citizens and the content of the criminal law may be costly. Anyone attempting to achieve reform of the criminal law must take note not only of the best normative view, but also of the constraints that in practice operate on the content of the criminal law that are imposed by the more or less reflective feelings and judgements of citizens. In the light of this, it is important too to consider how political structures can impact on criminalization and the criminal law: to attend, for instance, to the role of elected judges or

---

[17] Recent examples might include 'grooming' (Criminal Justice and Immigration Act 2008 s 63) or smoking in certain public places. This is discussed in P. Ferguson, '"Smoke Gets in Your Eyes...": The Criminalisation of Smoking in Enclosed Public Spaces, the Harm Principle and the Limits of the Criminal Sanction' (2010) 31 *Legal Studies* 259–78.

[18] eg Husak, *Overcriminalization* (n 4 above) *passim* on drug crimes.

prosecutors,[19] of pressure groups such as victims' movements,[20] or of second chambers or 'super-majorities'.[21]

The relationship between criminal law and social structures is even more complex and diffuse. Few would deny that criminal law must draw on social beliefs, and depends for its legitimacy on some minimum level of social acceptance, but it is much harder to unpack the content of such a claim, or to determine just how this relationship between criminal law and social structures and beliefs is mediated. This relationship has obvious implications for the definition of crimes. Claims about fair labelling, which have become commonplace in writing about the criminal law, depend on claims about the social meaning and acceptance of crime definitions.[22] Equally, much recent academic discussion about the extent to which offence definitions should be set in descriptive terms, or should use morally laden concepts, focuses on the audiences to whom those definitions can be seen to be addressed (judges, citizens?), and on how the law can best guide actors (judges, juries) involved in the decision-making process (Baron). These debates must appeal to claims about the 'fit' between legal doctrines and concepts on the one hand, and social attitudes and beliefs on the other (Robinson). But such claims about fit also raise deeper questions about the relationship between social and moral beliefs about wrongs on the one hand, and the criminal law's definitions of offences on the other—whether from the perspectives of moral and political philosophy, to which theories of criminalization so often appeal, or from the less familiar but no less important perspectives of criminology and social and political theory (McGuire, Ramsay).

Some of the central questions in this context are, roughly, empirical and sociological: in what ways do existing social attitudes, beliefs, and values influence the development or workings of the criminal law; how far can the criminal law shape such attitudes? Others, however, are clearly normative: how far should the criminal law aim to reflect, and how far to shape or to modify, the attitudes, values, and beliefs of citizens of the society whose law it is? What is the proper role of the criminal law in the political and social structure of what aspires to be a democratic polity (Ramsay, Robinson, Thorburn)? To what extent must the criminal law reflect the values of the

[19] W. Stuntz, 'The Pathological Politics of Criminal Law' (2001) 100 *Michigan Law Review* 506.

[20] M. D. Dubber, *Victims in the War on Crime. The Use and Abuse of Victims' Rights* (New York: New York University Press, 2002); V. Bergelson, *Victims' Rights and Victims' Wrongs. Comparative Liability in Criminal Law* (Stanford: Stanford University Press, 2009).

[21] D. Dripps, 'Overcriminalization, Discretion, Waiver: A Survey of Possible Exit Strategies' (2005) 109 *Penn State Law Review* 1155.

[22] eg A. Ashworth, *Principles* (n 3 above) 78–80; J. Chalmers and F. Leverick, 'Fair Labelling in Criminal Law' (2008) 71(2) *Modern Law Review* 217–46.

society in which it operates, and to what extent may it have a role in shaping those values?

This volume of essays addresses all of these issues. It opens up a range of questions in the philosophy of the criminal law, many of which have not adequately been addressed. At the same time, we recognize that there is much more work to be done to develop a comprehensive account of the internal structure of the criminal law, the way in which it operates in its institutional context, its place within the law in general, and its relationship with a range of social and political structures. Our aim, in collecting these essays together, is to advance our understanding of these issues, but also to stimulate further work—work which moves beyond traditional questions about the role of harm and wrongdoing and their relationship with the criminal law to questions about the forms of the criminal law and its place within broader social and political contexts.

2

The Standard of the Reasonable Person in the Criminal Law

Marcia Baron[1]

I. Introduction

> Will the reasonable person please stand up, and get out of this court-room! The common law is obsessed with reasonable people. These people are pinnacles of virtue–courteous, placid, gentle, timely, careful, perceptive–in short, complete figments of our imagination. Yet they are permitted to perform a hideous function within the criminal law. Although no one is really like them, they set the standard for judging our frailties. If we do not match their glorious perfection, we are cast into the shadow of ignominy and damnation. It is time to say: Off with their heads![2]

So begins an essay by Sharon Byrd, commenting on an article that likewise excoriates the standard of the reasonable person in the criminal law.[3] My immediate aim is to figure out what is supposed to be so bad about reliance in criminal law on the notion of the reasonable person. That there are problems working out how it should go I was well aware of,[4] but that it is thought to be

---

[1] I am grateful to Antony Duff, Dennis Klimchuk, Richard Lippke, Kenneth Simons, Victor Tadros, Malcolm Thorburn, and discussants at the 2010 Stirling Workshop for very helpful comments on earlier drafts of this chapter, and to Megan Mullett for editorial assistance. This chapter is part of a larger project, for which I benefited greatly from fellowship support from both the Indiana University College of Arts and Sciences Humanities Institute and National Endowment for the Humanities.
[2] B. S. Byrd, 'On Getting the Reasonable Person out of the Courtroom' (2005) 2 *Ohio State Journal of Criminal Law* 571, 571.
[3] O. Kamir, 'Responsibility Determination as a Smokescreen: Provocation and the Reasonable Person in the Israeli Supreme Court' (2005) 2 *Ohio State Journal of Criminal Law* 547.
[4] That reasonableness is sometimes required when it should not be I am also well aware of. I am thinking here of the preposterous position, affirmed by many courts in the US, that for the force

so errant that it should be cast into the rubbish bin I found perplexing. I try in this chapter to understand the objections, and when I see a way to do it, to rehabilitate them as needed; to separate out the objections that are serious, calling for more discussion than I can provide here, from those that I believe lack merit; and to uncover, in addition to some errors, some underlying disagreements about what the standard is, or at its best can be.

I intend this chapter to be in the service of a larger aim of (1) working out how the construct of the reasonable person should best be understood for the purposes of the criminal law and then (2) considering whether the standard should be retained, an aim towards which this chapter is only a first step. To date, literature on the standard either roundly dismisses it or assesses it thoughtfully but without considering what it can be at its best. My tentative view is that properly understood, the reasonable person standard is of considerable value, though its value varies depending on the area of the criminal law to which it is put to use. It needs, moreover, to be fleshed out differently depending on the defence or offence in question; that that does not generally happen is a deficiency in the way it is understood and utilized today.

Perhaps one reason the standard is thought by some to be hopeless is that they assume that to be useful, it has to be uncomplicated, a one-size-fits-all concept, whereas in fact 'reasonable', for the purposes of the criminal law, needs to be understood sometimes in terms of self-control in the face of intense emotion,[5] and sometimes in terms of reasonable belief (where this in turn reflects several concerns that may need to be elaborated, among them, that one apportion one's belief to the evidence, that one take appropriate steps to guard against error, and that one look around and take note of one's environment, including, of course, the words and demeanour of those with whom one is interacting).[6] One might claim that there is nothing that all these have in common, at least nothing having to do with reasonableness, or being a reasonable person. I disagree; what they have in common is

---

requirement for rape to be met, it is not enough that the victim was afraid and acquiesced because she was afraid, and that the defendant saw this and took advantage of her fear; her fear also has to be reasonable. (See for example *State v Rusk* 424 A.2d 720 (Md. 1981); by contrast, *People v Barnes* 42 Cal.3d 284, 303 n.20 (1986), allows that in 'some circumstances, even a complainant's unreasonable fear of immediate and unlawful bodily injury may suffice to sustain a conviction . . . if the accused knowingly takes advantage of that fear in order to accomplish sexual intercourse'.)

[5] This is the key idea of reasonableness for the provocation defence, though not the whole of it; being reasonable involves not only getting control of oneself, but also not being very quick to take offence in the first place.

[6] This is not intended as a complete list of the ways in which 'reasonable' needs to be understood for the purposes of criminal law.

self-governance (understood broadly to include not just self-control, but self-correcting so that one becomes, inter alia, more attentive to one's environment).[7]

But also fuelling the view that the standard is best abandoned is, I suspect, another assumption, viz, that the reasonable person is to be thought of as having a full panoply of qualities and ideally as someone we can picture to ourselves. To that later. Let's first take a look at Byrd's attack on the reasonable person standard.

II. Byrd's Attack

Since Byrd writes with levity and does not defend her assault on the reasonable person standard, one might think that it is unhelpful to cite. I cite it in part for its apparent assumption that no explanation is called for, and no convincing needs to be done.[8] It is as if we all know already that the reasonable person standard needs to be jettisoned. The rest of her paper is devoted to finding 'an objective normative criterion' for the provocation defence that 'avoids any use of the reasonable-person standard, a standard that Kamir rightly criticizes as opening the floodgates for courts to engage in normalizing'.[9]

Although Byrd doesn't argue for the position that the reasonable person performs 'a hideous function within the criminal law', her opening remarks do present a reason for rejecting the reasonable person standard (and the bit I quote in the paragraph above points to another reason, offered by Kamir and endorsed by Byrd, which I'll discuss later). The fictitious reasonable person, who sets 'the standards by which we are then judged,' is, according to Byrd, a pinnacle of virtue. Now, were this true, the standard would be far too high. But it is not true. There is room for argument about how high or low it

---

[7] That self-governance is involved in apportioning one's belief to the evidence may not be initially evident; but brief reflection on how hard it can be to face the disturbing evidence that not-p rather than hide from it, and not to allow oneself to believe p just because one badly wants to, should make the connection apparent. If not, see W. K. Clifford, *The Ethics of Belief and Other Essays* (Amherst, NY: Prometheus Books, 1999); for further discussion, see A. W. Wood, 'W.K. Clifford and the Ethics of Belief,' in Wood, *Unsettling Obligations: Essays on Reason, Reality and the Ethics of Belief* (Stanford: CSLI Publications, 2002).

[8] Another way it is instructive is that she makes it clear that she wants an objective standard (at least for the provocation defence, the subject of her discussion). This is instructive because criticisms of the reasonable person standard are so often presented as criticisms of objective standards as such, that one might be left with the impression that opposition to reasonable person standards (in context C) is part and parcel of opposition to objective standards (in context C).

[9] Byrd (n 2 above) 571.

should be, but it is a settled matter that the reasonable person in the criminal law is not to be understood as a pinnacle of virtue.

III. Rehabilitation of Byrd's Objection?

Taking into account that Byrd is obviously exaggerating in the quotation above, we should try to find a plausible version of the objection of which hers is a lighthearted version. I don't see one, though—nothing that is really *that* objection. There are objections to be made to the way the standard is sometimes applied that resemble her objection to the standard itself. Sometimes defendants *are* held to unduly high standards.[10] Relatedly, sometimes defendants are held to a standard that fails to give sufficient attention to relevant particulars of the situation, ie, that fails to ask, 'Might a reasonable person, worried about x/fearful of y/aware that z, have acted as the defendant did?' and only asks 'Might a reasonable person have acted as the defendant did?'

Here I need to be careful. It is tempting to say: the fact that a standard is sometimes badly applied is not itself a serious objection to the standard.[11] Although true, and worth mentioning, it is not the whole story. Objectionable applications of a standard cannot be dismissed as irrelevant to an evaluation of the standard itself. If there is something about the reasonable person standard that renders it very difficult to apply well, and if we have reason to believe that clarification and refinement of the standard cannot address the problems, the value of the standard is clearly quite limited.

I see nothing in the reasonable person standard as such that invites holding the defendant to too lofty a standard. Any standard—at least any that does not have built into it an indication that it requires only a bare minimum—carries that risk to some extent. There is no elevated risk here as long as the reasonable person of criminal law is not confused with the reasonable person of tort law. Moreover, we can guard against the risk—such as it is—by building a clarification into requirements in which a reasonable person standard plays a part. So, for example, the definition of 'negligently' in the Model Penal Code specifies a '*gross* deviation from the standard of care that a reasonable person would observe in the actor's

---

[10] See Kamir (n 3 above), esp. 549–50.

[11] We might, moreover, appeal to John Stuart Mill's acerbic remark that '[t]here is no difficulty in proving any ethical standard whatever to work ill if we suppose universal idiocy to be conjoined with it' (JS Mill, *Utilitarianism*, ed. George Sher (Indianapolis: Hackett ed., 1979) 23).

situation' (emphasis mine).[12] There are, to be sure, instances where a defendant is held to too high a standard; this was, as I see it, the case in *State v Williams* [P2d 1167 (Wash Ct App 1971)], where the appellants, whose 17-month-old child died after his abscessed tooth became infected, causing gangrene, had been convicted of involuntary manslaughter because of their failure to seek medical treatment for him. The conviction was upheld, relying (as the Washington statute dictated) on a simple tort negligence standard rather than a standard that required a gross deviation from the standard of care that a reasonable person would observe in the actor's situation.[13] Since a tort negligence standard was relied on, the appellate ruling provides less evidence than one might think that reliance on a reasonable person standard in criminal law is best avoided (or that negligence should not suffice for criminal liability).[14]

The objection concerning relevant particulars is more likely to tell against the reasonable person standard. The reason for this is that it is quite difficult to spell out (or give clear guidance as to) which particulars of the situation are relevant; and so it is not an implausible objection to the standard itself that it invites—without having a good way to address the problem—either inattention to relevant particulars or attention to irrelevant particulars. More on this serious issue shortly.

A comment is in order on the way I elaborated the objection concerning relevant particulars (in the opening paragraph of this section). I used the word 'might' where one might expect to see the word 'would'. The objection,

---

[12] The definition in full reads as follows: 'A person acts negligently with respect to a material element of an offense when he should be aware of a substantial and unjustifiable risk that the material element exists or will result from his conduct. The risk must be of such a nature and degree that the actor's failure to perceive it, considering the nature and purpose of his conduct and the circumstances known to him, involves a gross deviation from the standard of care that a reasonable person would observe in the actor's situation.' Model Penal Code (2nd edn) § 2.02.

[13] The manslaughter statutes involved in *Williams* were repealed in 1975. Ordinary negligence—simple tort negligence—no longer suffices for a manslaughter conviction. See Kadish et al, *Criminal Law and Its Processes: Cases and Materials* 8th edn (New York: Aspen Publishers, 2007) 421.

[14] It does, however, reflect the problem, discussed below, that relevant particulars may not be sufficiently taken into account in addressing the question of whether a reasonable person in the defendant's situation might have acted as the defendant did. In addition, it prompts the question (elaborated below in part IV. (d)) of whether what matters is deviation, gross or not, from the standard of care that a reasonable person would observe in the actor's situation, or instead, culpable indifference (often, but not invariably, reflected in that gross deviation). For discussion, see M. Moran, *Rethinking the Reasonable Person* (Oxford: OUP, 2003) 311–14; V. Tadros, *Criminal Responsibility* (Oxford: OUP, 2005) chs 9 and 13; S. Pillsbury, 'Crimes of Indifference' (1996) 49 *Rutgers Law Review* 105; K. W. Simons, 'Rethinking Mental States' (1992) 72 *Boston University Law Review* 463; and Simons, 'Culpability and Retributive Theory: The Problem of Criminal Negligence' (1994) 5 *Journal of Contemporary Legal Issues* 365.

I said, is that the question we are to ask, according to the reasonable person standard, is 'Might a reasonable person have acted as the defendant did?' when (if we are going to talk about the reasonable person at all) it should be 'Might a reasonable person, worried about x/fearful of y/aware that z, have acted as the defendant did?' Compare affirmative answers to these questions when 'might' is used, to affirmative answers to the questions if 'would' is used, and it is evident that the word choice matters. If we say that a reasonable person might have acted as D did, we recognize that a reasonable person might also have acted differently. By contrast, saying that a reasonable person would have acted as D did suggests that a reasonable person would have done precisely that. The use of 'would' suggests a definiteness about what a reasonable person would do, a definiteness that generally misleads,[15] suggesting that the reasonable person represents exactly one person-type. 'The reasonable person' can be many different people. This is easier to recognize if 'might' is used rather than 'would'. It is not as if the reasonable person is a sort of sage who always does precisely what one should do—if indeed there is exactly one course of action that one should take in a given set of circumstances. Depending on what x is, it may be the case that a reasonable person might do x in a given situation and might do ~x. (For example, a healthy, 45-year old reasonable person, leading a very full life, and satisfied with her life as it is, who discovers that she is unexpectedly pregnant, might opt to carry the pregnancy to term, or might opt for an abortion.) Indeed, this would be true even if the reasonable person *were* the pinnacle of virtue (or so I would hold, though certainly there is room for debate on that point).[16]

Asking 'Might a reasonable person have acted as D did?' rather than 'Would a reasonable person (or worse: *the* reasonable person) have acted as D did?' thus turns out to make a significant difference.[17]

---

[15] However, there are exceptions; as Victor Tadros reminded me, in situations where there is only one permissible option, 'would' is more apt.

[16] My thought here is simply that in many situations where a difficult choice has to be made, diametrically opposed options—staying married vs getting divorced, opting for an abortion vs going ahead and having the baby—may both be options that not only a reasonable person, but even a very virtuous person, might choose. Any temptation to think otherwise is, I suspect, due to some notion either that the very virtuous person picks the (more) self-sacrificial option, or that opting for a divorce is less courageous than opting to stay married and that opting for an abortion is less courageous than opting to have the baby. I don't think either is true; in addition, even if it is more courageous to choose x than to choose ~x, x might still not be a more virtuous choice.

[17] It might be objected that this makes the standard absurdly easy to meet: 'anyone might do anything!'. This can be addressed by clarifying that we are assuming that the reasonable person is not acting out of character. So, fully spelled out, the question is: 'Might a reasonable person in D's situation, not acting out of character, have acted as D did?'

IV. Giving the Particulars Their Due

(a) Let's look more closely at the problem concerning relevant particulars. There is more than one vantage point from which the problem can be formulated. One vantage point can be seen in the following question, posed by Mayo Moran: '[W]hich characteristics of the reasonable person really matter and which ones should be treated simply as default characteristics that can be displaced when that characteristic is not possessed by the person whose behavior is being judged?' I find this question disorienting. Why would there be default characteristics? What would they be? Shouldn't the idea be to conceive of 'the reasonable person' in abstraction from his or her various particular characteristics? (I use quotation marks as a reminder that, as Ross Parsons put it, the 'monism' in the formulation of the reasonable person standard is 'only a shell.'[18]) The characteristics, after all, would vary from one reasonable person to another. I see the task not to be that of displacing some of the reasonable person's characteristics, but that of determining, when we ask, 'might a reasonable person in D's situation have acted as D did?' *what counts as D's situation.* Is it, for example, part of D's situation that D has a very short temper?[19]

In this section, I explain the task set by the reasonable person standard (viewed as just described), some of the objections to which it gives rise, and a partial solution; later I'll return to the contrast between these two ways of understanding the reasonable person. On one view, the reasonable person is to be understood as having a full panoply of personal characteristics, and the task set for us by the reasonable person standard involves picturing that person with some of his or her characteristics replaced by some of the defendant's qualities.[20] As I see it, by contrast, we are to understand the reasonable person abstractly.

---

[18] R. Parsons, 'Negligence, Contributory Negligence, and the Man who Does Not Ride the Bus to Clapham' (1957–58) 1 *Melbourne University Law Review* 163, 169.

[19] One might think that it is because I use 'might' rather than 'would' (as explained above in part III) that I see the problem from a different vantage point than does Moran. That may enter in, but my vantage point also makes sense if we use 'would'; the question then is 'would a reasonable person in D's situation have acted as D did?' and the issue again is that of asking what features of D's situation count.

[20] The view is not altogether clear, and is not explicitly stated. I am piecing it together primarily from remarks of Mayo Moran's, together with various criticisms of the reasonable person that make more sense on my hypothesis that the critic, like Moran, takes the reasonable person to be someone we can picture, and who has such default characteristics as being male. The critics I have in mind include Kamir (cited in n 3 above) and Donavan and Wildman in 'Is the Reasonable Man Obsolete?

(b) To better understand both the task set by the reasonable person standard if it is understood in the way I endorsed above and challenges to the standard when thus formulated, consider the case of Bernhard Goetz. Two brief preliminaries: (1) in the US, unlike in England, self-defence requires that the defendant held a reasonable belief that the use of self-defensive force was necessary; (2) self-defence is generally understood to be a justification, not an excuse. There are some who think it should be understood as an excuse, but I will not take that up here, and will treat it as a justification.

Goetz, who in 1984 shot four African-American youths when they asked him for $5 in a NYC subway car, challenged the use of a reasonable person standard in a jury instruction. He argued that the instruction (offered in response to a juror's request for clarification of 'reasonably believes') to 'consider the circumstances of the incident and determine "whether the defendant's conduct was that of a reasonable man in the defendant's situation"'[21] would 'preclude a jury from considering factors such as the prior experiences' of the defendant. It thus requires a jury 'to make a determination of "reasonableness" without regard to the actual circumstances of a particular incident'.[22] His objection, in short, was that a reasonable person standard does not allow consideration of relevant particulars.

In rejecting his appeal (and overturning a lower court ruling), the New York Court of Appeals rejected his conception of reasonable person standards. Goetz's argument, the Court wrote,

falsely presupposes that an objective standard means that the background and other relevant characteristics of a particular actor must be ignored. To the contrary, we have frequently noted that a determination of reasonableness must be based on the 'circumstances' facing a defendant or his 'situation.' Such terms encompass more than the physical movements of the potential assailant . . . [T]hese terms include any relevant knowledge the defendant had about that person—including, for example, any information the defendant had concerning the assailant's prior acts of violence or reputation for violence. They also necessarily bring in the physical attributes of all persons involved, including the defendant. Furthermore, the defendant's circumstances encompass any prior experiences he had which could provide a reasonable basis for a belief that another person's intentions were to injure or rob him or that the use of deadly force was necessary under the circumstances.[23]

A Critical Perspective on Self-Defense and Provocation' (1981) 14 *Loyola of Los Angeles Law Review* 435.

[21] *People v Goetz* 497 N.E.2d 41, 47 (NY, 1986); the internal quote is from the instruction to the Grand Jury.

[22] Ibid 52.

[23] Ibid 52.

The court's approach avoids two extremes. One extreme is that of reading 'the defendant's situation' so broadly that it includes the defendant's prejudices, irrational fears, unwarranted anger, and vengeful desires. Clearly, the reasonable person standard should not be understood as directing us to ask whether a reasonable person who saw the world exactly as D did, had all and only D's attitudes, desires, reactive emotions, and so forth, might have acted as D did. 'Reasonable' has to be doing some work. The other extreme is that of excluding from 'the defendant's situation' such particulars as relevant knowledge the defendant had about the alleged assailant (now victim).

On the approach taken in *Goetz*, the following count as part of the defendant's 'situation' (in the context of self-defence): relevant knowledge the defendant had concerning the assailant's prior acts of violence, or reputation for violence; relevant physical attributes of all persons involved; and any prior experiences that provide a reasonable basis for a belief that the use of (deadly) force was necessary under the circumstances. The defendant's mental attributes are not on the list, and that should come as no surprise; as noted above, the idea is not to ask whether a reasonable person with the attitudes, reactive emotions, and beliefs of the defendant would have acted as the defendant did. That said, it is not hard to sympathize with those who suspect that sometimes, some of the defendant's mental attributes should indeed be considered part of the situation.

Some might react to the reasonable person standard, thus understood, by pointing out how much it does not decide. For example, how do we determine whether a particular experience provides a reasonable basis for the beliefs just mentioned? With respect to some experiences, the answer is obvious. That Goetz had on a previous occasion been beaten up by three young African-American men, leaving him with a permanent knee injury, may elicit some sympathy and help one understand his action (particularly against a background of racism); but it does not provide a rational basis for a belief that *these* men, who happen also to be African-American (and young), are going to do him harm. But, one might ask, suppose he had been repeatedly beaten up by young African-American men (and never by anyone else), and suppose the manner in which these men in the subway car addressed him was very similar to that of some of his previous attackers: would he then have had a rational basis for a belief that he was about to be attacked? (A further question, of course, is whether he needed to use deadly force to repel the attack, and whether deadly force was proportional to the attack he faced.) Insofar as the reasonable person standard leaves this and similar questions unresolved, one might think that the standard is deficient. But that misunderstands the nature of standards. No standard is going to dictate all the answers on matters to which the standard applies; there will always be a need for judgment.[24]

Thus far, in discussing the complaint that the reasonable person standard cannot do justice to the relevant particulars, I have (indirectly) addressed two objections. One, put forward by Goetz and addressed by the court, is that because it is an objective standard, it leaves no room for taking into account the actual circumstances of the defendant. The second objection is that although it leaves room for taking them into account, it does not tell us which circumstances should be taken into account. The court's response offers an answer. Some might regard it as inadequate since it does not provide a decision procedure for determining exactly what counts as the situation— does not, for example, spell out what it takes for prior experiences to provide a reasonable basis for a belief that self-defensive force was necessary in these circumstances. But a standard is not, and should not be, expected to provide a decision procedure.

(c) A more interesting objection is that because of what it does not include as part of 'the situation', the reasonable person standard (as portrayed in *Goetz*, and as I am understanding it) is unfair to defendants. The objection could focus either on experiences of the defendant's that would not count as part of the situation, or on mental attributes of the defendant's that arguably should be included. I will focus it on the former. This objection is best motivated by considering a more sympathetic sort of defendant than Goetz.[25]

---

[24] For a rich discussion of this issue in connection with moral philosophy, see A. W. Wood, *Kantian Ethics* (Cambridge: CUP, 2008) ch 3.

[25] But see S. Garvey, 'Self-Defense and the Mistaken Racist' (2008) 11 *New Criminal Law Review* 119. In addition, see Tadros' claim that the very fact that D had (recently) been the victim of violence should factor into a judgement of whether D acted reasonably (*Criminal Responsibility* (n 14 above) ch 13). Emphasizing that we should lower our expectations for someone who was recently the victim of violence, he claims that reasonableness should not be measured against the standard of what a reasonable person in that situation would (or might) do. Instead, the relevant question should be what is reasonable for someone who recently was the victim of violence. That we should lower our expectations is a plausible position, but I see no need to adjust what we consider reasonable in the light of what the person has recently suffered. (In addition, the approach Tadros puts forward leaves us with the question of which of many facts about the person that might affect how he or she now reacts should enter in. Could we ask what is reasonable for someone who recently learned that he has lung cancer? Or who recently had a miscarriage? Or who recently married, or divorced? Or who as a child suffered the loss of a sibling?) Instead, mitigation may be in order at sentencing (and in other circumstances, where, say, the defendant was involuntarily intoxicated, he should be excused altogether). My position reflects the (not unusual) view that excuses should not be conflated with justifications. Involuntary intoxication does not render one's conduct reasonable (except in a different sense of 'reasonable' according to which we might say, 'given that she was under the influence of that powerful drug administered to her without her knowledge, she did pretty well/made pretty reasonable choices'). But it provides an excuse; it blocks criminal liability.

Consider someone who was the victim of partner violence in more than one relationship and now is in a new relationship in which there has not, so far, been any violence. In an argument over whether she has used her partner's car without his permission, she sees a flash of anger in his eyes, and remembers that flash in another man's eyes, a flash that immediately preceded an attack that left her with two broken ribs and a broken jaw. Determined to thwart what she believes to be an impending, serious attack on her, she stabs him. For those who (unlike me) think that she should be acquitted on self-defence grounds, the reasonable person standard is most unfortunate. That another man badly beat her when he had that same look in his eye does not provide a reasonable basis for a belief that this man was going to attack her; that experience, therefore, cannot count as part of her 'situation'.

Lest it seem as if the reasonable person standard will have trouble with most or all cases of battered women who kill their batterers, note that if the man she stabbed had attacked her on previous occasions, the fact that he had the same look in his eye that he had on those occasions might, especially if conjoined with other indicators (such as the cadence of his speech), indeed be a reasonable basis for a belief that he was about to attack her again. (Whether it would be depends on whether he often had that look in his eye on non-violent occasions, as well.) The fact that to an observer, the look in his eye would not have any such significance is immaterial. What matters is not how the situation would be read by an observer who had no history with the man, or knew him only as a business partner, or a client, or even as a friend; what matters is how a reasonable person with her knowledge of his moods, his temper, and in particular, his manner just prior to attacking her, would (or might) view the situation.[26]

The objection under consideration takes hold in instances where there are past experiences that arguably should count as part of the 'situation' but which cannot so count, on the reasonable person standard as spelled out in *Goetz*, because they do not provide a rational basis for a belief that one needs to use self-defensive force. Relative to the defendant's belief, the conduct is reasonable; but the belief itself is not reasonable.

The most straightforward, and I believe the most compelling, way to develop the objection is to say that the fact that the belief is not reasonable

---

[26] See *People v Humphrey*, 13 Cal. 4th 1073 (1996), ruling that the jury instruction that evidence concerning battered woman syndrome could be considered only in deciding whether she believed that she needed to use self-defensive force, not in deciding whether her belief was reasonable, was in error; evidence that battered women become hyper-vigilant, and learn to recognize signs that an attack is impending, bears on the question of whether a reasonable person in the defendant's situation might have acted as she did.

should matter only if the defendant is culpable for holding that belief.[27] Otherwise, that the belief is not reasonable should not, for purposes of the law (and specifically, for self-defence) be held against the defendant. If the victim of partner violence in previous relationships is not culpable for misreading the present situation as one in which she is about to be attacked and needs to use self-defensive force immediately, then arguably she should not be criminally liable for acting accordingly. The mere fact that her belief that her partner is about to attack her is not reasonable should not, some will claim, be a barrier to a self-defence claim.[28]

This objection merits serious consideration.[29] Framed as it is in terms of self-defence, it is bound to be of less interest in the UK than in the US, since self-defence law in the UK does not require that the belief be reasonable.[30] But the same or similar objections arise in other areas of the criminal law. In the remainder of this section, I explain how such objections arise in connection with the *mens rea* of negligence.[31]

(d) The claim that an unreasonable belief should exculpate as long as the agent is not culpable for holding it—or put differently, that an unreasonable misreading of a situation should exculpate as long as the agent is not culpable for so misreading the situation—poses a challenge to the view that negligence suffices for criminal liability. Why should D be criminally liable just because D should have been aware of a 'substantial and unjustifiable risk'

[27] A different version of the objection, put forward by Garvey (n 25 above), holds that the fact that D culpably believed p should not preclude a self-defence claim *unless* the culpability can be linked to some obligation that the state can legitimately demand of D.

[28] This would of course be more plausible if we understood self-defence (as I don't) as an excuse rather than a justification. For a defence of the position that it should be understood as an excuse—but as a rational excuse—see C. Finkelstein, 'Self-Defense as a Rational Excuse' (1996) 57 *University of Pittsburgh Law Review* 621; for a reply, see H. Pendleton, 'A Critique of the Rational Excuse Defense: A Reply to Finkelstein' (1996) 57 *University of Pittsburgh Law Review* 651.

[29] It also calls for careful probing into 'reasonable' in this context: is the idea mainly epistemic? Or is it more closely pegged to what it is reasonable to expect of each other, or what we may legitimately demand of each other? See A. Ripstein's discussion of the reasonable person in his *Equality, Responsibility, and the Law* (Cambridge: CUP, 1999), and T. M. Scanlon's discussion of reasonableness in 'Contractualism and Utilitarianism', Sen and Williams, eds, *Utilitarianism and Beyond* (Cambridge; CUP, 1982) 103–28, and *What We Owe to Each Other* (Cambridge, MA: Harvard University Press, 1998) esp 192–7.

[30] It does require that the force used was 'reasonable in the circumstances as the accused believed them to be, whether reasonably or not', according to D. Ormerod, *Smith and Hogan: Criminal Law* 11th edn (Oxford: OUP, 2005) 329.

[31] Another important area where they arise is provocation law. However, there the issues are complicated by the fact that provocation is only a partial defence. If one passes a reasonable person test, it would seem that one should be fully exculpated; yet of course one is only partially exculpated if one succeeds in one's provocation plea. It would not be implausible to hold that the reasonable person standard should be utilized only for complete defences, not partial ones.

(to quote the language of the Model Penal Code, s. 2.02)? If D wasn't aware but is not culpable for not being aware, why should D be criminally liable?

I have put the challenge generously, arguably too generously; to be a challenge worth taking seriously, it should be developed so as to address a careful statement of what negligence is, preferably one authored by supporters (or at least by non-opponents) of the view that negligence, properly understood, can suffice for criminal liability. Let's restate it by reference to the MPC definition of 'negligently'. The objection then reads:

Granted, the 'risk must be of such a nature and degree that the actor's failure to perceive it, considering the nature and purpose of his conduct and the circumstances known to him, involves a gross deviation from the standard of care that a reasonable person would observe in the actor's situation';[32] but unless D is culpable for that gross deviation, why is D criminally liable for the harm or wrong he did through his failure to perceive a risk that he should have perceived?

Once we see it developed as it would need to be if negligence is understood as defined in the MPC, the objection is less compelling. Attaching criminal liability to failing to see a situation as one should sounds bad; but if the failure to see it as one should involves a gross deviation from the standard of care that should be observed in the situation, attaching liability to it no longer sounds so dubious. But even if less compelling, the objection does not go away. Although it is easier to imagine someone not being culpable for failure to see a situation as one should than to imagine someone not being culpable for grossly deviating from the standard of care that should be observed, the latter is also possible.

Two lines of thought motivate and lend support to the objection. One is that grossly deviating from the standard of care that should be observed does not suffice for criminal liability unless that gross deviation reflects culpable indifference. Now, as has been rightly pointed out, failures to meet a reasonable person standard generally do in fact show at least some lack of concern for the well-being of others. If I don't notice the risks that I am unjustifiably imposing on others, this usually means that I don't really care.[33] Still, there are cases where failures to see what one should see may not reflect a lack of care (and there are also cases where the failure to care enough is not something for which the agent deserves blame). I'll return to this first line of thought later.

---

[32] Model Penal Code § 2.02.

[33] See in particular R. A. Duff, *Intention, Agency, and Criminal Liability* (Oxford: Basil Blackwell, 1990) esp ch 7.

A second line of thought concerns not culpable indifference, but inca-
pacity. To quote H. L. A. Hart, 'even if the standard of care is pitched very
low so that individuals are held liable only if they fail to take very
elementary precautions against harm, there will still be some unfortunate
individuals who...could not attain even this low standard'.[34] And, the
thought continues, it is wrong to hold a person criminally liable for failing
to meet a standard that he or she is unable to meet (particularly, though
perhaps not only,[35] if the person is in no way culpable for being unable to
meet it).

What should we say to the objection that the reasonable person standard
wrongly imposes criminal liability on those who, despite their best efforts, are
unable to meet the standard? I cannot do justice to this objection here, and
am mainly concerned to single it out as an objection that, unlike some others
that I have noted, merits serious consideration. But a promising line of reply
suggested by Hart is worth mentioning here.

Acceptance of the reasonable person standard, Hart observes, does not
require that we *either* allow the 'situation' to include all the defendant's
personal qualities (such as being mentally ill) *or* hold criminally liable for
failing to meet the standard even those who were incapable of meeting it.

[W]hen negligence is made criminally punishable, this...leaves open the question:
whether, before we punish, both or only the first of the following two questions must
be answered affirmatively:

   (i) Did the accused fail to take those precautions which any reasonable man with
       normal capacities would in the circumstances have taken?

  (ii) Could the accused, given his mental and physical capacities, have taken those
       precautions?

Hart agrees with those who oppose criminal liability for negligence that it
would be wrong to hold that only the first question has to be answered
affirmatively. But the solution need not be to give up on an invariant
standard. Instead, keep (i) and (ii) as two distinct questions; answer
(i) without attention to (ii), and then if the answer to (i) is affirmative, we
move to (ii). We handle the problem—the worry that there will be some who
fail to meet the standard despite doing their best—by recognizing excuses,

---

[34] H. L. A. Hart, 'Negligence, Mens Rea, and Criminal Responsibility' in *Punishment and Responsibility* (Oxford: OUP, 1968) 154.
[35] If, due to reckless habits (drag car racing, perhaps, or biking at high speeds without a helmet),
I sustain a brain injury that renders me no longer able to size up a situation and recognize the risks
I am imposing on others, it is not clear what significance the fact that I am culpable for the
diminution in my mental capacities should have.

not by altering (i) by building into 'the circumstances' that the man is mentally ill, or by qualifying the term 'man' by the term 'mentally ill'.

One might argue, however, that there are cases where both (i) and (ii) are satisfied, yet where the defendant should not be held criminally liable. A defendant might, in doing x, grossly deviate from the standard of care that a reasonable person would have observed yet not be culpable for having done x, *without* it being the case that she was unable to meet the standard of the reasonable person. If there are such cases, then Hart's approach, even if it addresses the objection that the reasonable person standard wrongly imposes criminal liability on those who, despite their best efforts, are unable to meet the standard, fails to address this worry. The most plausible way to press this point is to say that culpable indifference is key, and this brings us back to the first line of thought limned above: the defendant whose conduct deviated (even grossly) from the standard of care that a reasonable person would observe should not be criminally liable unless his conduct shows culpable indifference.

I am not convinced that there in fact are cases where both (i) and (ii) are satisfied yet where the defendant should not be held criminally liable, but a somewhat promising candidate, pointed out to me by Victor Tadros, is *R v Adomako*.[36] Adomako, an anaesthetist, was convicted of involuntary manslaughter. He had failed to notice that the tube carrying oxygen from the ventilator to his patient had become disconnected and that the patient had ceased to breathe and was turning blue. Adomako did attend to the alarm from the blood pressure monitor (an alarm that is estimated to have sounded about four minutes after the tube became disconnected); he checked the monitor in an attempt to ascertain whether it was malfunctioning, and judging that it was not, administered a drug to raise the patient's blood pressure. Somehow he did not notice throughout this time that his patient was not breathing. It was only after the patient suffered cardiac arrest (some 11 minutes after the tube became detached) that Adomako realized that the tube was disconnected.

Although Adomako is less aptly described as having failed to take a precaution than as having failed to notice what any doctor should have noticed, it is reasonable to say that (i) is met. In addition, (ii) is met; there is no reason he could not have properly monitored the patient and the equipment whose functioning was crucial to keeping the patient alive. As Tadros observes, Adomako's conduct does not reflect indifference. *Adomako* is thus a good test case: if we think that holding Adomako criminally liable

---

[36] [1995] 1 AC 171. Tadros discusses *Adomako* in *Criminal Responsibility* (n 14) 84–5.

was appropriate, we are rejecting the position that criminal liability should require culpable indifference. Tadros maintains that he should not have been held criminally liable. My own sense is that there was no travesty of justice in finding Adomako guilty of manslaughter (though criminal prosecution and conviction seem to me decidedly less appropriate than civil action together with removal of his licence to practice medicine).[37] But there is certainly room for debate. In any event, this is about as strong a candidate for satisfying conditions (i) and (ii) and yet not meriting a judgment of criminal liability as we can expect to find.

I turn now to a rather different objection to the reasonable person standard, one that concerns the conflation of the reasonable with the ordinary.

V. The Ordinary and the Reasonable

'Reasonable' in the reasonable person standard is often understood as 'ordinary', with unsettling results, as Mayo Moran documented in her *Rethinking the Reasonable Person*. Indeed the standard is often articulated using the term 'ordinary' instead of 'reasonable', and the terms are very often used interchangeably in legal scholarship and in statutes and rulings. I share Moran's view that the conflation of the ordinary (and the normal, and the natural) with the reasonable is very unfortunate, but am far less sure than Moran is that this conflation constitutes a reason for doubting the value of a reasonable person standard.

Moran highlights two problems with this conflation of the reasonable with the ordinary. First, common expectations that benefit one social group over another seep into the law, raising 'profound rule of law concerns'.[38] This is illustrated by the disparity between the law's treatment of girls at play and that of boys at play when a child is injured by an attractive nuisance. Girls are thought to be more able to resist the allure of an abandoned house or boat than are their male counterparts; and, thanks to the way the reasonable person standard is applied, girls are less likely than boys to recover damages in an attractive nuisance lawsuit. The notion that 'boys will be boys' taints the reasonable person standard. Second, prejudices that shape our view of what is ordinary and natural likewise affect our view of what is reasonable. This is chillingly illustrated by *Plessy v Ferguson* (the 1896 US Supreme Court ruling that Louisiana's law requiring separate train cars for whites and blacks was

---

[37] And indeed criminal prosecutions of doctors for negligently causing the death of a patient are very rare, though not as rare in the UK as in the US. Thanks to Kenneth Simons for this point.

[38] M. Moran, *Rethinking the Reasonable Person* (Oxford: OUP, 2003) 198.

not unconstitutional).[39] According to *Plessy*, Louisiana was required only to establish that the regulation was reasonable, and 'in determining the question of reasonableness', the state was 'at liberty to act with reference to the established usages, customs, and traditions of the people . . .'.[40] Thus 'the treatment of different groups under the objective standard seems to mirror problematic differences in the treatment of those groups more generally', because 'the objective standard draws its notion of what is reasonable in large part from a conception of what is normal or ordinary'.[41] Expectations, in the predictive sense, morph into normative expectations.

To what extent do the gender inequities that Moran cites call into question reliance in the law on a reasonable person standard? It seems to me that they call only for greater care in applying it. The problem to which she draws attention lies in the fact that the courts did *not* rely on a reasonable person standard—or a reasonable child standard—but instead (perhaps without realizing it) on a reasonable girl standard and a reasonable boy standard. Unless it is (virtually) inevitable that the reasonable person standard will be applied in a way that transforms it, the cases she cites do not tell significantly— if at all—against the reasonable person standard.

That gender plays a role in the application of the reasonable person standard is nonetheless a worry; my focus being on criminal law, I think here especially of the provocation defence, where assumptions about masculinity, anger, and honour conspire to render the provocation defence rather easier to obtain for men than for women;[42] moreover, the assumptions themselves are in a sense validated by legal rulings in which they are reflected.[43] But the solution, as I see it, is to clean up the standard—to attain, and then disseminate, a better understanding of what reasonableness, for the purposes of the reasonable person standard, is (or should be). In the case of provocation, we may also want to stipulate that certain conduct, eg sexual infidelity, does not count as adequate provocation. This approach has been

---

[39] *Plessy v Ferguson* 163 U.S. 537 (1896).

[40] Ibid 550. In fairness I should mention that the rest of the sentence is as follows: 'and with a view to the promotion of their comfort and the preservation of the public peace and good order'. Moran puts it differently, and exaggerates slightly: she says that according to *Plessy*, reasonableness was 'to be gauged by conformity with "established usages, customs and tradition"' (296n).

[41] Moran (n 38 above) 195–6.

[42] See the English Law Commission's *Murder, Manslaughter and Infanticide* (Law Com No 304, 2006), and my 'Gender Issues in the Criminal Law' in J. Deigh and D. Dolinko (eds), *The Oxford Handbook of Philosophy of Criminal Law* (Oxford: OUP, 2011) 335–402.

[43] There are rulings in other areas of criminal law one could cite here, in particular in self-defence, as well as in other areas of law. Moran cites research suggesting that tort damages to female plaintiffs 'are routinely and significantly lower than awards to male plaintiffs', for example (Moran (n 38 above) 180, n 41).

adopted by England, in the Coroners and Justice Act 2009, and by at least one state in the US (Maryland).

In addition to disentangling the reasonable from the ordinary and customary, it will be important not to expect one explication of reasonableness to fit all criminal law contexts in which the reasonable person standard (or a requirement of reasonableness) is relied on, so reasonableness will need to be spelled out somewhat differently depending on whether the reasonable person standard is employed as part of the provocation defence, or self-defence, or negligent homicide, or something else. Too often reasonableness is discussed as if it is entirely about proper attention to risk, a reflection, I suspect, of a tort law conception of reasonableness seeping into criminal law. The use of 'prudent' as interchangeable with 'reasonable' has probably contributed to the confusion, because although 'prudence' means (to quote the OED), 'the ability to recognize and follow the most suitable or sensible course of action', it also means 'good sense in practical or financial affairs; discretion, circumspection, caution'.[44] In its broader meaning 'prudent' is closely enough aligned to 'reasonable' to be a tolerable substitute for that term; but in the narrower—and, I think, more common—sense, prudence has more to do with being cautious. To treat 'prudent' in that sense as interchangeable with 'reasonable' thus invites a picture of reasonableness as mainly concerned with not taking unnecessary risks. Using 'prudent' as interchangeable with 'reasonable' also invites a conflation of reasonableness with rational self-interestedness, thus obscuring a crucial component of reasonableness: being reasonable (unlike being rational) at t_1, with respect to x, is incompatible with being selfish at t_1, with respect to x.[45]

I want to clarify that in joining Moran in opposing the conflation of the ordinary and the reasonable, I do not mean to suggest that the ordinary has *no* bearing on the reasonable. Part of the work that needs to be done to clean up the problems attending the reasonable person standard is sorting out what bearing it properly does have. Here are some initial suggestions. The ordinary or customary can sometimes be brought in to support a claim that a reasonable person in D's situation might have acted as D did. A surgeon charged with negligent homicide should be able to cite the fact that she followed customary procedures in support of her claim that she did not act negligently, ie that the risk she overlooked or underestimated was not of such a nature that her failure to see it for what it was involved a gross deviation

---

[44] The OED also notes that 'in early use' it meant 'the wisdom to see what is virtuous'.

[45] I borrow this point from W. M. Sibley, 'The Rational versus the Reasonable' (1953) 62 *Philosophical Review* 554, a paper Rawls cites in his discussion of the rational and the reasonable in Erin Kelly (ed), *Justice as Fairness: A Restatement* (Cambridge, MA: Harvard University Press, 2001).

from the standard of care that a reasonable person would observe in the actor's situation. Ordinary procedures are relevant, for we won't know what the standard of care for a surgeon is unless we know something about the procedures surgeons are trained to follow and ordinarily do follow.[46] To avoid demanding perfection from surgeons (or paramedics, or intake personnel in emergency rooms, or airline pilots), we need some sense of what the ordinary, accepted practice is. We have to be careful not to hold them to too lofty a standard, something we might be prone to do with defendants who have special training and special responsibilities.

Things are a little different in a context where the responsibilities are those that every human (or every human over a certain age) has to every other human. Or are they? It will be argued by some that there too we need to ask what is ordinarily done. I disagree. Imagine that a 21-year-old male student at a fraternity party ignored the 'No' and the alarm on the face of the female student he found reclined on a bed, dozing, and raped her. He discounted her claim that she had gone to lie down in an acquaintance's room because she did not enjoy the party and wanted to leave, but had to wait for her roommate, so had retreated here, where she had then fallen asleep while reading; he told himself that he knew she flirted with him earlier in the evening, and he'd seen her eyeing him from across the room, so no doubt she went to a bedroom figuring that he would look for her and find her, alone on a bed. Would it be relevant to his claim that he did not act negligently (or recklessly) to cite data (supposing such data is indeed available) showing that young adult males, particularly at fraternity parties, very often do not take 'No' seriously and figure that mere presence at fraternity parties—especially if one goes alone to a bedroom—itself signals consent? As Moran argues, this should not be considered relevant. They (and he) are making a mistake of law about consent; mistakes of law (except regarding crimes that are *mala prohibita*) are no defence.[47] That they are making a mistake is evident from the fact that their notion of consent leaves virtually no room for the possibility of refusal.

Just how and where the ordinary bears on the reasonable is a large topic, not one to which I can hope to do justice in this chapter. The main point of this section has been that before we give up on the reasonable person standard, we should see how it fares once we undo the damage done by the frequent talk of 'ordinary or reasonable' that invites conflation of the two

---

[46] I take it that the reasonable person in the surgeon's situation is not a reasonable person who, for reasons not known to us, is present at the surgery; the reasonable person in this instance *is* a surgeon.

[47] See Moran (n 38 above) ch 7.

concepts. We need to clean up the language—in our academic and legal writings—and endeavour to get the statutory language cleaned up, too. In addition, judges need to bear in mind (and instruct juries when appropriate) that mistakes of law are no defence, and thus even if it is common to think that x constitutes consent, that is no excuse; and more generally that what is ordinary, or customary, or 'normal' is of limited relevance to the issue of whether a reasonable person in the defendant's circumstances might have acted as the defendant did.[48]

VI. Normalizing, Privileging, and the Reasonable Person Standard

Earlier I postponed discussing an objection Byrd endorsed, namely that the reasonable person standard opens 'the floodgates for courts to engage in normalizing'.[49] In this section I will say a bit about that objection, while exploring Moran's pessimism about the prospects for disentangling the reasonable from the ordinary. The objection and Moran's pessimism, I suggest, can be traced to the same source: an assumption that the reasonable person is to be thought of as someone we can picture, not as a mere abstraction.

Byrd was endorsing an objection raised by Orit Kamir: 'The sweeping use of any uniform "reasonable person" model, critics argue, is inherently unfair to certain distinct social groups... Nor is there an "average" Israeli person who could fairly be used as a role model (a "reasonable person standard") for the entire population.'[50] I take issue both with the assumption that the reasonable person is supposed to be a role model and with the idea that a reasonable person standard requires that there be a particular person (average or not; but requiring that the person constitute an average of some sort clearly compounds the problem) who serves as 'the' reasonable person. Certainly if the reasonable person standard did require what the critics Kamir refers to apparently say it requires, I too would want to jettison it.

---

[48] One quite legitimate use of the word 'ordinary' in this context bears mention: the term 'ordinary' may serve in some instances to remind us not to demand extraordinary attentiveness or self-restraint, or whatever it is that is called for in the situation at hand. When we offer a gloss on what, for the particular defence or offence, is intended under the rubric of 'reasonable' we may want to use 'ordinary' in front of (say) 'self-control'.

[49] Byrd (n 2 above) 571.

[50] Kamir (n 3 above) 549.

Moran discusses at greater length this supposed 'personification' of the reasonable person standard. The personification, she claims, is part of what we value insofar as we value having a reasonable person standard.[51] At the same time, she sees the personification to be very problematic. Moran writes:

Personification of the standard ... poses particular impediments to a more egalitarian conception of responsibility. This arises because of how the default characteristics of the reasonable person tend to mirror those of the privileged in our society— 'unmodified', the reasonable person is presumptively white, male, educated, an English speaker, literate, adult, employed, physically able and the like. This is not to say that he could not be made black, female, illiterate, physically disabled, and so on. The point is rather that the need to displace default characteristics (whenever they do not pertain) places a difficult burden on those who do not share those characteristics. Even identifying what might need to be displaced will be difficult— for such characteristics are rarely even recognized as such until they are challenged.

She adds:

It will always (and rightly) be difficult to justify employing a conceptual tool that is much more burdensome for some individuals than for others. But it is yet harder to account for why we would place that additional burden on the most disadvantaged. Effectively this is what we do when we insist that it is up to those who do not see themselves in the idealized agent to identify and displace all of its inapt attributes, while by contrast the privileged person who finds herself nicely paralleled by the normative and non-normative attributes of the idealized person faces no such difficulties. This feature of personification means that both the burden of reshaping the standard and the consequent likelihood of the standard going badly awry are far greater in the case of the disadvantaged than the privileged.[52]

If what I suggested earlier is correct, there is no need for all this personification. (Nor for idealization.)[53] Like the conflation of the ordinary with the reasonable, the personification problem Moran articulates is not a reason to jettison the standard of the reasonable person, but is a reason to take care not to present the standard in a way that invites such personifying.

---

[51] Moran (n 38) 301: 'The genius of the reasonable person is largely found in the way he seamlessly weaves together the normative components of the standard—attentiveness to others— with biographical or empirical qualities—age, intelligence, level of education, mode of transportation, etc. Thus constructed, the reasonable person has the undoubted virtue of making an otherwise abstract normative standard seem familiar and knowable.' She proceeds to explain, 'But these very virtues are inextricably linked to his most serious vices. . . .'.

[52] Ibid 306.

[53] Onora O'Neill points out that many objections to abstraction make sense only if abstraction is conflated with idealization. 'Abstraction, taken straightforwardly, is a matter of *bracketing*, but not of *denying*, predicates that are true of the matter under discussion.' See O'Neill, *Towards Justice and Virtue* (Cambridge: CUP, 1996), esp 40–4. The quotation is from 40.

VII. The Notional Person

Perhaps because of my Kantian leanings, I had, prior to reading Moran's book, assumed that the reasonable person in the reasonable person standard was strictly a notional person, someone we think of abstractly. That, at any rate, is what I think it should be. I suspect that those who do not so view it—like those who object to the very idea of decisions behind a veil of ignorance, and of the model conceptions of persons in the Original Position—have doubts about whether there is any sense in the concept of a person without a rich array of attributes. I'm reminded of a friend's anecdote: her young son, spotting a rotating image in front of a Dunkin' Donuts, asked, 'What kind of donut is that?' She answered, 'Oh, no particular kind. It's just a donut.' 'How,' the child countered, 'can it be a donut without being a particular kind of donut?' Surely we can talk about donuts as such, and about reasonable people as such. In both instances (though far more so with people than with donuts) it is important to remember that they come in many varieties; but as long as we keep this in mind and do not treat one type as the prototype, there should be no problem. Now, if the reasonable person standard is explained in a way that invites us to picture an 'average' or 'ordinary' person—whether by using those terms or by equating the reasonable person with the man on the Clapham omnibus—that is a problem. But again, the problem should not be assumed to be endemic to the reasonable person standard, and the solution should be to improve our articulation of it and refine it as needed, not to abandon it.

Moran's view seems to be that whether or not the concept of a notional person makes sense, we are not sufficiently able to conceive of persons abstractly, abstracting away from an array of traits, for notional persons to be helpful constructs. Referring to Lord Simon's remark in *Camplin*, 'A reasonable woman with her sex eliminated is altogether too abstract a notion for my comprehension, or I am confident for that of any jury', Moran comments, 'we need not accept all of the implications of Lord Simon's passage in order to admit the difficulty of conceiving of an agent without some implicit gender'.[54] She adds that it 'does seem to confirm a suspicion that creating an idealized person may not be the best way to capture the law's commitment to an objective reasonableness standard'.[55] It is not clear to me what the problem is supposed to be, however. The idea (apart from the fact that we are not creating an *idealized* person) is not that we are trying to

----

[54] Ibid 302–3.   [55] Ibid 303.

imagine reasonable persons as having no gender, but that we seek (1) to ignore their gender, and (2) to bear in mind that they will not all be of the same gender (or sexual orientation, or economic status, or intelligence, or ethnicity, and so on).

VIII. Concluding Remarks

Lurking in the background as we consider various objections to the reasonable person standard is the question of what the alternatives are. My remarks on this will have to be brief. First, something that is almost too obvious to bear mention but which I mention because the option has seemed promising to many: 'subjectification' of the standard (replacing it, for example, with standards of the reasonable woman, the reasonable man, the reasonable Italian-Australian, etc.) will, as Moran recognizes, only exacerbate the problems that she drew attention to concerning inequality. After all, the problem is that inequities infect legal decisions through such notions as that more can be asked of girls than of boys; if we relativize reasonableness to gender and ask whether a reasonable girl in the defendant's situation would (or might) have acted as the defendant did, we increase the probability that girls will be held to a higher standard. A reasonable woman standard applied to female defendants who claim to have killed in the heat of passion is very likely to work against them, since women are thought to be either less prone to extreme anger or more able to control it, expressing it in a way that does not involve (homicidal) violence.[56]

An option that Moran proposes is to drop 'person' but retain 'reasonable'. This seems unlikely to address the problem that 'reasonable' is understood to mean 'ordinary', however. The language in *Plessy* to which Moran drew attention was entirely about what is reasonable, not about what a reasonable person would have done. Moran seems to think that the substitution of 'ordinary' or' customary' for 'reasonable' is more likely when the question is whether a reasonable person in D's situation might (or would) have acted as D did than if we simply ask whether D acted reasonably. I doubt that is true; but in any case, the best solution is to address the conflation and clarify how 'reasonable' is to be understood. That said, I am open to the possibility that the reference to a reasonable person adds an unnecessary layer of complexity,[57] and

---

[56] For a bit more on this problem, see my 'Gender Issues in the Criminal Law' (n 42 above) 352.

[57] This is suggested by R. A. Duff in his 'The Virtues and Vices of Virtue Jurisprudence' in T. Chappell, *Values and Virtues: Aristotelianism in Contemporary Ethics* (Oxford: Clarendon Press, 2006) 94–6.

that we are better off asking whether the reaction, or the conduct, was reasonable.[58] My sense, though, is that this question—was the reaction, or the conduct, reasonable?—is too susceptible of being interpreted differently depending on how sympathetic we find the defendant. It leaves room for understanding 'reasonable' in a way that is relativized to the defendant . . . or not, if we are not eager to cut the defendant any slack. The reasonable person standard, despite its ample room for differing views of what can go into the 'situation', at least has a very clear intent: the standard is supposed to be invariant, not to be relativized to the defendant.

I have tried in this chapter to bring to light a disagreement about the reasonable person standard—ie whether the person is to be thought of abstractly, or pictured as an individual with a full panoply of qualities—by contrasting the approach taken in *Goetz* with that taken by Moran. The contrasting approaches represent competing views of the task set by the reasonable person standard. I also examined objections to relying in criminal law on the reasonable person standard, and sought to distinguish those that merit further consideration from those that do not, and to develop the former in the hope of advancing discussion of them. Those that most merit further consideration are the claims that (1) reliance in the criminal law on the reasonable person standard wrongly imposes criminal liability on those whose failure to meet the standard—even though their failure constitutes a gross deviation from the standard of care that a reasonable person would observe in the actor's situation—does not reflect culpable indifference, and (2) such reliance imposes criminal liability wrongly if the failure is due to an inability to do otherwise. One view is that an inability to do otherwise is key, and that even those who are culpably indifferent should not be criminally liable as long as they are unable to do otherwise; another is that culpable indifference is key. A third, but similar, view would specify not culpable indifference, but culpability for the unreasonable belief (in the case of self-defence) or for the failure to notice and to recognize as substantial and unjustifiable a risk that a reasonable person would have noticed and so recognized.

---

[58] Comparing the question: 'Might a reasonable person in D's situation have acted as D did?' with 'Was D's conduct reasonable?' I think the former is preferable; built into it is a reminder that there are many ways to be reasonable. We might consider, though, an alternative to both: rephrase the latter question negatively, as 'Was D's conduct unreasonable?' That, unlike 'Was D's conduct reasonable?', arguably provides a kind of reminder that all we are asking is that a threshold be met, not that the conduct meet a high standard, and that there is more than one way of not being unreasonable.

Claims that the reasonable person standard 'normalizes', demands perfection of us, and conflates the reasonable with the ordinary are useful as reminders that the reasonable person standard needs to be properly articulated, but do not constitute serious objections to the standard itself. All of the objections, however, aid us in the task of clarifying what we mean by 'reasonable' for purposes of the reasonable person standard in the criminal law and (of secondary importance, but also important) what bearing the ordinary should have on the reasonable.

3

Resultant Luck and Criminal Liability

Andrew Cornford[1]

I. Introduction

The causation of harm is an important factor in criminal liability, both as a ground for and as an object of it. That a person has acted in a certain way, or omitted to act in certain circumstances, is important in how the state will treat them as an offender, but it is not conclusive. The nature and extent of criminal conviction and punishment often rest on the harms that these actions and omissions bring about. Thus, in English law, the person who intentionally punches another and bruises his cheek will be guilty of assault, whilst the person who intentionally punches another and kills him, no matter how unwillingly, will be guilty of manslaughter.[2] This practice is so familiar that we rarely stop to question it. Indeed, in informal discussions of crimes, it is likely to be harm that predominates. For example, we would tend to say that the alleged manslaughterer is on trial for killing his victim, rather than for intentionally performing some unlawful and dangerous act that happened to cause the victim's death.

However, on reflection, criminal liability for resulting harm raises some troubling philosophical questions. In particular, it seems to be an instance of the problematic phenomenon known to moral philosophers as *moral luck*. Formally, moral luck occurs when the moral blame or judgement that is due to an agent can be influenced by factors outside of that agent's full control. If moral luck is ever 'true'—that is, if it ever occurs legitimately—then, as Thomas Nagel points out, it seems to present us with a paradox in our

[1] I am grateful to the editors and to the participants in the Stirling workshop for all their input. Particular thanks are due to Alan Norrie, Dan Priel, Massimo Renzo, and Victor Tadros for their more detailed comments, and to Vera Bergelson for her comments as my respondent.
    [2] *Newbury and Jones* [1977] AC 500 HL.

conception of morality. This is because morality is often thought, for reasons of fairness, to be subject to a *control principle*: that is, that the moral judgement or blame that is due to agents ought only to be influenced by factors that are *within* those agents' control.[3]

To illustrate the significance of this problem, consider the following example. Imagine first that a person is driving her car at 60 miles per hour through a residential area with narrow streets. This driver approaches a blind corner. She fails to slow down sufficiently and, as a result, mounts the kerb on the outside of the corner as she goes round it. Unfortunately, a pedestrian is walking down the footpath just as the driver goes round the corner. The car is travelling fast enough to kill the pedestrian instantly. Now imagine a variation of this case in which the same driver acts in exactly the same way: she drives through the same area at the same speed, fails to slow down in time for the same corner and mounts the same kerb. However, this time there is nobody on the footpath. Nobody is hurt and the driver reaches her destination safely.

Resulting harm would influence this driver's criminal liability in English law. In the first place, she would be liable for different offences depending on the harm that she causes. Whilst she would be guilty of dangerous driving in the harmless second case, she would be guilty of *causing death by* dangerous driving in the first.[4] In turn, since the driver would be liable for different criminal offences, she would also be liable to different levels of punishment. Dangerous driving carries a maximum penalty of two years' imprisonment, whilst the maximum penalty for causing death by dangerous driving is 14 years.[5]

The element of moral luck in this example consists in the fact that the driver lacks full control over the results of her actions. Certainly, as Nagel points out, it is intuitively plausible that whether or not the driver kills should influence the moral blame that is due to her.[6] However, the control principle is also plausible: we tend to adjust our moral judgements as we learn the various ways in which they are incompatible with it.[7] From the driver's internal perspective, the above cases are identical: her deliberations and volitions are the same whether or not she does harm. The fact that she encounters a pedestrian is (one might think) purely a matter of luck.[8]

---

[3] See generally 'Moral Luck' in T. Nagel, *Mortal Questions* (Cambridge: CUP, 1979).

[4] Road Traffic Act 1988 ss 1 and 2, as amended.

[5] Road Traffic Offenders Act 1988 sch 2 part 1, as amended.

[6] Nagel (n 3 above) 29–31.

[7] Ibid 27.

[8] Some dispute the use of the word 'luck' in this context, since its ordinary usage implies abnormality as well as a lack of control: see eg M. U. Coyne, 'Moral Luck?' (1985) 19 *Journal of Value Inquiry* 319, 321–2; K. Levy, 'The Solution to the Problem of Outcome Luck: Why Harm Is

Thus, if one subscribes to the control principle, one will think it unfair that harm should influence her criminal liability.

The type of moral luck on display in this case is often called *resultant luck*, because it is the results of the agent's actions that make the (putative) difference to the moral blame or judgement that is due to her. Whilst there are other forms of moral luck, I will only discuss resultant luck in this chapter.[9] Since criminal conviction and punishment are public forms of blame and censure, we should expect them to be subject, in at least some degree, to the ordinary conditions of moral judgement. However, as we have already seen, it can seem unfair on reflection that results should affect moral judgement or blame, because agents lack full control over their occurrence. Thus, criminal law incorporates the problem of resultant moral luck. Given the importance of resulting harm as a factor in criminal liability, this potentially poses a significant problem for the justice of the criminal law.

In this chapter, I do not pretend to offer another attempted 'solution' to the moral luck problem. Given the troubling questions that this phenomenon raises about moral agency and responsibility, their objects and conditions, I am sceptical that the problem can satisfactorily be solved.[10] However, I believe that it can be made much less daunting—at least in the context of resultant luck—if we identify more precisely wherein the problem lies. That is my aim in part II of this chapter. I will argue that, by distinguishing different senses of moral judgement and blame and the various ways in which results might affect these, the scope of the resultant luck problem is significantly narrowed. I will further argue that our intuitive reactions in resultant luck cases—which are often used to support the existence of true resultant moral luck—in fact only support, on their most plausible construction, a very different kind of resultant luck to the one that Nagel imagines.

In parts III and IV of the chapter, I turn to the question of what influence resultant luck should have in the specific institutional context of the criminal

---

Just as Punishable as the Wrongful Action that Causes It' (2005) 24 *Law and Philosophy* 263, 278–9; M. Moore, 'The Independent Moral Significance of Wrongdoing' (1994) 5 *Journal of Contemporary Legal Issues* 237, 254–6. Nothing in this chapter turns on the use of the word 'luck'.

[9] The other kinds of moral luck that Nagel identifies are constitutive luck, circumstantial luck, and 'luck in how one is determined by antecedent causes' (n 3 above) 32–5. The problems presented by these forms of moral luck are distinct from those presented by resultant luck, mostly reflecting more familiar problems of the compatibility of causal determinism with traditional conceptions of moral responsibility.

[10] For example, what kind or level of control is required for moral agency? And why should we judge that people are morally responsible for consequences at all? In this chapter, I assume (justifiably or otherwise) that there is some satisfactory answer to this second question. Suffice it to say for now that our morality (and, indeed, our self-understanding more generally) would look very different without this practice.

law. I begin in part III by arguing that harm can properly be a part of what the state communicates about specific criminal acts. To illustrate this, I consider the significance of resulting harm from three perspectives: those of offenders, victims, and the general public. I then go on in part IV to provisionally explore the practical consequences of this significance for particular determinants of criminal liability. I argue that resulting harm might properly influence how criminal offences are defined and conceivably even decisions to criminalize conduct in the first instance. However, the legitimate extent of its influence will depend on a number of variable countervailing factors.

II. Clarifying the Problem

Resultant moral luck is problematic because it reveals the apparent incompatibility of two intuitively appealing principles in our conception of morality. On the one hand, it seems plausible that harm should affect moral judgement and blame. On the other, it seems plausible that these should only be sensitive to factors that are within agents' full control. To resolve this paradox, it may seem necessary to jettison one principle or the other. However, the simple statement of the problem introduced above conceals several important ambiguities. For example, what do we mean by 'moral judgement and blame'? And precisely what kind of influence over these do we intuitively allow to resulting harm? Detailed answers to these questions will help us to better understand the resultant luck problem.

A. Moral judgement and blame

There are many different kinds of moral judgement that we might make about agents or their actions, including judgements about their blameworthiness. Despite employing similar terminology, such judgements can have quite distinct targets. For instance, consider two judgements that we might make about the case of the reckless drivers, introduced above. On the one hand, it seems that the driver who kills and the driver who is merely reckless are equally morally blameworthy. As we saw, these agents' actions are the same from their internal point of view; thus, it seems absurd to regard one as more morally culpable than the other. On the other hand, however, it seems that greater blame is appropriate in the case of the driver who kills. Unlike the merely reckless driver, the driver who kills is responsible for a death. As such, we might say that she is more blameworthy, because she is *to blame for* more.

Judith Thomson shows how we can explain these kinds of apparently paradoxical statements about resultant luck cases by distinguishing different meanings of the word 'blame' in moral discussion.[11] The first meaning Thomson identifies can be seen in the thought that the two drivers are equally blameworthy, because they are equally morally culpable. We might call this the *culpability* sense of blameworthiness. A person is blameworthy in the culpability sense when some action of his gives us reason to think badly of him. It is this sense of moral blameworthiness that informs the thought that there is no material difference between the two drivers: since their deliberations and volitions are identical, the fact that one driver has caused harm gives us no extra reason to think badly *of her*.[12] Indeed, it would be absurd if resultant luck were to influence judgements of this kind. The mere causation of harm gives us no reason to think badly *of agents*, other than as evidence of why their actions might have been wrongful in the first instance.

The second meaning of 'blame' that Thomson identifies can be seen in the thought that the two drivers are differently blameworthy, because only one is responsible for causing harm. We might call this the *attribution* sense of blameworthiness. A person is blameworthy in the attribution sense to the extent they are responsible for bringing about some unwelcome outcome, or are responsible for doing something which is unwelcome in itself. In this sense, the driver who kills is more blameworthy than the merely reckless driver because only she is *to blame for* a death.[13] By contrast to judgements of blameworthiness in the culpability sense, we would obviously expect judgements of attribution blameworthiness to be sensitive to resultant luck. We clearly cannot judge which outcomes agents are responsible for without asking what the results of those agents' actions were.

An important feature of both the attribution and culpability senses of blameworthiness is that they are simply a function of moral facts about agents and their actions. It is unsurprising that harm only influences judgements of attribution, for harm does not make a difference to how we should judge agents *qua* agents. Indeed, hardly anyone argues directly against *this*

---

[11] 'Morality and Bad Luck' (1989) 20 *Metaphilosophy* 203. Others make similar distinctions: for example, between 'scope' and 'degree' of responsibility (M. Zimmerman, 'Taking Luck Seriously' (2002) 99 *Journal of Philosophy* 553); between liability to blame and 'being responsible' for one's actions (J. Andre, 'Nagel, Williams and Moral Luck' (1983) 43 *Analysis* 202, 205); between 'verdictive' judgements of blameworthiness and the appropriateness of blaming actions (H. Jensen, 'Morality and Luck' (1984) 59 *Philosophy* 323).

[12] 'Morality and Bad Luck' (ibid) 209–11.

[13] Ibid 208–9.

position.[14] However, the idea that some kind of control principle should apply to judgements of culpability is entirely compatible with the idea that harm should influence judgements of attribution. That some consequence is attributable to an agent is, again, simply a judgement about another kind of moral fact. There is thus nothing paradoxical in claiming that more bad consequences are attributable to the driver who kills, whilst also claiming that the two drivers are equally morally culpable.

This distinction between different senses of blameworthiness may help to alleviate some of the perplexity that the resultant luck problem has caused to criminal lawyers. The debate over whether harm ought to influence criminal liability often seems irresolvable because it is framed as an argument about 'desert'.[15] Since the entire substance of this disagreement is whether or not harm affects desert, there seems to be little possibility of progress if the various parties simply base their positions on contrary intuitions. However, progress would be enabled if reflection were invited on the different kinds of moral blame that might influence legal liability. For example, one might reconstruct the belief that harm should not affect desert as a belief that criminal liability should only track culpability. Against this, one might argue that criminal conviction can properly reflect resulting harm without violating the control principle, for whilst it gives an account of attributable harms, it does not carry any implication that the person whose actions cause harm is more culpable than the person whose actions do not.

Such a relocation of the debate about the proper place of harm within criminal liability also highlights the truly problematic aspect of resultant moral luck. Judgements of culpability and attribution are simply judgements about moral facts. By contrast, the practices of criminal liability are blaming *actions* with potential negative consequences for those to whom they are directed. As such, they call for independent justification. Of course, one might still think that there are simple cases here. For example, one might think that the occurrence of harm entails an entitlement to act indignantly towards those who cause it, simply as a corollary of the fact that the harm is attributable to them.[16] Whether or not we accept this, however, the cases of

---

[14] Margaret Urban Walker at least appears to: see 'Moral Luck and the Virtues of Impure Agency' (1991) 22 *Metaphilosophy* 14. However, she does not distinguish between different senses of moral blameworthiness as I suggest here that we should.

[15] For example, Michael Moore believes that harm affects desert ('The Independent Moral Significance of Wrongdoing' (1994) 5 *Journal of Contemporary Legal Issues* 237), whilst Larry Alexander and Kimberley Ferzan believe that it does not (*Crime and Culpability* (Cambridge: CUP, 2009) chs 2 and 5).

[16] See eg M. Otsuka, 'Moral Luck: Optional, Not Brute' (2009) 23 *Philosophical Perspectives* 373.

criminal conviction and punishment are surely not this simple. Criminal conviction involves public stigmatization, whilst punishment involves the deliberate infliction of substantial deprivations. We should seek positive reasons for allowing the occurrence of harm to influence these practices.

I return to this issue in part III. For now, we need only note that defining blame more clearly locates the resultant luck problem more precisely. In particular, we should note that there can be no inherent objection to attributing harms to people who cause them, for we have no reason to apply a control principle to this kind of judgement. It follows from this that there can be no inherent objection to the state convicting harm-doers of different offences to similarly culpable non-harm-doers. The material question is instead whether, all things considered, the state is justified in doing so.

B. The intuitive significance of harm

Since the blaming practices of the criminal law potentially have negative consequences for those to whom they are directed, they require independent justification. As we have already seen, it seems intuitively plausible that the occurrence of harm should have at least some influence in this context. This intuitive response may be seen to provide compelling evidence of the existence of true resultant moral luck. However, as is so often the case with such intuitive responses, the precise content and motivation of this feeling is ambiguous. Must it really be construed as a feeling about the appropriateness of greater punishment or resentment? Or is it best understood as a feeling about something else entirely?[17]

Some obvious but important points are worth making about the psychological pressures that act on our intuitive responses to resultant luck cases. First, consider the motivation for anger that the occurrence of harm gives us. This motivation is quite independent from that generated by wrongful action alone. Certainly, we could probably expect to feel some kind of anger when we hear about the actions of the merely reckless driver. However, the driver who hits and kills a pedestrian has actually brought an undesirable circumstance into being. Given this, we are more likely to feel angry with this driver, and to a greater degree. Doubtless this will often be accompanied by a greater urge for retribution, especially if we have any kind of emotional attachment to the victim.

---

[17] I assume here that the best explanation of particular intuitive judgements is the one that can best be reconciled with our other, rational judgements and with our intuitive commitments as a whole. For an alternative approach—deriving a set of moral 'first principles' from our intuitive judgements about resultant luck cases—see Moore (n 15 above).

However, these retributive urges that the occurrence of harm tends to activate surely should not be taken to express any intuitions about justice or the appropriateness of moral blame. To illustrate this, consider first how these retributive urges are altered by emotional *detachment* from a case. If we have no attachment to the victim, any desire for retribution will likely be less strong and may not even be present at all.[18] Conversely, consider how we would react to those cases where we have an attachment to a specific person, who narrowly *avoids* being harmed by another person. For instance, say that our reckless driver mounts the kerb and misses a close friend of yours by a matter of inches. Here your reaction will more closely resemble your reaction to the case in which your friend is hit and harmed.[19]

Additionally, those retributive urges that we retain are often mitigated on reflection. As we acquire greater appreciation of the facts of a given case, our attitudes towards it are likely to change. For instance, the culpability of the driver who kills will be immediately obvious; by contrast, we may not appreciate how dangerous the merely reckless driver's actions were until it is pointed out to us. Once we learn how fast she was driving and where, that she took a blind corner without slowing down sufficiently, and so forth, we will appreciate how easily someone *could* have been hurt and adjust our judgements accordingly. Again, the converse case illustrates the same point: imagine how we would react if we found out that the driver who killed the pedestrian did nothing more dangerous than travel a few miles per hour too fast through a residential area, as many drivers do every day. Then we may be inclined to think that 'it could have happened to anyone'.[20]

These observations suggest that our intuitions about how we should react to people who do wrong are not related to the harm that they cause in any simple way. Such a relationship, if it exists, is likely to be more complex. One famous attempt to explain it can be found in Bernard Williams' essay on moral luck.[21] Williams argues that people can be expected to feel a special kind of remorse for those harms that they cause, even when they cause them entirely non-culpably.[22] As we have seen, we can expect people to develop a degree of critical detachment from such cases. However, surely even the most reflective and dispassionate observer would think something amiss if a driver who killed a pedestrian, even quite accidentally, simply shrugged it off as 'a

[18] R. Parker, 'Blame, Punishment and the Role of Result' (1984) 21 *American Philosophical Quarterly* 269, 273.

[19] Ibid 274.

[20] J. Andre, 'Nagel, Williams and Moral Luck' (1983) 43 *Analysis* 202, 203–4.

[21] 'Moral Luck' in B. Williams, *Moral Luck* (Cambridge: CUP, 1981).

[22] Ibid 28.

matter of luck'.[23] Rather, since this driver brought the harm about, we would expect them to feel remorseful about what they have done.

Williams calls this special kind of remorse *agent-regret*. Whilst agent-regret is a notoriously difficult idea to pin down precisely, Williams is clear about some aspects of it. For instance, he is clear that it is distinguishable from both general regret and the desire to have done otherwise than one did. Indeed, it is compatible with being *glad*, all things considered, to have done as one did. Rather, Williams eventually seems to settle on the idea that agent-regret is characterized by a desire to *think* better next time: to learn something from the experience that can inform future deliberations.[24] He is not clear on exactly how the appearance of agent-regret supports his conclusion that resultant moral luck is probably unavoidable. However, the clearest route to this conclusion seems to be that agent-regret is somehow uniquely obligatory for those who cause harm, and that we are justified in reacting differently towards harm-doers as a result of this.

There are several problems with using agent-regret as a way of linking resultant luck to our intuitive beliefs about the appropriateness of moral blame or judgement. First, why should those harms that are brought about entirely non-culpably prompt a resolution to 'think better next time'? Certainly, one might properly feel remorseful for having been in a position (albeit unwittingly) to avoid causing the relevant harm. However, this simply follows from the fact that it is good to be compassionate: to care about others' well-being and to feel bad when one avoidably harms them. It would be irrational to think that one's deliberations should have been better than they were if they were not faulty.[25] Indeed, one surely cannot be culpable in any degree for causing harm unless one had reason to know that one's actions carried a risk of causing that harm. As Nagel points out, there is nothing truly 'moral' about resultant luck unless it has this dimension.[26]

Moreover, if deliberative failure is the object of agent-regret, then it would be appropriate even when no harm is caused. 'Thinking better next time' is a fitting resolution in respect of any morally faulty action, whatever its consequences.[27] Doubtless, it is true that the occurrence of harm is *in fact* more likely to prompt such a resolution than its non-occurrence. However, this is

---

[23] M. U. Walker, 'Moral Luck and the Virtues of Impure Agency' (1991) 22 *Metaphilosophy* 14, 19.

[24] Williams (n 21 above) 28–33.

[25] D. Enoch and A. Marmor, 'The Case against Moral Luck' (2007) 26 *Law and Philosophy* 405, 420.

[26] 'Moral Luck' in his *Mortal Questions* (Cambridge: CUP, 1979) 19.

[27] Joel Feinberg makes a similar point to this. We can rightly feel morally guilty *whenever* we do wrong, including in those cases where our wrongful conduct makes no mark on the world: see

insufficient to prove a *necessary* connection between harm and agent-regret. To illustrate, consider again the case of the reckless driver who narrowly misses a specific pedestrian. In this situation, the risks of harm associated with that driver's actions are clearly revealed. Thus, she is likely to revise her plans about how to drive in future, even though she has done no harm.

Additionally, the examples that Williams uses to support his argument are defective, because they leave open how far the agents concerned can justifiably regard themselves as being non-culpable for the harms that their actions caused.[28] For instance, one important case for Williams' argument concerns a truck driver who kills a child that jumps out in front of his vehicle.[29] Perhaps we might expect this truck driver to question his own fallibility: did he really do everything that he could reasonably have done to avoid hitting the child? However, this feeling is not related to the appropriateness of blame, of whatever kind. If we ourselves are convinced of the truck driver's moral innocence, we surely would not oblige him to feel regret simply because he happened to have a certain kind of causal connection to the child's death.[30]

All of this suggests that our intuitions about the appropriateness of agent-regret are insufficient to support any commitment to resultant luck in our blaming practices. However, perhaps they are sufficient to support another kind of moral luck. After all, we surely retain the intuition that even the completely non-culpable actor who causes harm has a certain kind of special relationship with their victim after the fact. They are not like a mere bystander, even a bystander who was particularly proximate to the event: they *caused* the harm, however innocently. As we have already pointed out, we might think such a person callous if they felt no regret at all. More than this, however, many will think that they now owe certain duties to the person that they harmed that they did not owe before. For example, it is plausible that they have a duty to apologize for causing that harm.[31] Additionally, we might think that, all else being equal, those who cause harm should compensate their victims for the damage that is attributable to them.

The plausibility of such duties as apology and compensation suggests that we do have an intuitive commitment to a certain kind of resultant moral luck: namely, that the results of our actions can influence our moral obligations.

'Equal Punishment for Failed Attempts: Some Bad but Instructive Arguments Against It' (1995) 37 *Arizona Law Review* 117, 128.

[28] Enoch and Marmor (n 25 above) 418–19.

[29] Williams (n 21 above) 28.

[30] B. Rosebury, 'Moral Responsibility and "Moral Luck"' (1995) 104 *Philosophical Review* 499, 515–16.

[31] Of course, such an apology would amount to a mere expression of regret, without the usual acknowledgement of moral culpability.

However, we should not overestimate the significance of this finding. In the first instance, we should not be too surprised that the appearance of these duties is a matter of luck, since our everyday moral duties often arise in ways that are outside of our full control. For example, we cannot determine when our friends might need our help, or whether our unborn children might have medical conditions that will generate particularly stringent duties to provide for them.[32]

Moreover, this kind of resultant luck is not 'moral' luck as defined by Nagel and Williams. Whilst it is plausible that resultant luck might influence our moral obligations, this says nothing of any intuitive commitments about the appropriateness of moral judgement or blame. Neither does it say anything about the appropriateness of agent-regret. Certainly, the person who causes harm, no matter how innocently, may properly regret acting as they did. However, the occurrence of harm by itself gives them no cause to regret *deliberating* as they did, unless that harm was itself the result of faulty deliberation. Indeed, in many cases of innocently-caused harm—Williams' truck driver case is probably one—it will scarcely be appropriate to say that the actor is an *agent* of that harm at all. Rather, one is more like an instrument through which the harm was brought about.[33] Doubtless it is a deeply unpleasant feeling to have been instrumental in the occurrence of some terrible harm. However, this again reveals no intuitive commitment to using resulting harm as a basis of moral judgement or blame.

III. The Significance of Harm

We can draw two conclusions from this clarification of the resultant luck problem. First, whilst our blaming actions and their potential negative consequences stand in need of independent justification, there is nothing inherently wrong with attributing to agents the harms that they have caused. Second, whilst it is plausible that agents' moral obligations are altered by their having caused harm, the best construction of our intuitions does not support the subjection of our blaming practices to resultant luck. I turn now to consider whether, in light of these conclusions, the state has good reason to make resulting harm a target of criminal liability. I will argue that recognizing the communicative function of the criminal law leads to a positive answer to this question. However, before I turn to this argument, I wish to briefly

[32] M. U. Walker, 'Moral Luck and the Virtues of Impure Agency' (1991) 22 *Metaphilosophy* 14, 24.
[33] Rosebury (n 30 above).

dismiss two alternative lines of thought that have also been thought to justify criminal liability for resulting harm.[34]

The first of these is the *epistemic limitations* view. According to this view, the limited nature of the state's knowledge about offenders' mental states—and thus also their moral culpability—justifies treating harm-doers differently from non-harm-doers. Given such limitations, the occurrence of harm provides *prima facie* evidence of moral culpability of a kind that is not available when no harm is done.[35] This argument also has a normative dimension: acquiring further evidence about offenders' mental states would require undesirable levels of scrutiny, amounting to an unjust invasion of privacy. According to some advocates of this view, our moral integrity as a whole would be damaged if such interference were permitted, given the excessive blaming that would occur if all culpable people were punished to the full extent of their desert.[36] In light of these concerns, the epistemic limitations view holds that it is preferable for a system of 'social morality' such as the criminal law to be grounded in resulting harm, as a 'proxy' for moral culpability.[37]

This first line of argument fails because its premises are false. In the first place, whilst it is true that the occurrence of harm provides evidence of culpability, it is only one kind of available evidence. Others will often be present. For instance, consider again the case of the two reckless drivers: here, the culpability of the merely reckless driver can be inferred from clearly visible aspects of her conduct, even though she has not caused harm. The concern that the investigation of culpability would create unjust invasions of privacy is also unjustified. The ascription of *mens rea* (or 'guilty mind') is already an established part of criminal law; it is a long way from holding people responsible for 'thought crimes'.[38] Correspondingly, applying the same blaming practices to non-harm-doers as to harm-doers does not seem likely to damage our moral integrity. Certainly, it would be excessive if the state were to subject people to blame *every* time they did wrong. However, the same is surely not true if the state takes blaming action only against those whose conduct may legitimately be criminalized in the first instance.

A second common way of justifying the imposition of criminal liability for resulting harm is the *voluntary assumption of responsibility* view. This line of

---

[34] Moore convincingly rejects a number of less well-developed arguments: see 'The Independent Moral Significance of Wrongdoing' (1994) 5 *Journal of Contemporary Legal Issues* 237, 241–52.

[35] See eg N. Richards, 'Luck and Desert' (1986) 65 *Mind* 198; D. Enoch and A. Marmor, 'The Case against Moral Luck' (2007) 26 *Law and Philosophy* 405, 415.

[36] See eg H Jensen, 'Morality and Luck' (1984) 59 *Philosophy* 323.

[37] Rosebury (n 30 above) 522. 'Social morality' is Moore's phrase (n 34 above).

[38] Moore (n 34 above) 247.

argument holds that, in acting wrongfully, we voluntarily accept liability for any negative consequences that result. There have been various expressions of this argument, all couched in diverse terminology. However, they rely on a common idea: namely, that there is something significant about voluntary wrongful action such that, when we engage in it, we change our own moral position in a way that leaves our liability open to the effects of resultant luck.[39] This argument is often supported by an analogy with gambling. When we act wrongfully, it is like spinning a roulette wheel at a casino. By voluntarily performing such an act, we subject our desert to luck: we are licensed to act in our uncertain world and to reap the rewards when we 'win', but only on the condition that we accept the burdens when we 'lose'.[40]

This line of argument is also unsuccessful, because it begs the question. The conclusion that resultant luck can properly influence criminal liability only follows because it is assumed that voluntary wrongful action entails accepting responsibility for those consequences that flow from it. No advocate of this view offers any reason to accept this assumption. The gambling analogy is also a distraction. Certainly, acting wrongly is like placing a bet, in that the outcome of such actions is *in fact* a matter of luck. However, it is only *like* placing a bet. All else being equal, gamblers freely consent to subject their desert to luck. What is more, the element of luck provides part of the putative value of gambling. Neither of these statements is true of criminal liability, whose practices cannot be 'opted into'. This is not to deny that we may nevertheless be able to find some independent reason to impose criminal liability for resulting harm: indeed, I will argue that we can. However, if we are to take this path, then there is no need for the 'voluntary assumption of responsibility' device in the first place.

These brief remarks suggest that we will need to improve on previous efforts if we wish to justify imposing criminal liability for resulting harm. As I have already stated, my preferred alternative is a justification based on the communicative function of the criminal law. It is familiar enough that the criminal law has this function.[41] Besides aiming to prevent future harms, it

---

[39] See eg J. Gardner, 'On the General Part of the Criminal Law' in his *Offences and Defences: Selected Essays in the Philosophy of Criminal Law* (Oxford: OUP, 2007); B. Herman, 'Feinberg on Luck and Failed Attempts' (1995) 37 *Arizona Law Review* 143; J. Horder, 'A Critique of the Correspondence Principle in Criminal Law' [1995] *Criminal Law Review* 759; K. Levy, 'The Solution to the Problem of Outcome Luck: Why Harm is Just as Punishable as the Wrongful Action that Causes It' (2005) 24 *Law and Philosophy* 263; M. Otsuka, 'Moral Luck: Optional, Not Brute' (2009) 23 *Philosophical Perspectives* 373.

[40] A. M. Honoré, 'Responsibility and Luck: the Moral Basis of Strict Liability' in his *Responsibility and Fault* (Oxford: Hart, 1999).

[41] V. Tadros, *Criminal Responsibility* (Oxford: OUP, 2005) ch 3.

plays an important expressive role: it provides the moral voice of the political community, reinforcing that community's norms and condemning infringements of them. I suggest, however, that the communicative content of the criminal law can legitimately go beyond these familiar terms. Because of its role as the political community's principal moral institution, the criminal law has reason to account for a range of morally significant facts about the events that it deals with, including resulting harm. To illustrate this, I will consider three groups for whom communications about harm may properly be morally significant: offenders, victims, and the general public.

Consider first the significance of harm for offenders. Antony Duff has sought to explain criminal liability for resulting harm from this perspective, particularly as a way of communicating the appropriateness of either relief or regret on an offender's part.[42] Duff observes that only those offenders who have caused harm have actually brought some tangible evil into being and thus fully made their mark on the world as 'criminal agents'. Those offenders who have not caused harm correspondingly lack this status, which generates a reason for relief.[43] By contrast, where an offender's actions result in harm, he has no grounds for feeling relieved. Instead, regret and remorse are appropriate: both for having brought the harm about and for the faulty deliberations that led him to act as he did. By making criminal liability sensitive to harm, the state communicates these facts to offenders. It reminds those offenders who have caused harm of the regrettable consequences of their wrongful actions, whilst those offenders who have not caused harm are reminded of the consequences that their actions *could* have had.[44]

One might doubt that this line of thought provides a particularly strong reason to impose criminal liability for resulting harm. Ultimately, the aim of inducing either relief or regret is surely the same: namely, to produce an emotional response in offenders that will prompt them to realize the error of their ways. However, as we saw in part II above, it is plausible that causing harm has more significant moral implications for offenders than this. In particular, it might entail that their moral duties are altered: for example, they may acquire duties to apologize to or compensate their victims. This is not to say that the state should enforce such duties (at least through the criminal law): indeed, there may be persuasive reasons against this.[45] However, such

---

[42] 'Auctions, Lotteries and the Punishment of Attempts' (1990) 9 *Law and Philosophy* 1.
[43] Ibid 35.
[44] As Duff puts it: 'you tried to harm this person but, thank God, you failed' (ibid 36–7). We might equally put it: 'you endangered this person but, thank God, you did not harm them'.
[45] For example, it may be that forced apologies are of less value than those freely given.

duties are surely morally significant, and by imposing criminal liability for resulting harm, the state can at least confirm that they are owed.

These claims are admittedly open to disagreement. After all, I merely demonstrated above that the idea that harm alters our moral duties is *intuitively* plausible; I did not present an argument for this conclusion. Indeed, advocates of the control principle will probably argue that this intuition simply provides further evidence of the unthinking, retributive tendency to attach too great an importance to harm in our moral judgements of agents and their actions. These duties could instead be more sensitive to culpability: for example, we might demand that all culpable people contribute to compensating the injured. Given the uncertain foundations of the duty to compensate, it will be best to avoid this controversy for the moment.[46] It will suffice to note that these revisionist arguments are not currently widely accepted. Many will still be receptive to the idea that causing harm alters our moral duties, and thus also to the idea that criminal liability for resulting harm communicates something of moral significance for offenders.

Nevertheless, it will be worthwhile to devote greater attention to the significance of harm for victims and the public, for there is greater potential for convergence in these areas. Let us turn first to the significance of harm for victims. To state that resulting harm is significant for victims of crime is obvious; however, it is also important, for it highlights the way in which those cases in which harm is caused are most dramatically different from those in which no harm is caused. In contrast to the offender context, an advocate of the control principle could not reasonably expect to tell a victim who has suffered harm that they should care only about culpability. Whilst a system of criminal prohibitions generally serves to protect that victim's interests, those interests have only been interfered with *in fact* if the victim has suffered harm.[47] Indeed, from the victim's perspective, that they have suffered harm is probably the most significant fact that the criminal law *could* communicate about 'their' case.

Does the significance of harm for victims give the state good reason to account for that harm in its communications? Here is a strong reason to think that it does. As we just noted, the substantive criminal law generally serves to affirm the moral claims of citizens. However, the state has an additional reason to *re-affirm* the moral claims of those who have actually become

---

[46] To illustrate, see the following for three very different perspectives on the philosophical foundations of compensation: Honoré (n 40 above); N. MacCormick, 'The Obligation of Reparation' in his *Legal Right and Social Democracy* (Oxford: Clarendon Press, 1982); E. J. Weinrib, *The Idea of Private Law* (Cambridge, MA: Harvard University Press, 1995) chs 3–5.

[47] This is not to deny that we have an interest in our primary interests not being endangered; however, the value of this interest derives from the value of the relevant primary interests.

victims of crime. This arises from the moral humiliation that is characteristic of feelings of victimhood: the demeaning of one's moral worth that is inherent in unjustified injury to one's interests. Because those who experience this feeling have been made to doubt the value of their moral claims, the state has a reason to confirm publicly the significance of *their* interests specifically. Making harm an object of criminal liability is one way in which the state can achieve this, because doing so acknowledges that the harm that the victim has suffered is worth reporting, as well as the culpable behaviour of the offender.

Of course, the category of people who have suffered such moral humiliation does not coincide perfectly with the category of those who have suffered harm. As I will explore further in part IV, criminal acts can have specific victims even when they do not result in harm, thus giving the state a similar reason to re-affirm the moral claims of specific persons. However, as a matter of psychological fact, the characteristic feelings of victimhood are inevitably at their strongest when a victim's primary interests have actually been interfered with. Thus, even if one does not agree that the need to re-affirm specific moral claims militates strongly in favour of criminal liability for resulting harm, one can still agree that harm is a worthy object of state communication. By acknowledging the significance of harm, the state acknowledges the significance of *victims*, because what matters to them is seen to matter to the political community as a whole.

Approached from this perspective, one can see that taking account of harm in the practices of the criminal law is plausibly even a matter of justice. Certainly, the primary role of the criminal justice system lies in what it does to offenders: catching them, calling them to account for their actions, condemning and punishing them for what they have done wrong, attempting to prevent them from doing wrong again. However, as a social institution—especially one with a role as the moral voice of the political community—the criminal justice system owes a duty of fair treatment to *all* citizens.[48] A criminal law grounded only in volition, of the kind that some commentators propose,[49] may do best at accounting for the offender perspective, but it would leave little room for other important facts about criminal cases. Given that there is no inherent moral restriction on attributing harm to offenders, the state thus has good reason to acknowledge harm. As we will see, other considerations might sometimes defeat this. However, not accounting for the victim perspective at all is unfair and thus—in the context of a public system with this unique moral role—unjust.

---

[48] As Rawls famously opined, justice is 'the first virtue of social institutions': *A Theory of Justice* rev edn (Oxford: OUP, 1999) 3.

[49] See eg L. Alexander and K. Ferzan, *Crime and Culpability* (Cambridge: CUP, 2009).

I appreciate that this line of argument may prove troublesome for criminal law theory, given its traditional focus on criminal law's 'general part'—the doctrines of which serve almost entirely to make sense of the offender perspective on criminal action. Given the primary function of the criminal justice system as outlined above, doubters may wonder whether the victim perspective has any proper role within it, save an evidential one. They may worry that, by adopting this perspective, we risk going too far: say, by giving victims a say in the fate of offenders.[50] Certainly we should guard against such a possibility. However, we can distinguish (at least in principle) between the objective moral significance of harm to victims and those same victims' unreasoned retributive desires. 'Justice for victims' of the kind that I am urging here need not involve giving effect to the latter. Rather, I simply argue that we are morally entitled to attribute harms to offenders, and that the significance of harm to victims gives us reason to do so.

Similar things can be said about the significance of harm in the criminal law's communications to the general public. To illustrate, consider how harm might influence our reaction to the case of the dangerous driver. Whilst we will be angry upon hearing of the case in which no harm is caused, the case in which the pedestrian is killed will provoke additional responses: for example, sympathy for the victim's family, indignation at his undeserved suffering, or sadness at the loss of his future. Such reactions are uniquely appropriate to the case in which harm occurs. We may even wish to encourage them as expressions of fellow feeling, and therefore important foundational elements of our sense of justice.[51] Again, this is not to deny that there might also be undesirable reactions that we ought not to give effect to; the negative influence of retributive public sentiment on criminal justice policy is familiar enough. However, recognizing the ways in which harm is reasonably a matter of public importance need not involve this.

To understand why the public has a legitimate interest in communications of this kind, we must once again look to the moral role of the criminal law in public life. Crimes are often distinguished as public wrongs: they interfere with values which are shared or protected by the political community.[52] However, the criminal law is also public in nature because its *practices* are public. When people are charged with a criminal offence, they are called to

---

[50] The controversy surrounding the use of victim impact statements in sentencing decisions illustrates these concerns: see A. Ashworth, 'Victim Impact Statements and Sentencing' [1993] *Criminal Law Review* 498.

[51] Rawls (n 48 above) § 71.

[52] Compare R. A. Duff and S. E. Marshall, 'Criminalization and Sharing Wrongs' (1998) 11 *Canadian Journal of Law and Jurisprudence* 7; G Lamond, 'What is a Crime?' (2007) 27 *Oxford Journal of Legal Studies* 609.

answer to their fellow citizens, in the name of their fellow citizens.[53] In systems where criminal cases are tried by jury, it may also be their fellow citizens who pass judgement on them. Crimes are thus 'public' in the sense that their prosecution and punishment is carried out by the state, in our name. Because of this, we have a stake in how the practices of criminal justice are carried out, as well as the substantive contents of the criminal law. Again, this suggests that the state has reason to look beyond the culpability of offenders in determining what and how to communicate through the criminal justice process. So long as we are morally permitted to attribute harms to offenders, the demands of fairness to each citizen suggest that we may also be justified in doing so.

This further contributes to explaining what would be absurd about a criminal law that imposed liability only for volitions. It would seem odd— perhaps even offensive—for the state to act as if there were nothing materially different about cases in which harm occurs from cases in which it does not. To better understand this, we can consider a specific aspect of criminal law that would be different under a volition-based system. For example, imagine that the state began convicting people who kill intentionally not of murder but of 'acting with intent to kill'. Imagine further the trial of a person accused of this offence, when that person had succeeded in killing. Part of what we would find odd about such a spectacle is doubtless that it would differ greatly from what we are accustomed to. However, the greater part of the absurdity lies in the use of a criminal court—the foremost moral forum of our political community—to discuss a series of events whilst deliberately ignoring a morally significant aspect of them. Given the public nature of criminal justice, this would effectively amount to a wrongful denial of the significance of harm *to us*.

IV. How Harm Should Influence Criminal Liability

All of this suggests that the state has good reason to make criminal liability sensitive to resulting harm. Given that there can be no inherent moral objection to attributing harm to those who have caused it, criminal liability for resulting harm is therefore justifiable in the absence of competing considerations. In this final section, I will discuss precisely *how* harm should influence criminal liability. Due to constraints of space, this discussion will be generalized and undesirably brief. What follows should therefore be

---

[53] R. A. Duff, *Answering for Crime* (Oxford: Hart, 2007) ch 2.

understood as preliminary and exploratory, open to further comment and expansion. Nevertheless, I hope that it will prove worthwhile to at least begin contemplating the practical implications of the above theoretical analysis. In this spirit, I will consider the proper impact of resulting harm in two areas: namely, offence definitions and decisions to criminalize.

Of course, in considering these two areas I must inevitably neglect other contexts in which resulting harm can and does make a difference to criminal liability. Most obviously, I neglect to discuss liability to punishment.[54] This is regrettable, as punishment is the context in which the issues surrounding the justice of criminal liability for resulting harm are most vividly illustrated. However, both the justification of punishment and the criteria for its apportionment are notoriously difficult and contested topics.[55] Because of this, it is difficult to say much about how resulting harm should affect punishment that readers of different theoretical inclinations would agree upon. Punishment is therefore a more apt question to leave aside here than offence definitions or criminalization decisions. I take this option in the hope that doing so will not prejudice the remainder of this chapter.

Bearing these caveats in mind, let us turn first to offence definitions. What conclusions can we draw from our discussion so far about how resulting harm might legitimately affect these? First, recall that there is no inherent moral objection to attributing harms to those agents that cause them. Second, we have just seen that the state also has good reason to impose liability for causing harm, because of what this communicates to offenders, victims, and the public. One way in which the state can make liability sensitive to harm is to attribute that harm to offenders by convicting them of causing it, as well as of acting culpably. This requires including harm in the definition of offences. For example, the state might create distinct offences of dangerous driving and causing death by dangerous driving, or of assault and manslaughter.

As we saw in part III, considerations of justice seem to militate in favour of such an approach. However, we have also encountered a potential *injustice* associated with it: namely, the unjust societal treatment to which the state may expose those who it convicts of causing harm. Following the observations made in part II, it may not trouble us that the driver who causes harm is labelled as a killer. As we saw there, this is simply a reflection of the consequences that are attributable to her; it does not entail any judgement

---

[54] There are also other less obvious but nevertheless significant ways in which resulting harm might influence criminal liability: for example, through police and prosecutorial decision-making.

[55] For overviews of suggested principles of punishment, see R. A. Duff and D. Garland (eds), *A Reader on Punishment* (Oxford: OUP, 1994); H. L. A. Hart, 'Prolegomenon to the Principles of Punishment' in his *Punishment and Responsibility* 2nd edn (Oxford: OUP, 2008); N. Lacey, *State Punishment: Political Principles and Community Values* (London: Routledge, 1988) ch 2.

about her culpability. However, the state cannot hope to educate citizens in such fine points of moral theory. Because of the independent motivation for anger that the occurrence of harm provides, citizens may therefore unreflectively judge that the driver who kills is more culpable because of the harm that she has caused, and treat her accordingly. By including harm within offence definitions, the state risks encouraging such behaviour.

In choosing whether or not to include harm in offence definitions, the state is therefore faced with a choice between two possible injustices. On the one hand, by excluding harm, it fails to include morally significant information in its communications about criminal cases. On the other, by including harm, it risks exposing those offenders who cause harm to unjust treatment by their peers. Which option the state should choose will thus depend on which injustice is the least grave. We can expect this to vary from case to case. For instance, the kind of treatment that an intentional killer will receive when convicted of murder may not seem gravely unjust, particularly when compared to the likely treatment of attempted murderers. By contrast, we will probably be concerned about the fate of the 'one-punch killer' who is convicted of a homicide offence, compared to those who are convicted of similarly culpable assaults.

How might we explain the intuitive difference between these two cases? One possible explanation concerns the extent to which the respective offenders had adequate opportunities to avoid the excessive blame that the attribution of harm precipitates. Liability to such negative consequences—and thus also the inclusion of harm within offence definitions—is more easily justifiable to the extent that one had such opportunities. Generally speaking, offenders who are guilty of *attacks* might easily have avoided having resulting harms attributed to them. This is because attacks are, by definition, intended to cause harm.[56] Assuming that we are generally capable of choosing autonomously, it is thus ordinarily easy to avoid liability for harmful attacks; one can simply choose not to act in this way. Murderers come into this category. They are successful attackers. We may therefore feel that exposing them to excessive blame by attributing harm to them is not gravely unjust, for they chose to bring that harm about.

We can contrast attacks with *endangerments*. Unlike attacks, endangerments merely expose people to risks of harm; they are not aimed at causing it. Indeed, one might conceivably endanger another whilst desiring not to harm that other. Because of this feature, an offender's chance to avoid liability for endangered harm will often be inadequate. For example, consider the

---

[56] On the distinction between attacks and endangerments, see R. A. Duff, *Answering for Crime* (Oxford: Hart, 2007) ch 7.

one-punch killer. Although this offender attacks his victim's bodily integrity, he only endangers with respect to the victim's life. He may not even contemplate the possibility that death might result from his actions. As such, an offence that potentially imposes liability for death as a result of any endangerment of bodily integrity – such as the current English man-slaughter offence – may not present a fair chance to avoid liability for that harm. Such provisions make offenders liable to be treated as culpable killers by their peers even when they choose only some less harmful course of action.

Several factors will make a difference to our judgements of the fairness of offences of harmful endangerment. For example, how foreseeable must the risks imposed by the prohibited conduct be? And to what extent are defendants required to be aware of these risks? In English law, one need only act in a way which a *reasonable person* would be aware carries a risk of *some* harm in order to be guilty of manslaughter, if that conduct is unlawful and results in death.[57] Most will agree that such an offence does not give actors a fair chance to avoid being treated as a culpable killer. However, the precise limits of this sentiment are unclear. Must all elements of harm in the definitions of endangerment offences be accompanied by culpability requirements in order to be fair? If so, what level of culpability should be required? I will not attempt to answer these questions here.[58] It will suffice to say for the moment that, in contrast to offences prohibiting attacks, offences prohibiting harmful endangerment will often raise concerns of fairness regarding the societal treatment to which they expose offenders.

We can turn now to criminalization decisions. I argued above that the state has reason to make criminal liability sensitive to resulting harm. Given that the criminalization of conduct is a necessary condition of criminal liability for that conduct, might resulting harm legitimately influence decisions to criminalize? Again, the discussion so far suggests that it might. In part III, I argued that the class of cases in respect of which a re-affirmation of victims' claims may be due coincides—albeit not perfectly—with the class of cases in which harm occurs. Because the criminal law cannot play its role in confirming the moral worth of victims unless the conduct concerned is criminalized, there is thus often an additional reason to criminalize harmful behaviour.

As promised above, I will now go into a little more detail about the relationship between harm and the need to re-affirm the claims of victims. Once

---

[57] *Church* [1965] 2 All ER 72, CCA. The Law Commission's most recent proposals would improve on this only slightly, requiring a defendant to be 'aware' that his conduct 'involved a serious risk of causing some injury': *Murder, Manslaughter and Infanticide* (Law Com No 304, 2006).

[58] For consideration of the view that harm elements of criminal offences should always be accompanied by corresponding mental elements, see J. Horder, 'A Critique of the Correspondence Principle in Criminal Law' [1995] *Criminal Law Review* 759.

again, it will be helpful to distinguish here between attacks and endangerments. Consider attacks first. Recall that attacks are those actions which are
intended to cause harm. By their very nature, attacks will thus usually have
specific victims (or at least specific targets) even when they do not result in
harm. As such, the state still has the relevant additional reason to criminalize
failed attacks—or, in the terminology of the criminal law, *attempts.* Whilst we
have none of the corresponding reasons to document harm in attempt cases,
we will usually still have reason to re-affirm the moral claims of specific
persons.

We can contrast attempts with cases of harmless endangerment. Whilst
harmless endangerment can sometimes have specific victims, this is not
generally the case as it is with attempts. For example, consider once more
the case of the dangerous driver. When she goes round the blind corner, she
may endanger a specific pedestrian who narrowly avoids being harmed.
However, she may endanger only a general class of people: say, 'people
who might have been walking on the footpath at the relevant time'. In this
latter case, there is no need to re-affirm the claims of specific persons and,
correspondingly, no additional reason to criminalize the driver's conduct.
This suggests that we have no general reason to criminalize harmless endangerment of the kind that we have to criminalize attempts.

Of course, it does not follow from this that the criminalization of harmless
endangerment is unjustifiable. However, it does follow that there may be
some cases in which the occurrence of harm will make a difference to whether
some type of endangerment ought to be criminalized at all. We have already
seen that attacks are autonomously chosen in a way that endangerments need
not be; thus, offences prohibiting the endangerment of a given interest are
inherently more difficult to justify than offences prohibiting attacks against
that interest. Furthermore, harmless endangerment does not generally give
rise to a need to re-affirm the moral claims of victims. The case for criminalizing harmless endangerment is therefore doubly disadvantaged when
compared to the case for criminalizing attacks. When endangerment results
in harm, however, one of these disadvantages is not present. It is thus
conceivable that harmfulness may prove conclusive in the decision to criminalize such conduct.

There is much more detail to add here. I do not mean to suggest that every
token of attempted crime is justifiably criminalized, or that we should always
be sceptical about criminalizing harmless endangerment. Rather, I merely
mean to make some general observations about these two kinds of offence.
Nevertheless, these observations might prove important, as the law must
inevitably deal to some extent in generalizations. Generally speaking, the
state has reason to criminalize attempts of a kind that it does not always have

to criminalize harmless endangerment. This contributes to explaining the current state of English criminal law, in which there is no general offence of endangerment that corresponds to the general offence of attempt.[59] The criminalization of attempts is generally justifiable, because attempts usually have specific victims and the relevant prohibitions do not impact greatly on our autonomy. However, neither of these statements is true of harmless endangerment. We may therefore do best to continue to approach the criminalization of such conduct on a case-by-case basis.

V. Conclusions

In this chapter I have explored why and how the state may justifiably impose criminal liability for resulting harm. I began by exploring the problem of resultant moral luck, arguing that we should distinguish between the attribution and culpability senses of moral blameworthiness. I demonstrated that we have no reason to make attribution sensitive to what is within an agent's control, and thus that there can be no inherent objection to attributing to offenders the harms that they have caused. I also showed that the best construction of our intuitions does not support the subjection of our blaming practices to resultant luck. I then went on to argue that the communicative function of the criminal law gives the state reason to attribute harms to offenders, because of what doing so communicates to those offenders, as well as to victims and the general public. Regarding the latter two, I argued that justice may even compel such communication. Finally, I tentatively explored precisely how resulting harm might influence criminal liability in two contexts: offence definitions and criminalization decisions. I argued that it might properly affect both, but that different considerations will apply to attacks and endangerments in determining the proper extent of its influence.

---

[59] Criminal Attempts Act 1981 s 1. For an example of a more general offence of reckless endangerment—albeit one pertaining only to risks of death and serious injury—see s 211.2 of the American Model Penal Code.

4

Criminalizing SM: Disavowing the Erotic, Instantiating Violence

Sharon Cowan[1]

[T]he story of SM can be seen as a battleground for the transformation of intimacy.

Langdridge and Butt, 2004, p 48

I. Introduction

This chapter explores the issue of consent to sadomasochism (SM), and the effects of criminalizing consensual SM activities. Catherine Elliot and Claire de Than (2007) argue for a unitary and consistent legislative definition of consent across the criminal law. Alternatively, in applying both feminist and queer perspectives, I want to argue for a more localized and context-specific conceptualization and application of consent in the criminal law. This chapter focuses specifically on consent discourses that dominate the subject(s) of sadomasochist sex, and the extent to which they interact with other governing (liberal) concepts such as harm, privacy, and dignity.

To begin I should briefly clarify my terms. SM is shorthand for sadomasochism—sometimes also referred to as BDSM (bondage/discipline, dominance/submission, and sadism/masochism). I am consciously using both terms together—where both sadism and masochism are present there is a shared giving/receiving of pleasure that is not present where one party inflicts violence on another purely for their own sadistic pleasure and without any

[1] I am immensely grateful to Sandra Marshall and Victor Tadros for detailed comments on an earlier draft, and for feedback from participants at the AHRC-funded Criminalization Workshops. Thanks also to the volume's editors for their support and patience.

regard to the recipient's will or desire. The unilateral exercise of sadist cruelty, and its criminalization, is therefore not the focus of my chapter.[2]

SM is usually understood as an erotic interest in the giving and receiving of painful physical or psychological stimulation in a context of power and control. Sadism and masochism have both been the subject of psychiatric categorization (Krafft-Ebing, 1965) and appear in the American Psychiatric Association's Diagnostic Statistical Manual as psychiatric disorders (APA, 2000), though to be categorized as such, the person has to act on SM 'urges' with someone who does not consent, or they have to cause the 'sufferer' some distress. In the criminal cases that deal with SM (some of which are discussed herein), SM is portrayed as an extreme, minority sexual practice, and one that is in desperate need of criminal regulation. I have argued elsewhere that although there may be a need for some regulation, the current form of criminalization of SM is disproportionate, unnecessary, and probably unenforceable. Criminal law in Scotland and in England and Wales, as applied to SM, constructs responsible, heteronormative sexual subjects as distinct from irresponsible, risky sexual deviants (Cowan, 2010a).[3] In this chapter I will analyze further the regulatory effects of the criminalization of all SM, and the ways in which the erotic and sexual practices of sexual subjects are disavowed in favour of an understanding of SM as unlawful injury. The supposed 'moral magic' of consent (Hurd, 1996) will form a key part of the discussion to follow, as well as an analysis of the normative role that consent, harm, and to a lesser extent dignity and privacy, play in constructing and informing the criminalization of SM activities.

By accepting the current terms of the SM debate, that is, by accepting the regulatory framework produced by liberal conceptions of consent, harm, dignity, and privacy, we allow the criminal law to ignore the specificities of SM sexual expression and desire, and are in danger of limiting sexual freedoms only to responsible sexual subjects. Rather, the criminal law might acknowledge the ways in which sexual behaviours and desires defy neat binary

---

[2] I accept that like non-SM sex, SM can be enjoyed for monetary purposes as well as sexual pleasure in and of itself. I include these instances as consensual, shared, and mutual experiences of SM, in contrast to instances where the sadistic/masochistic pleasure is gained from the infliction of non-consensual violence.

[3] Briefly, by heteronormative I do not simply mean norms that promote heterosexuality as opposed to non-heterosexuality, but rather the normative structuring of (good) heterosexuality as familial, monogamous, reproductive, and so on, and the extension of this normative framework to certain kinds of non-heterosexuality. That is, those who may historically have been deemed deviant, such as transgender or homosexual individuals, are brought within the protective scope of law if they mimic this narrow, traditional model of heterosexuality. For discussion see Cowan (2009); Diduck (2001). The term homonormativity has also been used to describe a form of Lesbian, Gay, Bisexual, Transgender (LGBT) politics that fails to challenge heterosexual norms (Duggan 2003; Wilkinson 2009).

categorization such as normal/deviant, sex/violence, and so on. Criminal law decision-makers and policy-makers should pay more attention to feminist critiques of gendered, binary systematization of sex, gender, and sexuality, but also to queer legal theory critiques, which apply to law a particular blend of postmodern and post-structuralist social theories of sexuality, and problematize dichotomized thinking around issues of masculinity/femininity, sex/gender, heterosexuality/homosexuality, and so on (see for example Fuss, 1989; Duggan and Hunter, 1995; Stychin, 1995; Halley, 2006). It is also notable that decisions about criminalization in this area often occur without proper regard to sociological research that explores the range of complex socio-sexual practices that are labelled as SM, and the meaning of such practices to participants.

In short, while acknowledging the tensions between the two discourses (Fineman et al, 2009), I aim to bring feminist and queer perspectives to bear upon the question of how we criminalize SM, in order to better understand how the criminal law might promote respect for and protection of bodily integrity and sexual intimacy, while attempting to avoid the constraints of overly deterministic and dualistic categorizations. In order to explore these issues it is first necessary to say a brief word about the current rules on SM in the UK.

A. The regulation of SM in the UK

Unlike the approach in sexual offences, where a lack of consent is seen to be part of the substantive offence that the prosecution must prove, in non-sexual assaults the criminal law in the UK treats consent as a potential defence, depending on the level of assault. The question of whether it makes a difference to say that consent is a defence or part of the offence in SM cases will be discussed below.

In England and Wales, it was held under *R v Brown*[4] and subsequent SM cases such as *R v Emmet*[5] that—established exceptions aside (such as tattooing, sport, medical treatment, and 'horseplay')—assaults amounting to less than actual bodily harm could be lawful if valid consent was given, but that any injury amounting to, or more serious than, actual bodily harm could not be justified by consent. Presumably then those activities which risk actual bodily harm but which do not in fact cause such harm could be charged as attempted assaults. In Scotland, following the rule that one cannot consent to

---

[4] [1994] 1 AC 212.
[5] *The Times*, 15 October 1999.

an assault (*HMA v Smart*),[6] the court decided in *HMA v McDonald*,[7] the only criminal case in Scotland to address the permissibility of SM, that even assuming that his wife had consented, the accused could not plead a defence of consent to acts of extreme violence which had ultimately ended in his wife's death. For the purposes of this chapter I understand the 'no consent to assault' rule to operate across the UK, despite subtle differences in approach to and expression of this rule as between the two jurisdictions (Cowan, 2010a).

I now turn to discuss the concept of consent itself, and explore the ways in which the criminalization of SM demonstrates the difficulties of relying on consent as a threshold concept, where it is determinative of criminal liability. In what follows I will examine how consent interacts with other concepts currently relied upon in criminalization discourses—dignity, harm, and privacy—to produce an impoverished and discriminatory view of certain sexual subjects.

II. Consent

A. Consent as a threshold term—is it useful in the SM context?

According to Hurd, consent carries a certain kind of moral magic, and essentially distinguishes the morally permissible from morally impermissible: 'Consent derives its normative power from the fact that it alters the obligations and permissions that collectively determine the rightness of others' actions' (Hurd, 1996, p 124). Consent is therefore crucial both instrumentally and normatively, for assessing criminal wrongdoing. What part does consent play in the SM context?

While some argue that SM involves violence and harm to participants, and that consent is therefore irrelevant—what I will call the 'harm trumps consent' approach, others would argue either that a voluntary, self-regarding choice negates harm, or that harm that is consented to is not the kind of harm that should concern the criminal law—the 'consent trumps harm' approach.[8]

The harm trumps consent approach is problematic in that it is likely to be over-inclusive in its criminalization ambitions, overriding the autonomy of those who have freely chosen a particular path. Sometimes the criminal law is

---

[6] 1975 JC 30.

[7] 2004 SCCR 161.

[8] I have presented these as two opposing positions for ease of exposition, in full knowledge that there are more nuanced approaches. Thanks to Victor Tadros for reminding me of this point.

said to be warranted in its imposition of sanctions for willingly chosen actions, since the principle of paternalism allows for individual choice to be overridden in the actor's own best interests. But the debate over the permissibility of paternalism in the criminal law is a thorny one. First of all, there may be different kinds of actions and reasons for such action that get conflated within the term 'paternalism' (Sunstein, 1986, pp 1138–9; Feinberg, 1986, p 5). Secondly while pure paternalism seems generally to fly in the face of autonomous choice, there may well be individual instances where there are good reasons for paternalism to prevail, and some philosophers are arguing for assessment of specific examples of paternalism rather than a defence of paternalism per se (Husak, 1981). Others take the view that paternalism is not necessarily the 'enemy of autonomy and dignity' (Wright, 1995, p 1433), since paternalistic action by a parent or indeed by the state can in fact promote the long-term interests of the individual, interests such as freedom and autonomy. Personal sovereignty is not absolute, and can be measured in degrees, just like other values such as rationality and voluntariness (Shafer-Landau, 2005, p 190) and one has to balance, alongside the strong presumption against interference, other factors such as the gravity or irreparability of the harm caused, the probability and preventability of the harm, and the centrality of the activity to be controlled within the actor's life (Shafer-Landau, 2005, p 187). Nonetheless, it is accepted in these accounts that there is at least a prima facie objection to paternalism (Husak, 1981) and that there must be some limits to paternalistic intervention; indeed Sunstein advocates 'regulatory caution' when paternalism and autonomy are in conflict (1986, p 1169).

However the consent trumps harm approach also presents problems, since one's freedom and capacity to make a voluntary choice exist, as Feinberg accepts, in degrees. That is to say, consent is always constrained—to a greater or lesser extent, depending on your political perspective. Catharine MacKinnon, for example, has argued (1989) that under current social conditions of inequality, women's consent is always suspect. MacKinnon's theory of women's sexuality posits that since women are commonly subjected to coercive pressure about sex/gender roles and about sexual intercourse itself, it is impossible to know whether or not a woman who says she wants to be dominated, beaten, or forced to commit sexual acts, is only doing so because she has been conditioned to see her sexuality in a masochistic way (1989, see particularly chapter 7). More nuanced feminist accounts have critiqued the concept of consent as it applies across a range of areas of law, not just criminal law. Common legal understandings and uses of consent, it has been argued, do not capture either the wrongs that can be done to women or the ways in which they express desire, and construct women in particularly constraining ways (see the essays in Hunter and Cowan (eds), 2007).

Another strand of this approach is to suggest that even if the initial agreement to engage in SM is truly consensual, we ought not to respect that choice because such relationships are risky and open to abuse. This argument is somewhat akin to Feinberg's objection to slavery contracts (as discussed by Shafer-Landau, 2005, p 177). This latter kind of argument has been applied to the criminalization of SM along the following lines: even if the motive and intention of some may not be to harm as such, or may even be to promote the interests of participants, the criminal law cannot tell the difference between these interest-promoting cases and the truly harmful and abusive (that is, the coerced and non-consensual) cases, and so in order to protect as many people as possible, the law should treat all cases as assaults rather than consensual sex—'It is better that the law protect against amateurs and punish true sadists than condone intimate violence' (Hanna, 2001, p 288). In other words, it is better to prohibit some voluntary choices than allow sexual abuse. This is a pragmatic acknowledgement of the difficulties of ascertaining 'true' consent.

Obviously we should not take every claim of consent at face value. Even if SM were lawful, and the claim were to be one of 'lawful activity gone wrong', the jury might still judge the encounter to be non-consensual and convict the accused. Any claim of consent must be open to scrutiny and its context and meaning fully examined before being accepted, particularly where one party is not able to testify. In the Scottish case of *McDonald*,[9] the accused was originally charged with murder, and gave evidence that the couple had previously engaged in SM sex, that the wife had consented to this episode of SM, and that he had not realized that he had on this night in question 'gone too far'. However, these rather gruesome facts are hardly representative of the range and number of sado-masochistic encounters in which SMers engage. SM is also portrayed by the judges in *Brown* as inherently injurious and extreme, and participants are understood to be driven by sexual deviancy, even though none of the participants required medical attention. But clearly not all SM activity ends in death or serious injury. Weinberg et al note in their ethnographic study of SM over six years in San Francisco and New York that '[T]he traditional model generalizes to the whole of sadomasochism the activities and experiences of those persons most likely to come to the attention of clinicians' (1984, p 388). Researchers have shown that those participating in SM are involved in a wide array of activities, for a wide

---

[9] 2004 SCCR 161.

variety of reasons, and engage in acts that exist along a spectrum of pain. Participants in Beckmann's (2001) study of SMers saw their behaviour as less risky than 'regular' (ie penetrative) sex; as a response to HIV and AIDS, and, because of the focus on non-genital erogenous areas, SM was embraced as a way to promote safer sex. In this study, both heterosexual and gay male subjects also reported SM sex as a way of avoiding the normative constraints of penetrative sex. It is in this sense that Pa positions SM as part of the feminist project of exploring and creating a 'post-procreative sex jurisprudence' (2001, p 91).

And in any case, as Bergelson argues, the fact that a practice or a rule can be abused does not justify its prohibition (2007, p 188)—we do not outlaw all penile penetrative sex on the basis that there is some rape. The criminal law's task is that of separating out the consensual from the non-consensual. Thus, notwithstanding the (rare) extreme cases, SMers could look to law to protect those who really do not consent to SM sex in the same way that we look to law to protect those who really do not consent to 'regular' sex.[10]

Now, there might be good reason to be more suspicious of apparent consent in cases where more extreme injury is inflicted, and the question of degree of permissible injury is explored below. However, the main objection to the pro-consent position here is that sometimes, something that looks like consent is not. This reflects the concern about consent being given under pressure or coercion, or where there is a history of violence, threats, or abuse. Some would include here cases of SM sold through prostitution, since it is well established that some sex work takes place under circumstances of undue influence, psychological or physical pressure, or abuse, or economic desperation. But these issues are apparent in the non-SM context too. Feminists and others have struggled and argued about whether and how to rely on consent as a threshold concept. They have either advocated the rejection of consent as the defining concept in rape and sexual assaults because it cannot account for cases outwith the paradigm of force (eg MacKinnon, 1989), or attempted to reimagine the concept as a thicker concept that can allow for agency, and take underlying questions of capacity and coercion into account in a more nuanced way (eg Cowan, 2007; Munro, 2007; Scoular, 2011).[11]

Ultimately, despite arguments that, at least in sexual assault cases, it may be possible to imagine laws without consent (Tadros, 2006) I am not arguing here for a complete rejection of the concept of consent. Unlike George Wright (1995), I do not think that in the world as we know it, replacing

---

[10] The corollary of this position is that rules which outlaw rather than protect consensual SM behaviour are 'futile' because they don't change people's preferences anyway. See Sunstein (1986).

[11] For a neat history of feminist struggles around consent see Jeffreys (1993).

consent with a concept such as trust, will protect those who have been injured or wronged (even as I acknowledge that consent does not always do so either), nor do I accept that 'consent is the last refuge of the mutually alienated' (1995, p 1438). Jeffreys argues that any use of the concept of consent must only be strategic since it is the language that male-made law understands, but that long-term, we must 'reconceptualise sexuality so that consent will seem a bizarre and outdated notion' (1993, p 173). For the moment I take the pragmatic view that consent is the current language of law, and that in many circumstances it is the best tool we have (so far) to measure expressions of autonomy and choice and to delineate criminal from lawful actions, and that it might be possible to some extent to try to make it a richer, thicker concept that more fully reflects the complex nature of (dis)agreements (Cowan, 2007). What would such a reconceptualized consent look like? Monica Cowart (2004) argues, for example, that consent exists only where both the will and the action of both parties are positively present and converge. Where they do, the law can deem the behaviour consensual. This is of course only one model we could explore. But although the current definitions and implementations of consent fall short of ideal in their aims to enhance autonomy and protect the vulnerable, we can continue to use consent strategically. At the same time, feminists and others should aim to improve the criminal law's ability to properly discern in practice who is consenting and who is not, by exploring other models and concepts alongside consent, such as negotiation (Anderson, 2005).

Consequently, as we continue to use consent as a threshold concept, it must be possible for the criminal law to adopt a framework that could assess the validity of consent in SM. However, difficulties still remain in discerning consent in practice, often with respect to issues of criminal burdens of proof. Arguably because of its more explicitly contractual nature, this task may well be easier in (some) SM encounters, and therefore the law should not outlaw all SM on the basis that some encounters are not truly consensual. As Weinberg et al note, for many SMers, 'a person who was not consenting would be considered neither into SM nor sexually desirable' (1984, p 385). Many SM encounters take place under conditions of explicit agreement and boundary making. In this respect consent as it operates for many participating in SM goes beyond a formal or thin consent model towards the substantive realities of mutuality and communication.[12]

Nonetheless, the question of establishing (and in Scotland, corroborating) a lack of consent is a pressing problem in sexual assault cases, and feminists

---

[12] See Law Commission (1995) part 10. See also Archard (1998) ch 7.

have extensively critiqued the way that consent is arbitrarily operationalized by police, lawyers, judges, and juries (see for example Finch and Munro, 2005; Ellison and Munro, 2010; Kelly et al, 2005; Lees, 2002; Temkin and Krahé, 2008). Some critics have suggested that where a non-consensual SM encounter gets as far as court, the existing culture of disbelief that surrounds women who bring sexual violence claims will allow men who sadistically sexually assault women to rely on the same problematic discourses that allow rapists to evade conviction, thereby concluding that consent cannot in practice delineate those who play by rules from those who do not (Hanna, 2001). Consequently, although decriminalization may challenge the discriminatory heteronormative constraints of the current law, the effect in practice may be to further legitimize the violence that pervades coercive and abusive heterosexual relationships (Jeffreys, 1993). Contemporary research highlights the continuing relevance of these difficulties, and feminists have argued for, amongst other things, more in-depth training for the legal profession and judiciary, the use of expert witnesses in court, and more widespread public debate on the need for communication, respect, and conversations about sexual intimacy (Temkin and Krahé, 2008; Ellison and Munro, 2010). Notwithstanding these worries about the practical operation of the criminal justice system and problems of proof, if we are to keep the current legal framework for rape, where consent sets apart those acts that are lawful from those that are not, then we ought to be able to do the same to distinguish between consensual/non-consensual SM activities. For the time being at least, then, we could continue to strategically invest in the possibility of consent as an emancipatory concept, in the absence of anything better.

B. Consent as part of the offence or as defence?

Currently, consent operates as a potential defence to an assault charge, though, as *R v Brown* makes clear, only in certain well-established situations such as surgery, refereed sports, tattooing, and so forth. If we take criminal law to be reflective of (at least some) social views, currently we do not perceive SM to be a valued sexual choice or preference. Rather it is treated as unlawful violence. But this is a normative judgement as to the kinds of sex that society deems normal, meaningful, and thereby lawful. It has been argued forcefully (Bibbings and Alldridge, 1993; Bamforth, 1994) that SM should be treated in law as primarily sexual rather than violent behaviour. If we see SM as sex and not violence, when SM *is* non-consensual and the criminal law steps in, arguably consent should be part of the offence definition, as it is in other sexual offences. Having consent as part of the offence definition signals, as it does in the law of sexual offences generally, that because the behaviour is generally valued, (or at least tolerated), in society, and therefore the criminal law should not discourage it, it is prima facie lawful, unless consent is absent.[13] Where consent acts as a defence, the implication is that the act is not of value to society, that it should be discouraged, and is therefore prima facie unlawful, criminal sanction only being avoided if consent can be, and has been, secured. Therefore, there are normative implications of the position of consent here. 'Normal' sexual acts are, somewhat tautologically, defined as sex, and deemed to be lawful unless proven otherwise (via lack of consent), whereas deviant SM acts are assaults, and unlawful unless it can be proven that injuries experienced consensually were so minor as to amount to less than ABH. There are therefore two questions here—the normative positioning of consent in the current structure of criminal law; and the question of whether we should call SM sex or violence.

Firstly, and leaving aside the question of what degree of harm we could justifiably legitimize in the name of SM, discussed below, some might worry that if we were to make consent part of the offence and define SM as 'injury for erotic or sexual reasons without consent', this would mean that all assaults would require to have consent built in to the offence definition. Would this not send out the wrong signals, that assaults were deemed prima facie legitimate unless done without consent? The answer might be that only assaults that had a primarily sexual purpose would be treated in this way, because we value sex, but not assault. However this does not explain the issue of medical treatment—which is widely valued in society—where treatment that goes ahead without consent (and in the absence of a defence of necessity) is battery. The notion that perhaps we value the development of our sexual selves more than we value medical treatment does not seem very convincing. Perhaps my approach of recasting SM so that consent is part of the offence definition would lead us to reconsider whether other activities that are useful and valuable in society also ought to have consent as part of the offence definition rather than as a potential defence. While the objection may be made that this only involves further value judgements, it appears that judges already make these kinds of value judgements, in an unaccountable way, when deciding in cases such as *R v Brown* which assaults deserve to be exceptions to the 'no consent to assault' rule. By reconsidering the structural role of consent in SM cases, even if it leads to reconsideration of other

---

[13] This is in direct contrast to the kind of approach taken by Madden-Dempsey and Herring (2007) where sexual penetration per se requires justification.

'assault' cases such as medical treatment, we might at least prompt an open and transparent conversation about what sorts of activities we do value.

Secondly, can we with any certainty say that SMers are engaging in violence rather than sex? As discussed earlier, the courts in the UK (and in other jurisdictions) have taken the view that in SM cases, sex and violence are distinct and easily separable for the purposes of attributing liability; the majority decision in *Brown* is predicated on the idea that SM is primarily violence, not sex. Radical feminists writing about SM also argued that SM is not sex but violence. Indeed feminism was in the 1980s wrought by what has been called the 'sex wars'—a fierce debate over the question of, amongst other things, whether lesbian feminists who explored SM were escaping or indeed reiterating the problematic power dynamics of heterosexism. Feminists were divided—some saw SM as a challenge to existing sex/gender categories and roles (see eg Rubin, 1984), others believed it to be a re-enactment of heterosexual male dominance and an extension of masculinist models of sexuality into the lesbian world (Jeffreys, 1994). The latter position is based on the following sort of argument: since people's choices are socially constructed and constrained, what appear to be private, autonomous choices are in fact socially prescribed, and therefore these private preferences can be interfered with in order to promote long-term interests such as freedom and autonomy (the problem of course being in discerning the circumstances under which interference will promote rather than constrain such interests; see Sunstein, 1986, pp 1133, 1136).

In the particular context of the 'sex wars', radical feminists saw SMers as somehow suffering from false consciousness, and in particular that women who experienced a desire for submissive sex were in fact unconsciously constrained by the internalized norms of heterosexism, where male sexuality is seen to be more 'naturally' aggressive and domineering, and female sexuality is passive and recipient. For these feminists, patriarchy constrains 'the very structure of desire itself' (Hoople, 1996, p 194, citing Bartky). On the other hand, Wendy Brown (1995) has argued that feminists themselves, in asking for state intervention against institutionalized male dominance have here furthered the reach of institutional power to define certain acts as violence, and in so doing, have sacrificed emancipatory aims at the altar of (male) state regulation. A more 'sex radical' feminism[14] would read SM less as a result of the constraints of patriarchy and more as an opportunity for women to step outside traditional gendered socio-sexual scripts of passivity and victimhood, and away from gendered protectionism and paternalism (see

---

[14] For discussion see Cossman (2003, p 620).

Smart, 1995). Indeed pro-sex feminists of the sex wars era (and others since then) have argued strongly that for the most part, gender, sexuality, submission, and dominance play out in complex ways, and do not line up along simplistic, linear, heterosexual roles (see eg Califia, 1988; 2000).

Of course, this question of sex or violence is a complicated issue; feminists fought long and hard to have the offence of rape recast as an issue of gender violence and power relations, rather than an individualized problem of lust; they challenged the once (contemporary?) deeply held belief that rape was simply a problem of the oversexed male libido. Defining rape as violence has been a significant improvement in terms of highlighting men's accountability and responsibility for sexual violence. But while we should be wary of conflating sex and violence, the connection between sex and violence is evidenced in a number of ways. First there is no denying that rape is an act of violence which involves sex. Second, even if there is no overt physical force involved, sex without consent involves some level of inherent violence against the body (and psyche) of another—even 'normal' sexual intercourse can often cause pain and/or injury (for various physiological reasons).[15] Third, all too often we can see that in practice rape is often more easily evidenced by—and accredited through—signs of violence (indeed, a charge of rape historically necessitated proof of violence). Fourth, a more fundamental problem for the criminal law is that it is sometimes difficult to say precisely where sex ends and violence begins—by what criteria do we judge an act to be violence rather than sex? What are the elements of a sex act that distinguish it from an act of violence? How do we decide if an act belongs better in one category than another? If we cannot answer this question then it is difficult to see how the criminal law can justify drawing such a bright line between the two, and in doing so making normative judgements about what counts as healthy or 'good' sex.

The criminal law *could* take the step of allowing the participants themselves to make this judgement, by what Weinberg calls 'mutual definition' (1984, pp 386–7). There will clearly be cases where participants disagree, but the criminal law's job is to resolve such disputes, and so the stronger objection to allowing subjective labelling of sex/violence will be that the criminal law has an interest in setting down firm and clear boundaries for the purposes of transparency, consistency, and for communicative purposes. The problem is, however, that SM is not simply violence, and that to describe SM as violence and therefore criminal is to disavow not only the obvious sexual content and context of SM acts, but to disavow the erotic residue inherent within violence

---

[15] Indeed the late Andrea Dworkin believed that all penetrative sexual intercourse involved some level of 'violence'—see particularly Dworkin (1987).

itself. In 1953 Kinsey found that over 50 per cent of men and women have an erotic response to being bitten (Egan, 2006–7). Kinsey noted that scratching and biting frequently play a part in conventional sex, and that physiologically the response to pain is similar to orgasm (Weinberg et al, 1984).[16]

Thus, the only way to make normative sense of the criminal law's current treatment of SM is by separating sex and violence: by reading SM as a matter of violence rather than of sex, it can be placed within the category of criminal injury. Such a disavowal of the erotic is, however, quite unconvincing, since in SM violence and the erotic are inextricably bound up with each other; the violence cannot, without serious distortion, be separated from its erotic meaning. If we see sex and violence as truly separable, and we deem SM to be violence, *and* we treat consent as a potential defence rather than part of the offence definition, taken together these criminalization decisions highlight the process of heteronormative construction of certain kinds of sexual subjects as violent, perverted, and 'risky', as distinct from responsible non-SM sexual subjects, and as unworthy of the respect and protection of the criminal law.

III. Harm

A. Preventing harm to dignity or preventing 'private' choices?

Leaving consent aside for the moment, it is also important to interrogate the part played by harm in this debate. Of course there is a vast literature on the concept of harm and its use as a justification for criminalization.[17] As many theorists have demonstrated, however, the seemingly simple formula— prevent behaviour if it causes harm to others—is 'packed with ambiguity' (Sunstein, 1986, p 1131). If it were possible to consent to SM sex, it is not clear how the expression of these personal preferences could be harmful. This is not to argue that SM is a prima facie harm that can be transformed by the moral magic of consent, but rather, and in line with the argument above favouring consent as part of the offence definition, that consensual SM is lawful. The question remains then as to how there can be a setback to the interests of the 'victim' if the SM is desired, requested, begged for even?

---

[16] In contrast much of what we might recognize as BDSM does not cause physical pain or any form of injury at all (tying with handkerchiefs, verbal abuse, and humiliation in role play, etc).

[17] See of course the crucial work of Joel Feinberg, *The Moral Limits of the Criminal Law*. For cogent discussion see Duff (2001).

Those who support the criminalization of SM have also argued that the practice is harmful to participants' dignity, despite any apparent desire for SM. Drawing on the work of Antony Duff, Bergelson (2007) develops the argument that a person's chosen actions can be said to cause harm to the self even where they are freely chosen according to their own lights, and reflect a self-regarding furtherance of their interests. This is because such actions may yet involve harm to their dignity (or as Duff (1981) puts it, their 'humanity'), even where the participant themselves does not consider it so. Likewise, Wright (1995) argues that dignity should prevail over legally valid consent, since human dignity is a 'more fundamental value' than consent; a person cannot in any meaningful sense give up their dignity. While proper consent always invokes dignity considerations, dignity cannot be fully cashed out through consent alone.

The idea that certain kinds of behaviour can be degrading and therefore harmful, even if consented to, relies, as Bergelson says, upon an 'objective' notion of dignity rather than on the subjective state of mind of the consenting SMer (2007, p 217). This of course begs the question, as she acknowledges (2007, pp 217–18), of how to define dignity objectively, but it also illuminates the tension between allowing sexual subjects to define and construct their own sense of sexual selves, and the state's desire to limit the ways in which an individual can 'harm' herself (the most extreme examples of such harm are often said to be consenting to slavery, or death).

Frustratingly, dignity is frequently lacking in content in these sorts of accounts. The view that dignity is the overriding value is stated rather than explained and there is a lack of proper justification for the founding argument that the value of consent needs explaining in a way that the value of dignity does not (Wright, 1995, p 1424). There is also a striking similarity between the paternalistic and patronizing potential of these kinds of pro-dignity positions, and the false consciousness arguments of the radical feminists opposed to SM, discussed above. In short, there is a struggle, evident in the literature, between the need to allow for agency, and ensuring that a collective sense of social unease with certain apparently consensual practices is appropriately translated into prohibitions.

With respect to SM, whether or not a practice harms dignity or degrades and humiliates the participants may well be thought to be a question of the *degree* of injury or harm inflicted. However, treating the affront to dignity as a form of harm is more likely to invoke questions about of the *kinds* of sexual interactions that society values, and challenging what appears to be a circular justification for criminalization; it is criminal because it is humiliating because it is not the kind of sex we value. In other words, there are underlying and unstated normative principles driving the differentiation of normal (permissible, dignity enhancing) from abnormal (impermissible, degrading) sexual behaviours; *some* consensual encounters where activities result in injury (and in some cases even death)[18] are permissible (and do not harm dignity), *others* are not.

Is the state justified in restricting me from engaging in activity that it deems is harmful and degrading to me? Sunstein distinguishes between paternalism born out of society's request to the state to restrict its own preferences or what he calls society's 'second order preferences', (eg recent public smoking bans in the UK), from what he calls 'ordinary paternalism—a system in which majorities impose their will on minorities because they disapprove of the conduct in question' (1986, p 1141). The example of SM does not seem to be one where the majority, fearing weakness and susceptibility to temptation, has asked the government to criminalize SM for its own benefit. It is more like the 'ordinary' case that Sunstein refers to, where a majority wishes to prohibit behaviour of others, of which it disapproves.[19] Duff argues that criminalization is justified because the SM acts that participants have consented to have 'denied their humanity' even if the acts are not directly proscribed under the harm principle (2001, p 41). This kind of justification for paternalism is particularly at odds with the defence of SM as an expression of the kind of deeply held desires that reflect core values, or as 'exercises in human flourishing' (Deckha, 2007, p 457).

One critique of *Brown* then is that the law is not in fact preventing harm but rather is preventing the participants from acting in their own best interests since they are not allowed to exercise their sexual autonomy—and indeed this argument was made, via Article 8 of the European Convention on Human Rights, by the defendants in *Brown* at their appeal to the European Court of Human Rights.[20] Those who argue against criminalization, particularly with respect to *Brown*, have tended to argue (along Wolfenden[21] lines) that SM is a sexual practice that takes place in the privacy of the bedroom, a space where the law has no business being.

However, it must be possible to argue against paternalism without relying on privacy. Arguments in favour of the protection of individual autonomy and privacy are problematic for those who wish to undermine both the notion that sexuality be confined to the 'private' sphere, as well as those

[18] See the case of *R v Slingsby* [1995] Crim LR 570—for discussion see Cowan (2010a).
[19] Even if it were to be classified as a second order preference, where the majority seeks to bind itself, applying Sunstein's argument, arguably the criminalization of SM is 'objectionable or distorted' (p 1143).
[20] *Laskey, Jaggard and Brown v UK* (1997) 24 EHRR 39.
[21] The Wolfenden Committee Report (1957) recommended the decriminalization of homosexual acts committed in private.

who consider sexual autonomy an impoverished concept, incapable of escaping the overly individualistic, atomistic traps of liberalism. Feminists have criticized the application of both autonomy and the classic public/private divide to issues of sex/gender (see, for example, O'Donovan, 1985; MacKinnon, 1989; Olsen, 1993; Lacey, 1998). Likewise, while those in the queer camp recognize that the 'closet' of private life can work to protect non-heterosexuals from state intervention, and that life in the public sphere brings with it state regulation of behaviour, many still resist the trappings of a liberal rights discourse and demands for privacy. For example queer legal theorists such as Carl Stychin (1995) have argued strongly for the right to a public sexuality, and to sexual citizenship for marginalized minorities that does not depend on a liberal conception of privacy. Even though the language of rights is utilized, it need not necessarily invoke traditional liberal values; feminists and queers amongst others have tried to reimagine rights in less atomistic, more open-ended, relational, reflexive, and radical terms (see for example Herman, 1994; Stychin, 1995).

The central focus for queers then is 'our right to public *sexual dissent*' (Duggan, 1995, p 5), thus rejecting the language of private space, but rather claiming safe public space for sexualities (Richardson, 1996, p 15; see also Califia, 2000). As Beckmann (2001, p 71) (quoting Sarah Livitnoff) stated, 'we're not talking about what goes on in individual bedrooms, but about the acceptable public face of sex'. We are also not talking about 'toleration', but of presence, of challenge, and of confrontation. At its broadest, queer critics advocate 'resistance to regimes of the normal' (Warner, 1993, p xxvi). This resistance is not simply a negative reaction, but is also 'positive and dynamic and creative' (Halperin, 1995, p 66). One strategy in this project of publicizing of the lives of queers and sexual deviants such as SMers is to embrace and colonize the public debates prompted by cases such as *Brown*, in order to reflect a wider range of people's experience of sexual desire within legal discourse—what Mezey (1995, p 115) calls 'infiltration of the discourse'. According to this view, making the voices of SMers and others heard within public discourse allows for resistance against the normalizing and regulatory effects of laws based on assumptions about what counts as good and healthy sex.

However, in the battle to make SM more visible there remains a crucial question about *which* SM voices get heard in public debates. Some proponents of SM argue that criminalization not only directly punishes SMers but also contributes to the popular depiction of SM as immoral, transgressive, and so on, thus denying them sexual citizenship (Pa, 2001). On the other hand some critical scholars have recently pointed out that in popular culture, some types of SM have become more fashionable, and more mainstream.

Films such as *Secretary*, the press coverage of Max Mosley's libel suit,[22] music, literature, and adverts have all brought SM into the public imagination, and been vehicles for the portrayal of 'low-end' SM as kinky and titillating (rather than disgusting) (Wilkinson, 2009; Langdridge and Butt, 2004; Pa, 2001). However, Khan sees this popular culture embrace of kinky SM sex as having occurred only within 'particular heteronormative strictures' (2009, p 117) and that SM is more acceptable if portrayed as within heterosexual, monogamous, marital confines, as in *Secretary* itself (p 82). Likewise, Wilkinson warns against 'SM-normativity' whereby a 'heteropatriarchal' version of SM becomes the norm. Hanna (2001, p 286) argues that this process of mainstreaming has also problematically cast SM as an upper middle class activity, thereby also racializing it as white, despite the obvious racist connotations of slavery-type language that permeates SM discourses.

These questions of acceptability and transgression have also marked debates over other sexual 'anomalies'—for example, it appears that transgender people who behave and look 'just like us' are more likely to be socially tolerated (Cowan, 2009, p 116). In the SM 'community' those who do 'play by the rules' insist that (good) SM is 'safe, sane and consensual' (Pa, 2001, p 61), and as such are asking for assimilation within the law as responsible sexual citizens. Their claim is that 'extreme' SM is very much in the minority, and that SM is really about the eroticization of power relationships rather than violence in and of itself. This allows SMers to argue (in the same way that LGBT people have done) that really they are 'just like everyone else'—that their sexual preferences should not mark them out as different or transgressive. However SMers do not form a monolithic community and some remain marginalized even within the 'community' (Wilkinson, 2009, p 190). Alongside the call for legal and social acceptance, representing SM sex as an extension of the 'natural', there is a simultaneous move by others to represent the dissenting, transgressive, and oppositional face of SM (Langdridge and Butt, 2004). These are what Jeffreys (1993–4, p 182) calls 'rebel sadomasochists'.

Although the mainstreaming of (some) SM may be seen as domesticating, it is not unusual, as Jeffrey Weeks points out, for social movements to be seen

---

[22] *Mosley v News Group Newspapers Ltd* [2008] EWHC 1777 (QB). In 2008 Max Mosley, the president of the International Automobile Federation (which runs Formula One car racing) successfully sued the British tabloid newspaper *The News of the World* for breach of privacy when they reported on his SM sexual 'orgies' that were alleged to have Nazi overtones. Mr Justice Eady held that his activities were consensual, 'albeit unconventional', and thus he was entitled to privacy, and that there was no evidence of Nazi behaviour which would have justified disclosure in the public interest. Mosley received 'record' privacy damages of £60,000. See for example reports from the BBC at <http://news.bbc.co.uk/1/hi/7523034.stm>, last accessed February 2011.

as transgressive before moving to the point where they can and do make citizenship claims. Weeks emphasizes the dialectical nature of these kinds of claims—that each is in necessary conversation with the other, and that even in the claims to citizenship there are inherent trangressions and spaces for dissent, where both are essential for social change (Weeks, 1995).[23] It is therefore 'the proliferation of contradictory and often conflicting stories' (Wilkinson 2009, p 190) that will offer a route to challenging SM-normativity.

One issue that is ripe for exploration here, then, is the battle over representation of SM, and the question of whose voices are heard, who has the power to occupy public space in order to represent certain kinds of SM stories,[24] and how this plays in to the legal regulation of SM—should only those who mainstream, and play by the rules of advance agreement and consent, be said to engage in lawful activity? This is a challenging area, one which raises normative and practical concerns, since it is not clear whether 'consensual non-consensuality', or consent agreed upon after the event, would or should be legitimate even under more lenient SM laws.[25] But, as Hoople points out, even if SM practitioners *do* get to represent themselves, they may be read as stereotypical caricatures, because they are 'inserted into the dominant cultural codes that regulate the production of meaning within that field and which produce SM as kinky sex (eroticized misogyny, a cult of violence etc) in the first place' (1996, p 197). Other theorists are more optimistic about the potential of SM to upset dominant social norms and heteronormative codes of gender (as well as race and class), to reveal 'the performative status of the natural itself' (Butler, 1990, p 146).[26] Ultimately, these arguments illustrate the ongoing struggle within social discourse to define and represent SM. As such, the feminist/queer critiques of the criminalization of SM demonstrate the troubling ways in which law constructs and represents SM participants, ignores the specificity of their desires and experiences, and discounts the dissenting and confrontational voice of SMers who reject the mainstream, heteronormative, and strictly boundaried model of sexual citizenship on offer to them.

---

[23] Cited in Hines (2007).

[24] For a fuller discussion of power struggles in the representation of SM, see Hoople (1996).

[25] A similar issue has arisen in the context of rape; fierce debate over whether it is possible for someone to consent afterwards to sexual activity that was initiated when they were unconscious or asleep caused the Scottish Parliament serious drafting problems in the new Sexual Offences (Scotland) Act 2010. For comment see Cowan (2010b).

[26] However Butler does acknowledge that 'there is no guarantee that exposing the naturalized status of heterosexuality will lead to its subversion' (1993, p 231).

B. How much and what kind of SM harm should we criminalize?

The criminalization of SM might, simplistically, be said to aim at prohibiting violence and preventing harm. However, noteworthy in this kind of approach is the unhelpful interchangeability of terms such as harm, pain, injury, and violence. For example, is physical injury necessarily harmful? The answer must be 'Not always', since the courts recognize some injuries (such as those sustained through boxing, tattooing, and surgery) as not harmful or at least not the kind of harm that should be criminalized (it varies from case to case). Such injuries are inflicted consensually—indeed, in these examples, consent seems to be written into the action itself rather than formally operating as a defence, since allowing them is said to be in the public interest; the sportsmanship (sic) of boxing is commonly understood to be a good reason for deliberate violence.[27] And harm of course does not necessarily have to involve deliberate physical violence, since there can be a setback to one's other interests—mental health, property, autonomy, and other rights, for example—in the absence of physical violence.

Likewise, is causing pain violence? In the medical context, again painful treatment can be consented to, thus rendering it lawful and not battery. In the SM context, it seems counterintuitive to describe pain that is desired (for whatever end) as violence. Again, we return to the fundamental question of whether pain that is desired can ever be harmful, particularly if the pain is seen as a vehicle to another goal (treatment, or sexual pleasure) that is *generally* valued in society. Take for instance cosmetic surgery: the pain endured by those undergoing non-therapeutic facial cosmetic surgery can be consented to since the end result is the aesthetic (and thereby psychological) benefit to the patient. In SM the goal is sexual pleasure which generally speaking is a valued goal in society, though clearly this goal has historically been constrained by social expectations as to gender roles, the value of reproduction, and so on. However, to position pain as a justifiable means to the end of sexual pleasure, rather than trying to justify pain as a justifiable end leads us to assume that the law should allow SM acts in the context of sex, but prohibit those acts that are done for purely cruel sadistic or masochistic

---

[27] It seems clear that boxing is violent, while it may seem anomalous to describe piercing and tattooing as violent. Violence, as opposed to injury, seems to carry with it normative definitional power. It might be characterized, for example, as 'psychological or physical injury or attack *plus* intent to set back interests'. However the precise meaning of violence is beyond the scope of this chapter, and I follow Deckha (2007, fn 8) in bracketing this question in favour of focusing on the consent issue.

reasons. In other words, to use the terminology of the court in *Brown*, sex counts as a good reason for SM while pleasure in violence for its own sake does not.

But should there be a limit to the kind or extent of SM that the criminal law should allow? Should we be able to consent to any level of harm, to permanent injury, or even death? Unless we are willing to allow individuals to consent to any and all forms of harm, including requests for death, or for enslavement, the criminal law must draw the line somewhere. The English courts in *Brown* drew the line at actual bodily harm—injury causing (or surpassing) ABH cannot be consented to (unless in the context of one of the established exceptions). This seems inconsistent though with the later case of *Dica*[28] (which approved *Brown*), which stated that a person can risk the sexual transmission of HIV, if she knowingly consents to that risk. Applying *Brown* criminalizes not only the ABH caused through SM, but also the *risk* of infliction of ABH through SM. Those taking such risks could be prosecuted for attempted assault. That *Dica* allows consent to the risk of grievous bodily harm whereas *Brown* does not, seems to be because of the court's explicit assumption that the risk of HIV is just one of those risks that ('normal') sexual intercourse incurs (para 47). The law here is engaged in the (hetero) normative construction of certain kinds of sexual subjects; those who knowingly and consensually risk transmission of HIV (a potentially lethal disease) are depicted in *Dica* as normal, responsible sexual subjects who have made responsible choices, but those who knowingly and consensually risk injury through SM sex are portrayed in *Brown* to be irresponsible, deviant, out of control, and dangerous.[29]

Kelly Egan (2006–7) on the other hand has argued for decriminalization of injuries amounting to less than serious bodily harm, a position that would allow for most of the actions in *Brown* to be deemed lawful. Even if one accepts the argument for allowing consent to sexual activity that causes serious harm, consent to death or the endangerment of life is more problematic, arguments about euthanasia notwithstanding.[30] Sexual pleasure does not seem to offer a strong enough justification for causing death or endangering life. Here the balancing exercise of weighing up the individual freedom to act upon deeply held sexual desires against the state's power to intervene to protect a person from themselves allows some freedom for the individual, but not to the

---

[28] [2004] EWCA Crim 1103.
[29] See eg Lord Templeman's speech at p 235, para F; p 236 para G; or Lord Lowry's speech at p 255, para H).
[30] See Chapter 7.

point where they can consent to the most irreparable and permanent forms of self-harm.

Bergelson argues that the more serious the harm that one is ostensibly consenting to, the higher the degree of capacity and voluntariness we might expect from the person consenting to the act. This position could lead to the worrying conclusion that the most rational and voluntary among us could consent to being killed (though it might equally lead us to assume, somewhat circularly, that those requesting the most serious forms of apparently consensual self-harm such as withdrawal of treatment, do not have capacity at all). With respect to adult patients in the UK, the test laid down in the apposite case *Re C*[31] makes no distinction as between medical consent and refusal, and courts have been resolute in their commitment to the principle that a mentally competent patient can refuse treatment for good reason, bad reason, or no reason at all.[32] But are consent and refusal equivalent? It seems clear that a competent refusal of treatment should be respected. But what about the patient who requests and consents to a 'harmful' treatment? Those with apotemnophilia, who consent to a serious surgical intervention such as the removal of a healthy limb, are said to be suffering from body dismorphia, ie a psychological condition that impairs their capacity to judge the need for such an operation. The ethical basis for amputation is hotly debated in the UK but currently there is a strong argument being made that apotemnophiliacs ought to be able to access surgical amputation in order to 'treat' their condition (Dyer, 2000; Dua, 2010). Thus the notion that capacity tracks degree of harm does not necessarily follow.

Clearly there are distinctions to be made between decisions as to medical treatment, and consent to 'assault' through SM but one of those distinctions—that consent renders treatment but not assault non-criminal—is created by the criminal law itself. One might argue that medical treatment is a good in itself whereas physical harm to body for sexual rather than medical purposes (or other good reason) is not, but this simply restates the issue and begs more questions about the principled basis for the distinction. If we allow patients with capacity to make 'bad' choices for themselves, can we not also extend that to SMers?

---

[31] [1994] 1 All ER 819, the test of competence as to the refusal in question being that one has to be able to comprehend and retain treatment information, believe such information, and be able to weigh it in the balance to arrive at a choice.
[32] *Re T (Adult: Refusal of Medical Treatment)* [1992] 4 All ER 649.

IV. Conclusion

The current criminalization of SM demonstrates a neglect of the complex and nuanced specificities of people's sexual interactions. Contemporary criminal law appears to be trapped within unhelpful and often polarized debates about harm versus consent (Deckha, 2007) without taking into account the localized and the particular context of its sexual subjects. Unreflective criminalization of all SM is costly, painful, and may offend the integrity and sense of self that underpins our sense of humanity. Criminal law demonstrates a commitment to liberal legal subjects by limiting regulatory constraints on choice through overarching principles such as respect for autonomy, privacy, and the limitation of punishment to harmful acts. But these attempts to limit the power of the criminal law are disingenuous if the state then decides that only some autonomous actions—those performed by the responsible, non-risky, sexual citizens—get to count as private, non-harmful, and therefore non-criminal. Criminalization ought to be based on robust empirical evidence as well as sound normative principles. The criminalization of SM both ignores the sociological evidence as to the meaning and effects of SM activity, and through a misplaced application of harm, instantiates a heteronormative concept of violence to stand in for the erotic. As Janet Halley would say, one reason to engage with the criminal law, then, is to get "a better outcome for the pervert" (2003, p 636).

However, regulation of sexual behaviour such as SM is not only achieved through legislation, but also through social regulatory systems which introduce and perpetuate sex/gender norms, including socio-cultural representations and images which support hegemonic norms of sex roles and gendered behaviour, and undermine non-dichotomous or queer alternatives. It is in this sense that I would argue that law is 'not radically distinct from culture and politics, but is simply one of a number of ordering mechanisms and is thoroughly imbued with the dominant philosophies' (Davies, 1997, pp 32–3). Engaging with law therefore means engaging in public debate about the social regulatory norms underpinning law, and the representations of sexuality and sexual behaviour they spawn. In the context of SM this means taking—and making—opportunities to demonstrate the way in which criminal law, often based on common social misapprehensions, constructs risky and deviant, in contrast to healthy, responsible, sex.

References

American Psychiatric Association, *Diagnostic and Statistical Manual of Mental Disorders, Fourth Edition (Text Revision)* (Arlington: American Psychiatric Publishing, 2000)

Anderson, M., 'Negotiating Sex' (2005) 78 *Southern California Law Review* 101–38

Archard, D., *Sexual Consent* (Oxford: Westview Press, 1998)

Bamforth, N., 'Sado-Masochism and Consent' (1994) *Criminal Law Review* 661

Beckmann, A., 'Deconstructing Myths: The Social Construction of "Sadmasochism" Versus "Subjugated Knowledges" of Practitioners of Consensual "SM"' (2001) 8(2) *Journal of Criminal Justice and Popular Culture* 66–95

Bergelson, V., 'The Right to be Hurt: Testing the Boundaries of Consent' (2007) 75 *George Washington Law Review* 165

Bibbings, L. and Alldridge, P., 'Sexual Expression, Body Alteration and the Defence of Consent' (1993) 20(3) *Journal of Law and Society* 356

Brown, W., *States of Injury: Power and Freedom in Late Modernity* (Princeton, NJ: Princeton University Press, 1995)

Butler, J., *Bodies that Matter: On the Discursive Limits of 'Sex'* (New York: Routledge, 1993)

—— *Gender Trouble: Feminism and the Subversion of Identity* (New York: Routledge, 1990)

Califia, P., *Public Sex: The Culture of Radical Sex* (Berkeley, CA: Cleis Press, 2000)

—— *Sapphistry: The Book of Lesbian Sexuality* (Talahassee, Florida: Naiad Press, 1988)

Committee on Homosexual Offences and Prostitution *Report of the Committee on Homosexual Offences and Prostitution* (London: Her Majesty's Stationery Office, 1957)

Cossman, B., 'Gender, Sexuality and Power: Is Feminist Theory Enough?' (Parts I and IV) (2003) 12 *Columbia Journal of Gender and Law* 610

Cowan, S., 'All Change or Business as Usual? Reforming the Law of Rape in Scotland' in Clare McGlynn and Vanessa Munro (eds), *Rethinking Rape Law: International and Comparative Perspectives* (London: Routledge, 2010(b)) 154–69

—— 'Choosing Freely: Theoretically Reframing the Concept of Consent' in Hunter, R. and Cowan, S. (eds), *Choice and Consent: Feminist Engagements With Law and Subjectivity* (Oxford: Routledge-Cavendish, 2007) 91–105

—— 'The Pain of Pleasure: Consent and the Criminalisation of Sadomasochistic "assaults"' in Chalmers, J., Farmer, L., and Leverick, F. (eds), *Essays in Criminal Law in Honour of Sir Gerald Gordon* (Edinburgh: Edinburgh University Press, 2010a) 126–40

—— '"We Walk Among You": Trans Identity Politics Goes to the Movies' (2009) 21 *Canadian Journal of Women and the Law* 91–118

Cowart, M., 'Consent, Speech Act Theory, and Legal Disputes' (2004) 23 *Law and Philosophy* 495–525

Davies, M., 'Taking the Inside Out' in Naffine, N. and Owen, R. (eds), *Sexing the Subject of Law* (Sydney, Law Book Company, 1997)

Deckha, M., 'Pain, Pleasure and Consenting Women: Exploring Feminist Responses to S/M and its Legal Regulation in Canada through Jelinek's *The Piano Teacher*' (2007) 30 *Harvard Journal of Law & Gender* 425–459

Diduck, A., 'A Family By Any Other Name . . . or Starbucks Comes to England' (2001) 28 *Journal of Law and Society* 290–310

Dua, A., 'Apotemnophilia: Ethical Considerations of Amputating a Healthy Limb' (2010) 36 *Journal of Medical Ethics* 75–8

Duggan, L., 'Introduction' to Duggan, L. and Hunter, N. (eds), *Sex Wars: Sexual Dissent and Political Culture* (New York, Routledge, 1995)

—— *The Twilight of Equality?: Neoliberalism, Cultural Politics, and the Attack On Democracy* (Boston, MA: Beacon Press, 2003)

Duff, R. A., 'Harms and Wrongs' (2002) 5 *Buffalo Criminal Law Review* 13–45

Dworkin, A., *Intercourse* (New York: Free Press, 1987)

Dyer, C., 'Surgeon Amputated Healthy Legs' (2000) 320 *British Medical Journal*, 332 (available at <http://www.bmj.com/content/320/7231/332.1.full>)

Egan, K., 'Morality-Based Legislation is Alive and Well: Why the Law Permits Consent to Body Modification But Not Sadomasochistic Sex' (2006) 70 *Albany Law Review* 1615

Elliot, C. and de Than, C., 'The Case for a Rational Reconstruction of Consent in the Criminal Law' (2007) 70(2) *Modern Law Review* 225–49

Ellison, L. and Munro, V. E., 'A Stranger in the Bushes or an Elephant in the Room?: Critical Reflections on Received Rape Myth Wisdom in the Context of a Mock Jury Study' (2010) 13(4) *New Criminal Law Review* 781–801

Feinberg, J., *Harm to Self: The Moral Limits of the Criminal Law*, vol 3 (New York: OUP, 1986)

Finch, E. and Munro, V. E., 'Juror Stereotypes and Blame Attribution in Rape Cases Involving Intoxicants' (2005) 45(1) *British Journal of Criminology* 25–38

Fineman, M., Jackson, J. and Romero, A. (eds), *Feminist and Queer Legal Theory: Intimate Encounters, Uncomfortable Conversations* (Aldershot: Ashgate, 2009)

Halley, J. 'Gender, Sexuality and Power: Is Feminist Theory Enough?' (Parts III and VII) (2003) 12 *Columbia Journal of Gender and Law* 610

—— *Split Decisions: How and Why to Take a Break from Feminism* (Princeton, NJ: Princeton University Press, 2006)

Halperin, D., *Saint Foucault: Towards a Gay Hagiography* (New York: Oxford University Press, 1995)

Hanna, C., 'Sex is not a Sport: Consent and Violence in Criminal Law' (2001) 42 *Boston College Law Review* 239

Herman, D., *Rights of Passage: Struggles for Lesbian and Gay Legal Equality* (Toronto: University of Toronto Press, 1994)

Hines, S., '(Trans)Forming Gender: Social Change and Transgender Citizenship' (2007) 12 *Sociological Research Online*, available at: <http://www.socresonline.org.uk/12/1/hines.html>

Hoople, T., 'Conflicting Visions: SM, Feminism, and the Law—A Problem of Representation' (1996) 11 *Canadian Journal of Law and Society* 177–220

Hunter, R. and Cowan, S. (eds), *Choice and Consent: Feminist Engagements with Law and Subjectivity* (London: Routledge-Cavendish, 2007)

Hurd, H., 'The Moral Magic of Consent' (1996) 2 *Legal Theory* 121

Husak, D., 'Paternalism and Autonomy' (1981) 10(1) *Philosophy and Public Affairs* 27–46

Jeffreys, S., 'Consent and the Politics of Sexuality' (1993) 5 *Current Issues in Criminal Justice* 173–83

——*The Lesbian Heresy: A Feminist Perspective on the Lesbian Sexual Revolution* (London: The Women's Press, 1994)

Kahn, U., 'A Woman's Right to be Spanked: Testing the Limits of Tolerance of SM in the Socio-Legal Imaginary' (2009) 18 *Law and Sexuality* 79–119

Kelly, L., Lovett, J., and Regan, L., 'A Gap or a Chasm? Attrition in Reported Rape Cases' (Home Office Research Study, 2005) 293

Krafft-Ebing, R. Von, *Psychopathia Sexualis* (1886, reprinted New York: Arcade Publishing, 1998)

Lacey, N., *Unspeakable Subjects: Feminist Essays in Legal and Social Theory* (Oxford: Hart, 1998)

Langdridge, D. and Butt, T., 'A Hermeneutic Phenomenological Investigation of the Construction of Sadomasochistic Identities' (2004) 7(1) *Sexualities* 31–53

Law Commission *Consent in the Criminal Law* (Law Com Consultation Paper 139) (London: Her Majesty's Stationery Office, 1995)

Lees, S., *Carnal Knowledge: Rape on Trial* revised 2nd edn (London: Women's Press Ltd, 2002)

Linden, R. et al (eds), *Against Sado-masochism* (CA: Frog in the Well, 1982)

Madden Dempsey, M. and Herring, J., 'Why Sexual Penetration Requires Justification' (2007) 27 *Oxford Journal of Legal Studies* 467–91

Munro, V., *Law and Politics at the Perimeter: Re-Evaluating Key Debates in Feminist Legal Theory* (Oxford: Hart Publishing, 2007)

O'Donovan, K., *Sexual Divisions in Law* (London: Weidenfeld and Nicolson, 1985)

Olsen, F., 'Constitutional Law: Feminist Critique and the Public/Private Distinction' (1993) 10 *Constitutional Commentaries* 319–27

Pa, M., 'Beyond the Pleasure Principle: The Criminalization of Consensual Sadomasochistic Sex' (2001) 11 *Texas Journal of Women and the Law* 51–92

Richardson, D., *Theorising Heterosexuality: Telling it Straight* (Buckingham: Open University Press, 1996)

Rubin, G., 'Thinking Sex: Notes for a Radical Theory of the Politics of Sexuality' in Vance, C. (ed), *Pleasure and Danger: Exploring Female Sexuality* (London: Routledge & Kegan Paul, 1984)

Scoular, J., *The Subject of Prostitution: Sex/Work, Law and Social Theory* (London: Routledge-Cavendish, 2011)

Shafer-Landau, R., 'Liberalism and Paternalism' (2005) 11 *Legal Theory* 169–91

Smart, C., *Law, Crime and Sexuality: Essays in Feminism* (London: Sage, 1995)

Sunstein, C., 'Legal Interference with Private Preferences' (1986) 53(4) *University of Chicago Law Review* 1129–74

Stychin, C., *Law's Desire: Sexuality and the Limits of Justice* (London: Routledge, 1995)

Tadros, V., 'No Consent: A Historical Critique of the Actus Reus of Rape' (1999) 3 *Edinburgh Law Review* 317–40

—— 'Rape Without Consent' (2006) 26(3) *Oxford Journal of Legal Studies* 515–43

Temkin, J. and Krahé, B., *Sexual Assault and the Justice Gap: A Question of Attitude* (Oxford: Hart, 2008)

Weeks, J., *Invented Moralities: Sexual Values in an Age of Uncertainty* (Cambridge, Polity Press, 1995)

Weinberg, M. S., Williams, C. J., and Moser, C., 'The Social Constituents of Sadomasochism' (1984) 31 *Social Problems* 379

Wilkinson, E., 'Perverting Visual Pleasure: Representing Sadomasochism' (2009) 12 (2) *Sexualities* 181–98

Wright, R. George, 'Consenting Adults: The Problem of Enhancing Human Dignity Non-Coercively' (1995) 75 *Boston University Law Review* 1397–439

5

Constitutionalism and the Limits of the Criminal Law

Malcolm Thorburn[1]

I. Introduction

Establishing limits to the scope of legitimate criminal law has been one of the central projects of liberal reformers for several centuries. In the twentieth century, most liberal reformers were of a utilitarian bent. As a result, they dealt with criminal justice as just another policy instrument—albeit a particularly coercive one—to be understood in terms of the net benefits it produced. And like all coercive policy instruments, they assumed that the scope of the criminal law should be limited by J. S. Mill's harm principle.[2] In recent years, the utilitarian liberal enterprise has come under attack on two fronts. On the one hand, the harm principle has been criticized for failing to constrain the massive expansion of the criminal law in recent decades.[3] And on the other hand, the very idea of a utilitarian account of criminal justice has come under attack as fundamentally illegitimate. Because utilitarians treat the criminal justice system as just another policy instrument for minimizing the incidence of undesirable conduct, they are unable to justify the way that the criminal justice system singles out particular individuals for censure and punishment in service of that end.

[1] Thanks to Antony Duff, Larissa Katz, Claes Lernestedt, and Arthur Ripstein for extremely valuable comments on an earlier version of this paper. Thanks also to the Social Sciences and Humanities Research Council of Canada for financial support. Responsibility for the faults of this chapter lies solely with the author.
[2] *On Liberty* (1859).

[3] Bernard E. Harcourt, 'The Collapse of the Harm Principle' (1999) 90 *Journal of Criminal Law and Criminology*, 109; R. A. Duff, *Answering for Crime* (Oxford: OUP, 2007) 138: 'the Harm Principle itself... can do little work in limiting the expansion of the criminal law'.

From the failures of the utilitarian project, a new school of criminal law theory has arisen. Two of the most influential criminal theorists of our time, Michael Moore and Antony Duff, have proposed accounts of the criminal justice system based on newfangled versions of legal moralism. They have suggested, each in his own distinctive way, that although we are not entitled to single out particular individuals for censure and punishment merely in order to deter undesirable conduct (as many utilitarians would have it), we *are* entitled to do so as a way of recognizing genuine moral wrongdoing on the part of that individual. Instead of treating that person as a means, the actions of the criminal justice system can then be understood to be respectful of the offender's agency, holding him responsible for his moral wrongdoing.

In short, Moore and Duff have given new life to the old idea that the criminal law's business is to enforce the demands of morality. And their newfangled legal moralism has the virtue not only of justifying the law's treatment of specific offenders; it also provides new tools for setting out limits on criminalization. If we are only justified in convicting and punishing offenders as a way of recognizing their moral wrongdoing, then it follows that criminal offences must all identify forms of genuine moral wrongdoing. Otherwise, we would find ourselves treating as moral wrongdoers individuals who had not actually committed any moral wrong at all. As we shall see later in this chapter, Moore and Duff add a number of other limitations on the scope of the criminal law that they take to flow from their core arguments, but the point for present purposes is that their new take on legal moralism provides new and promising tools to limit the scope of the criminal law— tools that were unavailable to the utilitarian liberal account. Because their accounts open up so many new possibilities and because of the depth and sophistication with which these two writers have developed their accounts, it is not surprising to find that legal moralism has become the new orthodoxy in English-language criminal law theory.

In this chapter, I argue that notwithstanding the many merits of Moore and Duff's legal moralism, their projects fail as accounts of the criminal justice system as we know it. Although they might be morally attractive accounts of something, they are not plausible candidates as theories *of criminal justice* because the institutions they describe are too different in certain key respects from the ones we see in operation across the common law world. The central problem I identify with Moore's account is its inability to explain the law's deep-seated aversion to vigilantism. Because he sees the criminal justice system as just one particularly effective mechanism for delivering deserved punishment, it seems that non-state actors might be entitled to deliver criminal justice wherever they are able to do so effectively. That is, Moore has no tools available to explain why it *must be* the state and *only* the state that delivers criminal justice. And yet the law is quite clear that this must be the case. Duff's account, because it is fundamentally relational, is not susceptible to the same criticism: he makes clear that we are answerable in the relevant way only to the polity (and not to private vigilantes) for our crimes (which he calls 'public wrongs'). But because Duff's account models criminal justice on the practice of a community calling its members to account for wrongdoing, it is unable to account for the criminal law's fundamentally coercive nature. We might be answerable to our private moral communities—friends and colleagues, religious communities, and social clubs—for certain wrongs we commit, but those private communities do not have the legitimate authority to impose coercive punishments on us for our wrongs in the same way as the state routinely does through the criminal justice system.

In light of the failure not only of utilitarian liberal accounts of criminal justice but also of these two well-developed accounts of legal moralism, we find ourselves still in search of an account of criminal justice that can show it to be a morally justifiable institution and that can generate moral limits to criminalization. In part III of this chapter, I sketch an account that I believe is capable of doing all this. In order to understand the workings of the account I propose, however, we need to see that its moral justification cannot be spelled out by analogy to some familiar morally justified practice. Indeed, a crucial step of the account I propose is the recognition that the state's coercive practices of criminal justice, though morally legitimate, are justifiable in a way that is wholly unique. The sort of account that I have in mind is liberal, but Kantian rather than utilitarian, and it is part of a larger story about liberal constitutionalism.[4]

The moral justification of the criminal justice system's coercive practices begins with the justification of the state's coercive powers more generally. We begin with the thought that the sort of freedom that should matter to us most in political affairs is that which is best understood in opposition to slavery. The slave is not unfree because of any particular impediment in his way or because of any particular disability; rather, he is unfree because every aspect of his situation (what he may or may not do, possess, etc) is entirely *dependent* on his master's arbitrary choice to permit it. Now, in the absence of law and state, everyone is radically unfree in the same way as the slave:

---

[4] As Alan W. Norrie—no friend of liberal political theory—points out, 'there is something essentially Kantian about the criminal law, and[. . .]this is not susceptible to moral criticism because it is enshrined in the historical structure of modern legal form that it begins with an abstract, formal individualism' in his 'Alan Brudner and the Dialectics of Criminal Law' 14 *New Criminal Law Review* 449 at 451.

everything we do, possess, etc is dependent on the will of others to permit it. And in this sort of context, all of our conduct takes on a sinister cast. Nothing we do is just an exercise of our freedom; we are always simultaneously imposing our unilateral will on others and thereby undermining their claims of freedom. In order to make it possible for us to interact with others in a way that is respectful of everyone's freedom, we need an entity that can put in place a rightful context for our actions. That entity must set out general rules that demarcate everyone's sphere of freedom and it must (in the name of us all) resist any attempt to supplant the law's rules with private preferences. That entity is the liberal constitutional state. The ground of the liberal constitutional state's legitimacy is the simple fact that it—and it alone— can provide the conditions of freedom for all. On this account, the role of the criminal law is to identify when individuals are attempting to supplant the law's rules with their own preferred arrangements and to regulate the use of state power to resist such attempts.

As I shall argue in part IV of this chapter, the liberal constitutionalist account of criminal justice not only fits well with existing practices and puts them into a larger framework within which they are morally justified; it also generates a number of important moral limits to the process of criminalization.

II. Michael Moore and Antony Duff's New Legal Moralism

A. The demise of utilitarian criminal law theory

Michael Moore and Antony Duff developed their positions on the nature and limits of the criminal law in large part as reactions to the failure of traditional utilitarian liberal accounts. In recent years, the failure of utilitarian liberalism that has attracted the most attention has been what Bernard Harcourt has called 'the collapse of the harm principle'. The attacks on the harm principle have come from almost every conceivable angle—we need not linger on the details of the many well-worn arguments. Some charge that it is hopelessly under-inclusive, citing serious forms of harmless or consented-to wrongdoing that it would not cover. Others point out that once we recognize that it is legitimate to criminalize the conduct that creates the risk of harm, the harm principle becomes so broad that it cannot provide meaningful limits to the growth of the criminal law.[5] Yet others have pointed out that the harm principle has become so empty that it is now routinely used by the very

---

[5] These challenges are elegantly summarized in Duff (n 3 above) ch 6, 123ff.

people that utilitarian liberals are meant to be arguing against: those who wish to expand the reach of the criminal law to include forms of private sexual conduct and the use of intoxicants of which they morally disapprove.[6] Now, whether or not any particular argument against the harm principle succeeds, the overall picture is bleak: it appears to be both over- and under-inclusive and it has now become a rhetorical tool in the hands of the enemies of liberal restraint in the use of the criminal law.

Another important failure of the utilitarian liberal account—and one that goes not only to its usefulness in limiting the scope of the criminal law but also to its ability to provide a justification of the criminal process at all—is its inability to justify the way in which particular individuals are singled out, censured, and punished as criminal wrongdoers. Even the most sophisticated utilitarian accounts of criminal law and punishment, such as the one set forward by H. L. A. Hart, do not address the crucial question of when an individual *deserves* the criminal punishment we impose upon him. Instead, they are really just accounts of when it is *useful* to us to punish individuals for the sake of some desirable social goal, such as deterring future wrongdoing. In his famous essay, 'Prolegomenon to the Principles of Punishment',[7] Hart purports to provide a way to satisfy both the utilitarian liberal's concern with forward-looking reasons for the institution of punishment and the need to provide a justification of punishment that the particular offender could not reasonably reject. As Hart puts it, a system of punishment could be utilitarian in its general justifying aim while remaining 'retributivist'[8] in its principles of distribution. Hart argues that so long as we refrain from punishing whenever the offender did not have a fair opportunity—whether by absence of *mens rea*, or on account of a defence such as duress, necessity, or insanity—to conform his conduct to the law's demands, we can rest assured that those who are punished genuinely deserve it.

But Hart's attempt to save the utilitarian liberal account of criminal punishment simply misses the point. What Hart needs is a positive rationale for the punishment of specific offenders that could ensure that those who are

---

[6] Harcourt (n 3 above).

[7] Reprinted in *Punishment and Responsibility: Essays in the Philosophy of Law* 2nd edn (Oxford: OUP, 2008).

[8] I put the term 'retributivist' in quotation marks here to indicate that Hart is re-defining what retributivism is all about in this essay. Rather than concerning himself with moral culpability as a positive reason for punishment (the central claim of traditional retributivists), Hart is concerned with fair choice to have done otherwise as a constraint on the use of punishment for utilitarian reasons. For more, see John Gardner's introductory essay in *Punishment and Responsibility* (ibid). See also my 'Three Models of Criminal Law: Deterrence, Accountability, and the Rule of Law' (forthcoming in *University of Toronto Law Journal*).

punished actually deserve the punishment they receive. But all that he provides is a principle to ensure that *no further injustice* is done by punishing those who did not have a fair opportunity to conform to the law's demands.[9] Simply because no further injustice is done in this way does not show that it is just to punish within these constraints. Hart is unable to provide any positive rationale for punishing offenders besides its deterrent effect—and this, as we have seen, is simply a tool for promoting our policy objectives. Hart's account of criminal law, like its utilitarian forebears, simply *uses* the punishment of the offender as a deterrent to future criminality. It is first and foremost in order to address this problem with the moral justification of the criminal justice system's treatment of particular offenders that writers such as Moore and Duff have turned to legal moralism.

B. Moore's retributivist moralism

In *Placing Blame*, Michael Moore argues that we should think of the criminal justice system as what he calls a 'functional kind'—a thing that is defined in terms of the function it is to serve—the function of which is 'to attain retributive justice...[by] punish[ing] all and only those who are morally culpable in the doing of some morally wrongful action'.[10] That is, the very point of criminal law has nothing whatever to do with its deterrent value (or any other future benefits that might accrue as a result of its operation). Rather, its point is simply to give moral wrongdoers what they deserve simply because they deserve it. This move—the retributivist argument that we should punish wrongdoers *just because they deserve it*—is an old and familiar one that was long seen as a retrograde impulse to be avoided by a civilized system of punishment. H. L. A. Hart famously rejected retributivism in the following terms:

It represents as a value to be pursued at the cost of human suffering the bare expression of moral condemnation, and treats the infliction of suffering as a uniquely appropriate or 'emphatic' mode of expression. But is this really intelligible?...[It] is uncomfortably close to human sacrifice as an expression of religious worship.[11]

But Michael Moore embraces this position on the grounds that it and it alone can justify the institution of criminal punishment. Far from being barbaric,

---

[9] John Gardner makes a similar point in the introduction to Hart (n 7 above) xxv. Indeed, he goes so far as to say that Hart's account is not actually an account of punishment at all, even by the very definition of punishment Hart himself set out.

[10] *Placing Blame* (Oxford: OUP, 1997) 33–5.

[11] H. L. A. Hart, *Law, Liberty and Morality* (Palo Alto, CA: Stanford University Press, 1962) 65.

Moore argues, it is a sign of respect for persons that we only punish them when they personally deserve such punishment, and not merely as a tool for some future good to come of it.

Objectionable as some utilitarian liberals might take retributivism to be, it has now become a well-accepted position within criminal law theory. Indeed, as John Braithwaite and Philip Pettit point out, 'the new retributivism has sounded the death-knell of traditional, consequentialist approaches to criminal justice'.[12] If this is the case, of course, then it becomes crucially important to the moral justification of punishment that the criminal law should track the demands of morality fairly closely—for it is only morally justifiable on the retributivist picture to punish those who have actually engaged in morally wrongful conduct. For this reason, Moore embraces a newfangled form of legal moralism. But we should make clear that Moore's legal moralism is radically different from another position of the same name espoused by Patrick Devlin in the twentieth century (and by James FitzJames Stephen before him in the nineteenth century). Whereas Devlin thought that the criminal law could legitimately be used to enforce the morality of a given society in order to prevent societal collapse (irrespective of whether its demands in fact reflected the demands of true morality), Moore takes the fit of criminal law with the demands of true morality to be crucial. That is, whereas Moore is concerned with the enforcement of morality as such, Devlin is interested in the enforcement only of *what people take to be* the demands of morality as a means to the pursuit of his real end, which is preserving social cohesion. In this way, Devlin is not really a legal moralist in Moore's sense at all.

Although Moore's position is sharply different from Devlin's, it is nonetheless deeply illiberal. At best, it is what he quite candidly calls 'liberal-in-content if illiberal-in-form':[13] it provides illiberal arguments for designing a system of criminal law that would look a lot like the sort of system of which a liberal would approve. Moore goes to great lengths to ensure that his position is not obviously illiberal in its content: he is quick to supplement his legal moralism with other limits on criminalization: (1) it is morally worthwhile to allow people to make some choices for themselves even if they make the wrong choice (the autonomy principle); (2) it may be too costly to criminalize some kinds of moral wrongs, say, because this might induce contempt for the criminal law if they are never enforced (the utility principle); and (3) legislators should be modest in their view of their own ability to determine

---

[12] John Braithwaite and Philip Pettit, *Not Just Deserts: A Republic Theory of Criminal Justice* (Oxford: OUP, 1990) 209.
[13] Moore (n 10 above) 80.

what is genuinely morally wrong conduct (the epistemic modesty principle).[14] Nevertheless, Moore's *argument* is deeply illiberal in its basic structure. According to his account, the point of criminal law is not to protect individual liberty but to interfere with it in the grossest ways imaginable in order to enforce the demands of morality.

C. The problem of vigilantism

There are good reasons of political theory for liberals to be suspicious of Michael Moore's retributivism, but there are other reasons to reject his view that should be of interest to criminal law theorists of any political stripe. That is, even if we were to accept Moore's claim that the criminal justice system is a tool for enforcing morality and that we impose criminal punishment simply because people morally deserve to suffer for their wrongdoing, we ought still to be sceptical of his enterprise on grounds of lack of fit with existing doctrine. Put another way, even if we think it is an attractive theory, it is not a theory *of criminal justice* in a form we can recognize. The problem of fit that is most problematic for Moore is raised by the phenomenon of vigilantism. If Moore is right that the criminal justice system is simply a tool for bringing about retributive justice, then what reasons might we have to object if private citizens were to take it upon themselves to hold trials and to punish offenders? It seems that there is no reason in principle why we should object: so long as the vigilante 'gets it right' and punishes only those who have committed moral wrongs (and does so for that reason and in proportion to the offender's desert), it seems that Moore would have no principled reason to object to this practice.

Of course, there might be reasons of administrative efficiency to insist that we ought usually to defer to the authorities in such matters: police officers are usually better trained than ordinary citizens in the use of force; they usually operate as part of a large and well-organized team that will carry out its purposes more efficiently than private citizens acting on their own initiative; and offenders (and others) might reasonably rely on the fact that it is the state's agents and not others who administer criminal justice. Notwithstanding all of these considerations, however, it remains an open question for Moore, to be decided on the balance of reasons in the particular case, whether the state or private citizens should be the one to run trials, and to punish wrongdoers. And it would seem that in some situations, at least, these reasons of efficiency and coordination will be outweighed by reasons of retributive

---

[14] Ibid 75ff.

justice. Where we know that a serious moral wrongdoer will escape punishment unless we carry it out, for instance, it seems that we have a good case to make for taking the law into our own hands.

As I have argued at length elsewhere, however, the law in virtually every common law jurisdiction is deeply hostile to vigilantism.[15] It is not just that the balance of reasons usually favours a state monopoly of legitimate violence; rather, it appears to be a central commitment of the legal system to maintain this state monopoly.[16] Whereas the criminal law treats duly authorized state officials who carry out the procedures of criminal justice as fully justified—whether they are police officers effecting wiretaps, searching for evidence, or making arrests or whether they are corrections officials administering punishment—it treats the efforts of private citizens to do any of these things as serious crimes. And the few situations where the law permits private citizens to take the enforcement of the law into their own hands are closely circumscribed. The right of a private citizen to use force to prevent the commission of an offence, to effect an arrest, or to prevent the destruction of life or property is much narrower than the powers of duly authorized state officials to do the same. In the few cases where private citizens are entitled to do these things, it turns in virtually every case on the unavailability of state officials. There is a clear trend in the criminal law of the English-speaking world toward treating private citizens who carry out any of these functions as mere emergency stand-ins for state officials—not as individuals who are equally entitled to carry out retributive justice, as Moore's model might suggest.

D. Antony Duff's 'calling to account' model

Antony Duff's account of the criminal justice system, like Moore's, is born of dissatisfaction with the traditional utilitarian liberal account's inability to justify the way we single out specific offenders for censure and punishment. But it is importantly different from Moore's position in at least two crucial respects: (1) whereas Moore's argument is focused on punishment as rendering retributive justice, Duff's emphasis is on the trial as a locus for calling individuals to account; and (2) in Duff's relational account of criminal

[15] See 'Reinventing the Nightwatchman State?' (2010) 60 *University of Toronto Law Journal* 425; see also 'Justifications, Powers, and Authority' (2008) 117(6) *Yale Law Journal* 1070. But see John Gardner's reply to the latter article in which he challenges this claim: 'Justification under Authority' (2010) 23 *Canadian Journal of Law and Jurisprudence* 71.

[16] The sociologist Max Weber famously stated this point as follows: 'Today, however, we have to say that the state is a human community that (successfully) claims the monopoly of the legitimate use of physical force within a given territory'; Max Weber, 'Politics as a Vocation' in H. H. Gerth and C. Wright Mills (trs and eds), *From Max Weber: Essays in Sociology* (New York: OUP, 1958) 78.

justice, we are answerable *only to the polity* (and not to other private actors who might take the law into their own hands) for 'public wrongs' that violate the basic values of the polity. Together, they give Duff's legal moralism an altogether different cast from Michael Moore's, allowing him to avoid both of the major problems with the Moore account.

Duff's most basic point, which is at the root of both of the differences with Moore identified above, is that we should not think of the criminal justice system simply as a delivery mechanism for deserved punishment. It is just not obvious, Duff maintains, that morality *requires* that wrongdoers be punished—and therefore, it is not obvious that the state is simply carrying out what needs to be done when it punishes wrongdoers. But we can make sense of the criminal justice system as a morally justified enterprise without recourse to this highly controversial retributivist premise, Duff argues, if we think of it not as a punishment-delivery mechanism but as an institution for holding one another accountable for our violations of shared moral values. Where individuals live together in a moral community—be that a family, a community of scholars, a religious group, a polity, etc—part of what this means is that we are thereby committed to living according to a certain set of values. And this, in turn, means that we are committed to holding one another responsible for conduct that violates these basic values. Calling members of the community to account for violating those norms is just part of what it means to hold those values as defining norms of our community. If we were regularly to see such a wrong committed and not to do anything, this would mean that our community is no longer defined in terms of those values. And if we were regularly to see a particular person violate the norms of our community but fail to call him to account for his conduct, we would be failing to treat his as a responsible agent. It is only those whom we view as not responsible—small children, animals, the insane, etc—whom we do not call to account for their conduct. It is just part of what it means to stand in a moral community with someone to be committed to holding one another accountable for wrongs against the defining values of that community.

If we think of the polity as an unusually large, institutionalized, and formalized moral community, then Duff's two key differences with Moore are clear to see. It is the trial rather than punishment that is the core of the criminal justice system because the basic point of criminal justice is for the polity to call its members to account for their wrongs and it is at trial that the polity presents individuals with evidence of their wrongdoing and asks them to answer for their conduct. Duff's account of the criminal trial is highly nuanced, but his main point is that it is not simply a mechanism for determining whether or not punishment is appropriate (as retributivists such as Moore would suggest) but is, rather, an end in itself—for it is in carrying out the process of the trial that the community calls the accused to account and that the accused is given an opportunity to answer the charges made against him.

Duff's second difference from Moore is at least a partial answer to the problem of vigilantism. That is, because he argues that moral answerability is a relational concept, Duff is able to explain why it must be the political community as a whole acting through the state that brings individuals to justice in criminal law. Although we might all have our opinions about the conduct of others—our friends may think worse of us for failing to do our duty to our children, our students, or our spouse—we must stand in the right relationship to hold someone to account for their wrongdoing. For example, our friends cannot properly call us to account for wrongs done to our students, our children, or our spouse because they are not party to those moral communities; they do not have the standing to accept or reject our answers for why we acted as we did, nor to absolve us for our wrongdoing. Similarly, the vigilante may have his opinions about the public wrongs of others, but he lacks the standing to call us to account formally for those wrongs. It is only the polity as a whole to whom we are answerable for our public wrongs.

It is this emphasis on the relational nature of accountability that provides Duff with a new and promising criterion for limiting the scope of the criminal law. Whereas Michael Moore was forced to add further constraints on the criminal law based on autonomy, utility, and epistemic modesty in order to ensure that it could be 'liberal in content' (if not in form), Duff builds in a more robust limit to the scope of the criminal law from the very beginning. We are not even *in principle* answerable to the polity in the criminal law for all of our moral wrongs, Duff insists. We are answerable to the polity in criminal law only for those wrongs that are 'violation[s] of the core values by which we define ourselves as a polity'.[17] Accordingly, it is *ab initio* inappropriate to criminalize conduct that is not a violation of those core political values. Clearly, respect for life, individual autonomy, and property are all defining values of the liberal polity, so wrongs against these are proper subjects of criminal law. But other important moral values—truthfulness, respect for other persons, animals, and the environment, and so on—will be a good deal more controversial and more difficult to convert into robust limits to the criminal law. But perhaps this is all we can ask from a theory of criminalization: although he does not provide any bright-line rules about

---

[17] Duff (n 3 above) 141.

what is in and what is out, Duff at least sets out a plausible set of principles that can guide our discussion about the limits of the criminal law.

E. Coercion vs calling to account

Duff's account of criminal justice is rich and highly nuanced and, as we have just seen, it is able to solve quite neatly the two major problems with Moore's retributivist moralism. According to Duff's account, we can still make sense of criminal justice without having to endorse the controversial retributivist claim that the guilty deserve to suffer and we can also explain why it is that the criminal law is so averse to vigilante action. But Duff's account is nevertheless vulnerable to a somewhat different problem, for the fact remains that we are answerable in the criminal process quite differently from the way in which we are answerable to anyone else for wrongdoing. So long as our attention in criminal justice is on the trial alone, Duff's account seems highly plausible. But at some point, we need to recognize the crucial role played by coercive punishment. The process of calling to account might have a close analogue in our ordinary moral life—our friends, our spouse, our students, and others may have the moral standing to identify relevant wrongs and to demand an answer from us for them—but criminal punishment seems to have no parallel in ordinary life. Although we might say that we are being 'punished' by our friends, spouse, business associates, religious community, etc for our wrongdoing, this should be understood to be a categorically different sort of reaction from the punishment that the state is able (and, I argue, entitled) to mete out to criminal wrongdoers. Outside the criminal process, individuals may withhold benefits from us or withdraw from associating with us, etc, but they are not entitled to take away our vested entitlements or to deprive us of liberty as the state may do in response to crime. An account of the criminal justice process must be able to explain its uniquely coercive nature. So although there is much to recommend Duff's account of criminal justice, it seems to take as its object an institution that is too different from the modern criminal justice system we know to be anything we could call a theory *of criminal justice*.

III. Constitutionalism and the Criminal Law

In this part of the chapter, I set out a different account of criminal justice from both the utilitarian liberal account of H. L. A. Hart and the moralist accounts of Michael Moore and Antony Duff. In setting out my alternative, however, I draw a number of lessons from Moore and Duff's important contributions. First, I recognize that I must be able to demonstrate how the criminal justice system's treatment of individual offenders is consistent with respect for their personhood. It is not enough, as the utilitarian does, simply to show that the coercion and censure endured by offenders (and even by criminal suspects who turn out to be innocent) is able to bring about substantial social benefit and that the costs of bringing about that benefit are fairly distributed.[18] Criminal justice is not just a policy instrument for sharing the costs of bringing about a social good; rather, it is an instrument for identifying wrongdoers and censuring them as such. Our account of criminal justice must make sense of that practice. Second, I also draw lessons from the failings of Moore and Duff's efforts. However attractive it might be to analogize the criminal justice process to a familiar morally justifiable practice, that temptation is to be resisted. There are features of the criminal justice system—most importantly, its state-dominated character and its coerciveness—that make it unlike other moral practices. Accordingly, any successful account of the criminal justice system is going to have to establish its moral legitimacy in an altogether different way from other practices, according to a form of argument that does not simply rely on an analogy.

The sort of argument that I believe can establish the legitimacy of a criminal justice system of the familiar kind begins by establishing the place of criminal justice within a larger framework of constitutionalism. Since we cannot simply analogize its operations to familiar moral practices of calling to account or private 'punishment', we should, instead, see it as part of the operations of a legitimate constitutional state. Before we return to the structure and justification of the criminal justice system, then, let us turn briefly to some larger questions in the foundations of the state's legitimacy.

A. Constitutionalism

Within the liberal political tradition, there is an important camp that sees law and the state not as instruments for bringing about specific outcomes (maximizing utility, punishing wrongdoers, etc) but rather as setting out the necessary context within which we can be free and independent persons even as we live together with others. A familiar way in which this argument is often introduced is with the thought that in the state of nature—ie in the absence of law and state—individuals can never be their own masters. The

---

[18] It is this second aspect of the utilitarian account that Hart believed could save it from the charge that we were simply using individuals in furtherance of our social project.

sort of unfreedom we suffer in the state of nature, according to this way of thinking, is akin to the unfreedom of the slave. Whether or not the slave's master actually restrains him from acting as he chooses to act, the slave is dependent on his master simply to allow his self-chosen arrangements to stand. Similarly, in the state of nature, whether or not we are actually restrained from doing certain things and whether or not those around us actually make our lives miserable by taking things out of our possession, injuring us, and so on, everything we do, possess, fail to do, etc is dependent on the arbitrary choice of others to let it stand. The trouble is that in such a context, the meaning of all our conduct is the same: we can never just exercise our own freedom in a way that is consistent with the equal claims of freedom of others. Because there is no system in place to demarcate each person's sphere of freedom, every act we undertake is an assault upon the freedom of others. We can make this point in a number of different ways. The philosopher Immanuel Kant states that 'any action is *right* if it can co-exist with everyone's freedom in accordance with a universal law, or if on its maxim the freedom of choice of each can coexist with everyone's freedom according to universal law'.[19] But we may put the point slightly differently to much the same effect by saying that to live in moral community with others, we need assurance not only that we are free in the relevant way, but that others with whom we associate are free as well.

In short, we need a systematic answer to a systematic problem, and law and state provide that answer. Unlike any private actor, the state claims to speak in the name of everyone's claim of freedom equally. For this reason, the state is the unique instrumentality through which we may collectively ensure our freedom as independence. It speaks for us all together in setting down general laws that define the scope of everyone's freedom in the same way, but it does not speak for anyone in particular—and so, in that way, the state's actions are not to be confused with the partisan choices of some particular individuals. We also act through the state in order to ensure that no-one shall fall into a situation of such poverty that he is entirely dependent on the charity of others in order to live his life, or that anyone should be so ignorant of the ways of the world that he should be dependent on others to live his life, etc. In short, we act together with others through the instrumentality of the state in order to secure for *all* of us the conditions of freedom as independence. We need to act through the state to do all this because only if we do so may we be sure that all those with whom we come into contact shall be secure in their freedom in the

---

[19] *The Metaphysics of Morals* in Mary Gregor (tr and ed), *Cambridge Edition of the Works of Immanuel Kant; Practical Philosophy* (New York: CUP, 1996) 387.

same way—and therefore, our interactions with them will be as free and independent moral agents, a precondition of right action.

The point of the constitutional state, then, is not to accomplish some important moral task such as maximizing utility or punishing moral wrong-doers. Rather, its purpose is the much more basic one of setting the frame-work within which we may interact with others in a way that preserves the freedom and dignity of all. The state in this model takes no role in ensuring that individuals exercise their freedom in the best way possible. Indeed, part of the liberal project is precisely to allow individuals to make that choice for themselves—to give them what Jeremy Waldron calls 'a right to do wrong'.[20] But that does not mean that the state's work is morally neutral—far from it. Because the state's existence is necessary in order for any of us to interact with others as free and equal moral agents, it is a matter of moral necessity. Without the framework of law and the state in place, our conduct—no matter how well-meaning—must always be an imposition of our private will on others, undermining their freedom and dignity.

In order to carry out its morally necessary task, it is not enough for the state merely to use its moral authority to guide individuals to the right way of acting. For the point is not for the state to guide individuals to the right acts. Rather, its purpose is to set in place a framework within which our conduct can have a certain meaning. And to set out that framework, it is necessary for the state to ensure that the conditions of equal freedom *actually obtain* between people. And, as we have seen, this means that the state's role is not simply that of an authority indicating to us how we ought to act that might require some coercive enforcement as backup; rather, it is *ab initio* a coercive role. In order for my conduct to be consistent with the freedom of all, I must be assured that I am acting in a certain sort of normative context—so it is up to the state to ensure that that normative context is in place. And this, as we shall see, requires the state to use coercive force.

B. Constitutionalism and the criminal law

According to the liberal constitutionalism story as I have been spelling it out so far, the two features of the criminal law that were missing from Moore and Duff's accounts come out as central features not only of the criminal law but of the legal order more generally: it is uniquely a matter of state action (for when private actors start enforcing the rules, this undermines the equality of all, rather than supporting it), and it is fundamentally coercive (for the point

[20] 'A Right to do Wrong' in *Liberal Rights: Collected Paper 1981–1991* (New York: CUP, 1993).

of the legal order is not simply to guide people toward what they ought to do but, rather, to ensure that a certain set of arrangements *actually obtains*). But what is the special role of the criminal law in this picture?

Within a liberal constitutional order, there are several different sorts of legal regulation. One sort of legal regulation is concerned with setting out and enforcing the boundaries between individuals' private rights claims. Private wrongs are acts that violate the terms of equal freedom that the state has put in place through the legal order. Thus, when one person culpably causes injury to another's person or property (whether intentionally, or through negligence), he has wronged that person. Through the institutions of the private law, the state ensures that the victim of such an injury may obtain compensation for any resulting injury from the wrongdoer in order to undo any factual injury to the rights claim. It is crucial to the framework of rights that we have such a system of private law in place and that the state back it up with its coercive power, for it is primarily through this mechanism that we are able to ensure that each person's sphere of freedom is sacrosanct. A second sort of legal ordering arises in the area of public law, where the state establishes programmes designed to ensure the independence of all, such as progressive income tax, public education, public health care, the regulation of markets, etc. In order for those programmes to function properly, it is often necessary to attach penalties to conduct that is at odds with its proper operation. But because these penalties—usually in the form of fines for regulatory offences—are imposed primarily as incentives to action, they are often (quite appropriately) imposed without any fault standard at all. Their purpose is not punitive as such; they are designed merely to encourage the desired behaviour.

The criminal law is not directly concerned with either of these sorts of regimes. Rather, in criminal law, we are concerned with the efforts of private actors who try to supplant the law's neutral ordering with their own favoured arrangements. The wrongs of criminal law, on this model, are not primarily concerned with the fact that an injury has been done to some specific individual or that the requirements of a particular regulatory regime have been violated. Rather, the criminal law's concern is with someone's efforts to undermine the whole system of equal freedom itself. The difference can be seen clearly in the distinction between civil negligence, which is a matter for compensation in private law, and criminal wrongdoing, which usually re-quires a higher fault standard. Criminal wrongs are those that demonstrate a willingness on the part of the offender to displace the legal rules themselves— they are concerned not merely with an injury to some specific rights claim, but to the very idea of living together under law rather than subject to the wishes of specific individuals. The criminal actively disregards the law's requirements and substitutes his own preferences; the tortfeasor may be guilty of nothing more than a culpable failure actually to conform to the law's requirements.

In an important sense, then, the criminal law truly is what Nils Jareborg calls *ultima ratio*.[21] But it is *ultima ratio* (a last resort) not merely in the sense that we ought to use regulatory instruments other than the criminal law to control behaviour if we can—that criminal law is the bluntest and most dangerous regulatory instrument at the state's disposal. It is *ultima ratio* in the deeper sense that it is a necessary last resort (or backstop) to the whole project of living together with others under law. For it is all very well to have in place a set of laws that demarcate each person's sphere of rights and even to have a legal regime in place enabling individuals to seek damages to undo the effect of wrongs done to them. But unless we have in place a system to address those who would disregard the whole system—whether by supplanting their will for some particular legal arrangement or by flouting some specific order from a court requiring the payment of damages or enjoining a certain course of action—no other part of the legal system can perform its part in setting out the framework of equal freedom for us all.

On the constitutionalist account of criminal law, then, it is not the point of the criminal law (as Moore or Duff might argue) to bring people to account or to punish them simply for doing things that we could identify as morally wrong on our own, nor is it simply to minimize the incidence of undesirable conduct at the lowest cost (as utilitarians might suggest). Rather, its role is tied tightly to the very survival of the framework of rights that makes it possible for us to interact with others on terms of equal freedom. So the criminal law's legitimacy is, ultimately, tied to its morally necessary role as ultimate guarantor of that moral ordering. But the *way* in which we establish the moral legitimacy of the criminal law is quite different from the methods proposed by Moore, Duff, and other legal moralists. The criminal justice system is morally legitimate not because it is analogous to some other, familiar, morally acceptable practice. Rather, it is morally legitimate because it performs a morally necessary function that is unlike that performed by any other practice.

One final point is worth mentioning before we turn to the limits of the criminal law under the liberal constitutionalist account. That is, some might argue that an account of criminal law that is concerned with attempted usurpations of the law's authority to establish the relations that obtain between persons does not fit with our settled understanding of what makes

---

[21] Nils Jareborg, 'Criminalization as Last Resort (Ultima Ratio)' (2004) 2 *Ohio State Journal of Criminal Law* 521.

conduct criminal in the first place. Surely (one might argue) the core crimes of murder, rape, assault, theft, and so on are of concern to the criminal law not simply because the offender sought to supplant the law's terms of interaction with his own will, but for the much more straightforward reason that he wronged someone very seriously by killing her, raping her, etc.[22] Of course, it would seem odd in the extreme to suggest that the law was indifferent to the wrong done to the particular victim and was merely interested in maintaining its own position of authority in all these cases. But that is not my suggestion. Rather, what makes all such conduct wrongful for the purposes of the criminal law is that the offender has intentionally undermined the possibility of interacting with others as free choosers who are entitled to live under the terms of interaction set out by the law. He has done so by treating that person as a mere object who may be dealt with in whatever way he wishes. The wrong of rape—and of murder, assault, etc—is precisely the objectification of one person by another, but that objectification is of concern to the state because it is the state's job to ensure the survival of the system that makes it possible for us all to interact on terms that preserve the status of us all as free and equal moral agents.

IV. Constitutionalism and the Limits of the Criminal Law

In this section, I conclude with a round-up of some of the more important implications of the constitutionalist account of criminal justice for debates on the limits of the criminal law. Although there are many more,[23] I shall focus on two: the enforcement of moral norms against selfishness and the role of subjective *mens rea*.

A. Immorality and selfishness

Thinking of criminal law in the way I suggest renders certain aspect of criminal law a good deal less problematic than they would otherwise be. Those who, like Moore and Duff, take it to be a system for enforcing the demands of morality directly often have difficulty explaining why the

---

[22] Thanks to Antony Duff for raising this issue with me.

[23] As indicated in the discussion of part III, one further implication is that the criminal law—and the law generally—should be directed at securing the conditions of independence for all, and *only* at that end. I do not treat this point here only because it is too large a topic. However, it is probably the most powerful and most radical implication of the constitutionalist story for the limits of criminal law.

criminal law is so averse to punishing selfish behaviour and why it is so willing to punish those who engage in morally laudable civil disobedience. But once we recast the role of criminal law in terms of its function as enforcer of last resort of the legal order as a whole, it becomes a good deal clearer why the law refuses to enforce certain moral demands.

According to the liberal constitutionalist story set out above, law's role generally is not to guide us (much less to coerce us) to exercise our free choice in one way or another. Indeed, the whole point of the story is to set out a framework within which we may exercise our free choice as we see fit. Whereas morality is concerned first and foremost with *guiding the exercise* of our free choice to decide what we shall do with ourselves and with what is ours (whether to be generous with our property or not; whether to be courageous in the use of our bodies or not, etc), law concerns itself with *defining the scope* of our powers to decide such questions. Thus, the law tells us that we are not entitled to be 'generous' with the property of another because it simply does not belong to us; and we should not choose to be 'courageous' in dealing with a wrongful attacker when we have a clear avenue of escape because this is the job of the police department; and so on.

When we think of the criminal law as concerned with the enforcement of the law rather than with the enforcement of morals, we are able to make sense of these apparent conflicts a good deal more easily. The law gives us a 'right to do wrong' with our own bodies and property—to disregard the requests of others for assistance (whether this is donating money, lending property, or offering physical assistance with our bodies).[24] But the law also prohibits us from doing what seems like 'the right thing' when it is not our business (as it prohibits vigilantes from bringing wrongdoers to justice or Robin Hoods from using the property of others to be generous to the needy). Although there is clearly a sort of moral ideal—an ideal of freedom as independence— at work in the law's articulation of rights, it is a moral ideal about the appropriate starting points for the operation of ordinary individual morality, not its conclusions.

B. Mens rea

Traditional criminal law jurisprudence insists that true crimes must be defined in terms of subjective fault.[25] Now, if the criminal law were truly a

---

[24] For a longer list of examples, see my chapter: 'Criminal Law as Public Law' in R. A. Duff and Stuart Green (eds), *The Philosophical Foundations of the Criminal Law* (Oxford: OUP, 2011).

[25] See eg, Jerome Hall, 'Negligent Behaviour Should be Excluded from Penal Liability' (1963) 63 *Columbia Law Review* 632.

repository of moral norms, this insistence would seem to be out of place: moral norms are very often defined in terms of objective fault or, in many cases, no fault at all. If I knock over your valuable vase, I am answerable to you morally for doing so even though I took every reasonable precaution to avoid doing so (and my answer will consist simply in pointing out that I took such precautions and perhaps adding that I feel something like what Bernard Williams called 'agent-regret').[26] But I am not answerable in criminal law for this sort of occurrence. It is not simply that I ought not to be punished if I took every precaution to avoid the injury to your vase; there is not even a criminal wrong here for which I ought to provide some defence. This suggests that there is a significant difference between the sorts of wrongs that concern us in criminal law and ordinary moral wrongdoing. Although liability to moral criticism (like liability to criminal punishment) is not usually strict, there is nevertheless a sharp disconnect between the way we define a prima facie moral wrong and the way we define a prima facie criminal wrong.

In recent years, of course, one of the ways in which the criminal law has expanded so quickly has been to include prohibitions where the fault standard is objective, where responsibility is strict, or (increasingly) where even liability to punishment is strict.[27] So it would be grossly inaccurate to suggest that today's criminal law pays much attention to the criminal law requirement of subjective *mens rea*. Nevertheless, part of the idea of criminal law for many years—part of what distinguishes it from other areas of the law that deal with wrongs such as tort law—has been its insistence that subject fault is, if not the required fault standard, at least the norm.[28] A principled insistence that crimes ought to be defined in terms of subjective fault would provide a significant mechanism for limiting the scope of the criminal law.

The focus of attention for prominent legal moralists such as Michael Moore and Antony Duff has been on strict liability and strict responsibility. Both Moore and Duff have argued (rightly) that we ought not to be liable to criminal punishment (indeed, we ought not even to be obliged to answer for our conduct) without some showing of fault on our part. But their arguments

---

[26] Bernard A. O. Williams, 'Moral Luck' in *Moral Luck: Philosophical Papers, 1973–1980* (New York: CUP, 1981). On agent regret, see also David Enoch, 'Being Responsible, Taking Responsibility, and Penumbral Agency' (unpublished manuscript on file with author).

[27] See Andrew Ashworth, 'Is the Criminal Law a Lost Cause?' (2000) 116 *Law Quarterly Rev* 225 for examples.

[28] When we say that subjective *mens rea* is required for true crimes, this does not mean subjective *mens rea* with respect to consequences. All that is required is subjective awareness that one is engaging in conduct that one ought to have known was criminal. For a thoughtful consideration of the need for subjective *mens rea* in true crimes, see Alan Brudner, 'Subjective Fault for Crime: A Reinterpretation' (2008) 14 *Legal Theory* 1.

do not go far enough. The point that flows from the constitutionalist position on criminal law goes much further than simply insisting on *some* fault requirement in criminal law. The insistence of the constitutionalist position is that criminal law, unlike tort and most other areas of law, is concerned with conduct that is designed to supplant the law's norms themselves. We are not criminally liable merely for violating the law's demands; rather, we are criminally liable only when our conduct is best understood as an attempt to supplant the law's norms and to replace them with our own preferences. And this requires at the very least proof of subjective *mens rea*.

V. Conclusion

Over the past 30 years, criminal law theory has moved away from the utilitarianism that dominated so much legal thinking in the twentieth century toward a newfangled legal moralism that models the structure of criminal law on that of moral wrongdoing. The moralism of Michael Moore and Antony Duff shows criminal justice to be an enterprise that takes seriously the offender's right not to be used as a mere tool for the deterrence of undesirable conduct. But, as we have seen, their accounts are of practices so different from the criminal justice system as we know it today that it is difficult to call them theories *of criminal justice* at all. Instead, in this chapter, I have proposed an account of criminal justice that takes it to be part of a larger project of liberal constitutionalism. In this way, I argue that criminal justice can be vindicated as the state-dominated, coercive institution it is. Moreover, this account of criminal justice is able to generate a number of meaningful limits on the expansion of criminal law, as well. I identify two such limits in this chapter— the criminalization of selfishness in the exercise of private rights and the requirement of subjective *mens rea*—but there are others, as well. Of course, like any plausible account of the limits of criminal law, my account does not provide a clear criterion for exclusion that can be neatly applied to specific cases. Instead, it provides only a way of thinking about questions of criminalization and about the role of criminal justice in our lives. When it is the state's job simply to preserve the conditions of freedom for all (rather than to guide us to the morally right path in our private conduct), it stands to reason that the scope of the criminal law should be fairly narrow.

6

International Crime: in Context and in Contrast

Adil Ahmad Haque[1]

An appreciation for structure is perhaps the greatest contribution criminal law theory has made to normative philosophy. The ethicist's favourite question ('what ought I do?') naturally tends to flatten the moral landscape and narrow our moral vision. For when we occupy the deliberative perspective, when we seek to guide our own conduct or those of others, the only moral categories that seem to matter are those of the permissible, the impermissible, the obligatory, and perhaps the supererogatory. Only when we adopt the evaluative perspective, when we seek to judge the conduct of others or our own, does the need become apparent to distinguish in a rigorous way between harm and culpability; offences and defences; justifications, excuses, and denials of responsibility. Such concepts are indispensible if we are to intelligently attribute responsibility, affix blame, and apportion punishment. It is therefore unsurprising that the deep structure of wrongdoing is primarily explored within criminal law theory and only sparingly incorporated into mainstream moral philosophy. It is also fitting that this volume should be devoted to exploring the structure of criminal law.

The topic of this chapter is the structure of international crimes, which differs from the structure of national crimes in two important respects. First, international crimes typically include—in addition to their conduct, result, and attendant circumstance elements—a contextual element that national crimes rarely contain. For example, the killing of a civilian will be considered a war crime if '[t]he conduct took place in the context of and was associated with' an armed conflict; a crime against humanity if 'committed as part of a widespread or systematic attack directed against any civilian population, with

[1] Thanks to Massimo Renzo and to all the participants in the Glasgow and Stirling workshops for their many excellent suggestions.

knowledge of the attack'; or an act of genocide if 'committed with intent to destroy, in whole or in part, a national, ethnical, racial or religious group, as such'. The first task of this chapter is to explain how this unfamiliar structure relates the values at stake in international crimes to one another. More specifically, the task will be to determine whether the contextual element of each international crime contributes to the moral wrongfulness of the offence or to the justification for subjecting the offence to the jurisdiction of international criminal tribunals.

In addition, to the extent that international crimes and national crimes display parallel structures, the parallel structures they display organize similar values in dissimilar ways. For example, international crimes such as attacking civilians are defined in terms of conduct; national crimes that implicate similar values such as murder are typically defined in terms of result. International crimes such as causing excessive civilian death include justificatory concepts in the definition of the offence; national crimes typically exclude such concepts, which instead appear in the definition of affirmative defences. The second task of the chapter is to determine whether these international crimes place the relevant values in their proper orientation toward one another, or whether they should be restructured along the lines of national criminal law. In particular, it must be determined whether these international crimes reflect a viable alternative structure according to which crimes are constituted by or related to either an attack or an endangerment.

Two brief prefatory remarks are probably in order. The definition and elements of the international crimes discussed will generally be drawn from the Rome Statute of the International Criminal Court, the multilateral treaty that established that tribunal, as well as the Elements of Crimes, a document approved by the signatories to the Rome Statute to guide the tribunal's interpretation of the Rome Statute. The rulings of other international criminal tribunals will be referred to only where they shed light on the provisions of the Rome Statute or the Elements of Crimes or where those provisions appear to deviate from customary international law. On a terminological note, I will use the term 'wrong' to describe the violation of a right or duty and will use the term 'wrongful' to describe the blameworthy commission of a wrong.

I. International Crimes in Context

In its Preamble, the Rome Statute of the International Criminal Court states that the world's first permanent international criminal tribunal will assert jurisdiction over 'the most serious crimes of concern to the international community as a whole'.[2] To a significant extent, this one clause sets the agenda for international criminal law theory. Specifically, a theory of international criminal law must do at least two things. First, it must account for the *seriousness* of international crimes, by identifying the features of international crimes that contribute to their moral gravity and by explaining the contribution made by each feature. Second, such a theory must explain why these crimes are *of concern* to the international community as a whole, by identifying the features of international crimes that justify the assertion of jurisdiction over those crimes by international tribunals (and perhaps by the national courts of uninvolved states). Sometimes, these two tasks will coincide, since sometimes the moral seriousness of international crimes justifies the assertion of international jurisdiction over them. But sometimes the features of international crimes that justify international jurisdiction do not contribute to the wrongfulness of those crimes, and sometimes features of international crimes which both contribute to their wrongfulness and justify international jurisdiction over them do not justify international jurisdiction in terms of the wrongfulness of the crimes.

The purpose of this part is to determine whether the so-called contextual elements of war crimes, crimes against humanity, and genocide contribute to the wrongfulness of these crimes or justify international tribunals in asserting jurisdiction over these crimes. In the language of the Model Penal Code, the question is whether we should view each contextual element as a material element or as a non-material element of the respective offences.[3] The question is of tremendous theoretical importance because it is primarily the contextual elements that differentiate international crimes from domestic crimes as well as from one another. International crimes typically contain a list of constituent acts preceded by a single 'chapeau' provision containing the contextual element that each of the constituent acts must satisfy in order to constitute an international crime. The constituent acts of each international crime are mostly familiar crimes such as murder, torture, and rape, or necessarily involve such crimes. It is the fact that such crimes are committed

---

[2] Rome Statute of the International Criminal Court, 17 July 1998, Preamble, UN Doc A/CONF.183/9 [hereinafter Rome Statute].

[3] American Law Institute, *Model Penal Code and Commentaries* (1985) § 2.02 (defining material elements as 'those characteristics (conduct, circumstances, result) of the actor's behavior that, when combined with the appropriate level of culpability, will constitute the offense'). Ibid. § 1.13(10) (defining non-material elements as those which 'relate exclusively to the statute of limitations, jurisdiction, venue or to any other matter similarly unconnected with (i) the harm or evil, incident to conduct, sought to be prevented by the law defining the offense, or (ii) the existence of a justification or excuse for such conduct').

in the context of armed conflict, or as part of an attack on a civilian population, or with the intent to destroy a group, that makes them international crimes. To understand the rationale of this unique constituent-act/contextual-element structure is to understand the essence of international criminal law.

A. War crimes

War crimes are serious violations of the laws and customs of war, which are derived primarily from the 1949 Geneva Conventions as well as the 1977 Additional Protocols to the Geneva Conventions. The laws and customs of war only apply to acts committed during armed conflict, which may involve the resort to armed force between states or protracted armed violence between states and armed groups or between such groups. Moreover, the laws and customs of war can only be violated by members of an armed force, by civilians who take direct part in hostilities, or by civilians who are linked to an armed force by a relevant position of *de jure* or *de facto* authority or responsibility.[4] Finally, the laws and customs of war are only violated by acts that are committed in furtherance or as a result of armed conflict.[5] The Elements of Crimes reflects these requirements when it states that an act only constitutes a war crime if it not only involved the requisite conduct, result, or attendant circumstance but also 'took place in the context of and was associated with' an armed conflict.[6]

The prescriptive jurisdiction of international law to define the laws of armed conflict seems relatively easy to justify. It seems desirable to regulate armed conflict by a shared set of legal norms applicable to all potential parties, and this could not be achieved through domestic legislation and military doctrine alone. Such a shared standard is necessary to prevent a race to the bottom, in which parties to armed conflict gain tactical advantage by legally permitting or otherwise adopting means and methods of warfare that their adversary legally forbids or otherwise forswears.[7]

Similarly, the adjudicative jurisdiction of international tribunals to try defendants for legal wrongs committed during armed conflict has several

---

[4] *Prosecutor v Clement Kayishema & Obed Ruzindana*, Case No ICTR-95-1-T, Judgment, para 175, 617 (21 May 1999).

[5] *Prosecutor v Kunarac et al, Case No* IT-96-23-A & IT-96-23/1-A, Judgment, para 58 (12 June 2002).

[6] UN Preparatory Commission for the International Criminal Court, Finalized Draft Text of the Elements of Crimes, arts 8(2)(a)(i)(4), 8(2)(c)(i)-1(4), UN Doc PCNICC/2000/1/ADD.2 (2 November 2000) [hereinafter Elements of Crimes].

[7] Whether international criminal law has set the bar correctly is a question for another paper.

plausible justifications. States will often be unwilling to prosecute war crimes committed by their own forces and unable to prosecute war crimes committed by enemy forces. Moreover, states that prosecute their own forces may scapegoat low-ranking personnel while the high-ranking officials most responsible for war crimes enjoy impunity. Finally, states that prosecute enemy forces may impose (or appear to impose) 'victor's justice', resulting in (or appearing to result in) false convictions, disproportionate sentences, and violations of due process.

The more interesting question is whether the context of armed conflict compounds the wrongfulness of the conduct, result, and circumstantial elements of the various war crimes. For example, it is an element of every war crime that '[t]he perpetrator was aware of [the] factual circumstances that established the existence of an armed conflict'.[8] Ordinarily, defendants need not posses any mental state with respect to merely jurisdictional elements, and this might seem to suggest that the context of armed conflict is intended as a material element instead. However, the Elements of Crimes elsewhere makes clear that it requires only that level of awareness 'implicit in the terms "took place in the context of and was associated with" [an armed conflict]'.[9] It is necessary but not sufficient to satisfy the contextual element that an act occurred during the same time period and in the same geographical area as an armed conflict. There must be some causal relationship between the act and the surrounding conflict, and the Elements of Crimes suggests that causal relationship must be mediated by the actor's awareness of the context. The awareness requirement clarifies but does not add anything to the contextual element, and indicates nothing about its materiality or non-materiality.

I believe that the key to understanding the moral significance of the contextual element is to recognize that, while other international crimes only supplement domestic criminal law, war crimes can either supplement or displace domestic criminal law, depending on the legal status of the perpetrator and the victim. For example, an individual who intentionally kills another person may be charged with murder under domestic criminal law. If that killing was part of an attack on a civilian population the perpetrator may also be charged with the crime against humanity of murder under international criminal law. By contrast, if the perpetrator and victim were members of opposing armed forces then the perpetrator typically may not be charged either with a war crime under international criminal law or with murder under domestic criminal law. There are two reasons for this result. The first reason is that it is generally not a war crime to intentionally

---

[8] Elements of Crimes, arts 8(2)(a)(i)(5), 8(2)(c)(i)-1(5).
[9] Elements of Crimes, art 8, Introduction.

kill members of an opposing armed force (except for religious and medical personnel) who pose no immediate threat to oneself or others and who probably will never pose such a threat. Such killings generally require neither justification nor excuse under international criminal law. The second reason is that members of an organized armed force who wear a distinctive mark or uniform and who carry arms openly may raise the affirmative defence of lawful combatancy if charged in domestic criminal courts with ordinary crimes such as murder. If the domestic crimes with which a lawful combatant is charged are not also war crimes then he or she enjoys 'combat immunity' from prosecution under domestic criminal law. By contrast, no such immunity is extended to civilians who take direct part in hostilities or to unlawful combatants who either fail to wear a distinctive mark or uniform or fail to carry their arms openly. These two categories of defendants may be prosecuted under domestic criminal law (whether or not their acts constitute war crimes) as well as under international criminal law for any war crimes they commit. The law of war can serve either as a basis for or as a bar to prosecution.

War crimes are therefore best understood not as acts that are wrongful because they are committed in armed conflict, but rather as wrongs that are specifically exempted from a lawful combatant's general immunity from prosecution in national courts. A parallel situation would arise if foreign diplomats enjoyed general immunity from prosecution in domestic courts but this immunity did not apply to particularly serious offences such as murder, rape, and arson. Similarly, lawful combatants enjoy general immunity for acts committed in the context of and in association with armed conflict, save for those acts defined as war crimes. The contextual element references the potential application of the general immunity, while the material elements establish an exemption from the general immunity. Sometimes an exemption is explained by the intrinsic seriousness of the wrong exempted, but often the exemptions are explained by pragmatic considerations or historical processes.

Take, for example, the war crime of intentionally directing an attack against civilians not taking direct part in hostilities.[10] When committed outside the context of armed conflict, for example by a terrorist organization, attacking civilians is among the most serious moral wrongs human beings can commit. Does such an attack become more wrongful when launched in the context of armed conflict? It is hard to see how. By contrast, it is easy to see why such a serious wrong should be exempted from the general immunity

---

[10] Rome Statute art. 8(2)(b)(i).

enjoyed by lawful combatants. This is true despite the fact that it is not entirely clear what, if anything, justifies the doctrine of combat immunity in its current form. For any plausible defence of combat immunity will either claim that combatants are justified in killing any member of an opposing armed force; or that they are justified in killing some members of an opposing armed force but not others and they are excused or not responsible for failing to distinguish between the two; or that they are justified in killing some or all members of an opposing armed force only if the killing serves a just cause and they are excused or not responsible for failing accurately to judge whether their cause is just or unjust. None of these possible defences seems to apply to intentionally attacking civilians not taking direct part in hostilities.

For example, Jeff McMahan has argued that the strongest reasons for not holding combatants responsible for fighting on behalf of an unjust cause are pragmatic and epistemic rather than moral in a deep sense. McMahan argues that we lack clear legal rules and authoritative legal bodies to distinguish between just and unjust causes. Moreover, since both sides of an armed conflict tend to think they fight for a just cause, any legal restrictions on those fighting for an unjust cause will be ignored by both sides while any legal permissions granted to those fighting for a just cause will be exploited by both sides. McMahan concludes that international law should not permit behaviour, such as attacking civilians, that will rarely be necessary to achieve a just cause and that would be intolerable if used in furtherance of an unjust cause.[11]

There are, of course, some war crimes that cannot be committed except during armed conflict, such as the crime of compelling nationals of the opposing party to take part in military operations against their own country.[12] However, in such cases it seems that the context of armed conflict is not a wrong-making feature of the war crime but rather a wrong-enabling feature. What makes it wrong to compel someone to fight against their country is that, in addition to forcing them to participate in killing others and risk their own lives, one thereby compels them to violate their own moral obligations of loyalty in a uniquely egregious way. It would not be possible to force them to act disloyally in this uniquely egregious way if there were no armed conflict in which one could compel them to fight, but the existence of the armed conflict does not itself contribute to the wrongfulness of compelling them to fight in it. Instead, the wrongfulness of compelling individuals to fight against their own country, combined with its limited military utility, justifies exempting this wrong from the scope of combat immunity.

---

[11] Jeff McMahan, *Killing in War* (New York: Oxford University Press, 2009) 108–9.
[12] Rome Statute art 8(2)(b)(xv).

It is also true that certain war crimes share morally significant features with crimes that are *mala prohibita*. For instance, treacherous or perfidious killing typically involves pretending to be wounded or a civilian and then attacking enemy soldiers who lower their defences. Such killings involve the manipulation of other rules of international law in order to obtain an unfair advantage in combat. International humanitarian law grants the wounded and civilians the benefit of immunity from attack so long as they do not participate in hostilities. Similarly, soldiers waving a flag of truce, as well as employees of the United Nations and Red Cross/Red Crescent, are protected persons who may not be attacked during armed conflict. When soldiers pretend to be protected persons they gain the benefit of immunity from attack without assuming the corresponding burden of foregoing participation in hostilities. Such treachery is a kind of free-riding—on rules designed to protect the lives of civilians, the wounded, and humanitarian personnel—and one could characterize the punishment of treachery as an attempt to annul the unjust advantage gained by treachery.

Certainly, treacherous killings are more wrongful that non-treacherous killings since the means of causing death involve not only deception but also the manipulation of laws that protect important interests as well as the exploitation of the victim's obedience to those laws. The full wrongfulness of treacherous killing could not be explained without reference to positive law, so to that extent there is a *malum prohibitum* component to the wrong. Indeed, the wrong-making force of this *malum prohibitum* component may justify exempting this wrong from the general immunity afforded to lawful combatants. But it would be misleading to characterize the war crime of treacherous killing as *malum prohibitum* without qualification. After all, treacherous killings are a subset of intentional killings, and intentional killings not justified by self-defence or defence of others are considered *mala in se* when committed by ordinary criminals or by unlawful combatants. What is remarkable about the law of war is not that it forbids treacherous killing of enemy combatants but that it permits lawful combatants to non-treacherously kill enemy combatants who pose no immediate threat to anyone.

Similarly, international criminal law prohibits the use of certain weapons per se, irrespective of their impact on civilians, such as poisons, gases, and expanding bullets.[13] It is not clear that dying from such weapons is substantially more horrific than dying from flamethrowers, shrapnel-laden explosives, or other non-prohibited weapons. The list of prohibited weapons is in large measure a historical artefact reflecting the repugnance felt toward such

---

[13] Rome Statute art 8(2)(b)(xvii–xix).

weapons following the horrors of World War I. There is no intrinsic reason (that is, no reason based on their intrinsic properties) why these weapons should be prohibited while equally horrible weapons are permitted. But it does not follow that the war crimes of employing these weapons are *mala prohibita*. Employing any weapon except in self-defence or defence of others is ordinarily *mala in se* and is criminal when committed by an unlawful combatant. Again, the remarkable thing about international criminal law is not that it prohibits the use of certain weapons but that it permits lawful combatants to use any other weapon against enemy combatants even if they pose no immediate threat. Lawful combatants are permitted to employ any weapon that is not specifically prohibited by international law, while unlawful combatants are prohibited from employing any weapon absent justification.

In conclusion, the contextual element of war crimes can help justify the jurisdiction of international tribunals over war crimes but does not directly contribute to their wrongfulness. On the contrary, the context of armed conflict generally serves to bar prosecution of lawful combatants for the acts they commit in violation of national criminal laws. The moral gravity of war crimes lies in their material elements, including those material elements that are only possible to satisfy in the context of armed conflict or that make essential reference to other laws and customs of war. War crimes are serious moral wrongs which have been exempted from the general immunity from prosecution enjoyed by lawful combatants and which are liable to prosecution as distinct international crimes as well as ordinary domestic crimes. The reason for their exemption from combat immunity is a function of their moral wrongfulness, their military utility, and historical accident.

B. Crimes against humanity

Crimes against humanity are inhumane acts 'committed as part of a widespread or systematic attack directed against any civilian population, with knowledge of the attack'.[14] These inhumane acts include murder, enslavement, deportation or forcible transfer of population, imprisonment in violation of international law, torture, rape and other forms of sexual violence, persecution, enforced disappearance of persons, and apartheid.[15] The Rome Statute additionally provides that such an attack must involve 'the *multiple commission* of [inhumane acts] against any civilian population, *pursuant to or*

---

[14] Rome Statute art 7(1).

[15] Ibid. Crimes against humanity also include '[o]ther inhumane acts of a similar character intentionally causing great suffering, or serious injury to body or to mental or physical health'. Ibid art 7(1)(k).

in furtherance of a State or organizational policy to commit such attack'.[16] This additional provision has a questionable basis in customary international law,[17] and seems inconsistent with the notion that such an attack may be *either* widespread *or* systematic. In any event, it is this contextual or (more precisely) participatory element that distinguishes crimes against humanity from ordinary crimes.

It is relatively easy to see how a widespread or systematic attack on a civilian population, particularly by a state or organization, could justify international tribunals in exercising jurisdiction over participants in the attack. States are more likely to be unwilling or unable to prosecute inhumane acts if they are committed by state officials or by organizations that have broken the state's monopoly on violence, co-opted state officials, or represent dominant social groups.[18] Moreover, the widespread or systematic nature of such an attack justifies the expenditure of the limited political capital and institutional resources of international tribunals.

The more interesting question is whether an inhumane act committed as part of a widespread or systematic attack on a civilian population is more wrongful than a similar inhumane act considered in isolation. For example, David Luban and Larry May have independently argued that attacks on a civilian population necessarily involve harming individuals based on their group membership rather than their individual characteristics.[19] Yet the moral significance of such non-individualized treatment remains somewhat obscure. Of course, it is always presumptively wrongful to harm someone who has personally done nothing to deserve or make themselves liable to be harmed. But neither Luban nor May explain why harming someone based on their membership in a civilian population is worse than harming someone based on any other fact that makes them neither deserving nor liable to be harmed. Moreover, since a civilian population may be targeted for reasons that are strategic rather than ideological, the extent to which such targeting is 'group-based' may be quite attenuated. For example, a civilian population might be attacked in order to deter or demoralize an opposing armed force, or to prevent members of an opposing armed group from hiding among the civilian population.

---

[16] Rome Statute art. 7(2)(a) (emphasis added).

[17] *Prosecutor v Kunarac*, Case No IT-96-23/1-A, Judgment, para 98, n 114 (12 June 2002) (concluding that 'no such requirement exists under customary international law').

[18] A. A. Haque, 'Group Violence and Group Vengeance: Toward a Retributivist Theory of International Criminal Law' (2005) 9 *Buffalo Criminal Law Review* 273.

[19] D. Luban, 'A Theory of Crimes against Humanity' (2004) 29 *Yale Journal of International Law* 85; L. May, *Crimes against Humanity: A Normative Account* (New York: Cambridge University Press, 2005).

Along different lines, Alison Danner has suggested that crimes against humanity deserve greater punishment than war crimes involving the same constituent acts because the perpetrators likely 'took encouragement, comfort, and resolve from the violent context in which they acted'.[20] One could imagine why greater punishment might be thought necessary to deter inhumane acts committed in groups, counteracting the psychological dynamics of collective action by threatening greater individual punishment.[21] What is harder to imagine is why it is worse to commit an inhumane act in conformity with the conduct of others than in any other circumstances in which one's moral, social, or temperamental inhibitions are temporarily weakened. More precisely, it is unclear how the weakening of one's inhibitions in particular circumstances adds to the wrongfulness of one's subsequent behaviour.

It seems more promising to argue for the converse position, namely that participation in a widespread or systematic attack on civilians is likely to *give* encouragement, comfort, and resolve to other actual or potential participants. More precisely, it is plausible to suppose that, if one commits an inhumane act as part of an attack on civilians, one thereby creates a substantial and unjustifiable risk that one will thereby encourage others to do the same. The imposition of this risk could, in turn, compound the wrongfulness of the inhumane act one commits.

However, there are two serious problems with such an account of the wrong-making force of the contextual element. First, on such an account crimes against humanity would be, in part, crimes of 'implicit endangerment' that do not explicitly refer to the risks they typically impose.[22] Such crimes are easier to prove in court, provide greater clarity to individuals seeking to conform their conduct to the law, and lend themselves to more consistent application than crimes defined in terms of risk, recklessness, or dangerousness.[23] However, because crimes of implicit endangerment permit conviction without proof that the relevant risks were in fact created by the defendant, they seem to permit punishment in excess of actual wrongdoing.

---

[20] A. M. Danner, 'Constructing a Hierarchy of Crimes in International Criminal Law Sentencing' (2001) 87 *Virginia Law Review* 415, 495.

[21] Similarly, if the harm or evil that one seeks to prevent is not the commission of the constituent crimes but only their widespread or systematic commission then one plausible prevention strategy would be to impose individual criminal liability for knowing or intentional participation in a widespread or systematic attack.

[22] R. A. Duff, *Answering for Crime: Responsibility and Liability in the Criminal Law* (Portland, Oregon: Hart Publishing, 2007) 166.

[23] Ibid 167.

Second, on such an account crimes against humanity would also be, in part, crimes of indirect endangerment that create a risk that another person will commit a wrongful or harmful action.[24] Such crimes are also difficult to justify, because typically one person can only be held responsible for the wrongs of another if the first person causally contributes to the other person's commission of the wrong with the intention or with the knowledge that the other person will commit that wrong.[25] Moreover, it seems illegitimate to hold someone responsible for creating a risk if they could not be held responsible for the materialization of that risk. It therefore seems problematic to hold one person responsible for creating a risk of encouraging the crimes of others unless they did so with the intent or with the belief that those further crimes will occur.

To conclude, the contextual element of crimes against humanity provides a substantial basis for asserting international jurisdiction over constituent acts committed in that context. However, the contextual element provides at best a problematic basis for considering acts committed in that context more wrongful than they would be outside that context. The distinction is practically quite important because it suggests that crimes against humanity should not always be punished more severely than war crimes involving similar constituent acts.

C. Genocide

Genocide is 'any of the following acts committed with intent to destroy, in whole or in part, a national, ethnical, racial or religious group, as such:

(a) Killing members of the group;

(b) Causing serious bodily or mental harm to members of the group;

(c) Deliberately inflicting on the group conditions of life calculated to bring about its physical destruction in whole or in part;

(d) Imposing measures intended to prevent births within the group;

(e) Forcibly transferring children of the group to another group.'[26]

---

[24] Ibid 163–5.

[25] Under customary international law, knowingly contributing to the crimes of others may be sufficient to make one complicit in those crimes. *Prosecutor v Anto Furundzija*, Case No IT-95-17/1-T, Judgment, paras 236, 245 (10 December 1998). The Rome Statute generally requires purposeful facilitation to be responsible for the crimes of others. Rome Statute art. 25(3)(c). However, one is also responsible under the Rome Statute for a crime if one contributes to the commission of the crime by a group acting with a common purpose with knowledge of the group's intention to commit the crime. Ibid art 25(3)(2).

[26] Rome Statute art 6.

Each of the five constituent acts either describes or necessarily involves crimes under domestic criminal law, including murder, assault, and kidnapping.[27] These familiar domestic crimes constitute the international crime of genocide only if they are committed with the intent to partially or totally destroy the group of which the immediate victim is a member. This specific intention is both the substantive and the structural essence of the crime of genocide.

Genocide is a form of instrumental violence in which the constituent acts serve as means to an end. Importantly, the constituent acts may be either a causal or a constitutive means to achieve the intended outcome. The partial or total destruction of a group may be the intended causal consequence of preventing births within the group, while killing members of the group in sufficient numbers may have the partial or total destruction of the group as its non-causal result. Additionally, the intent required to commit genocide may be the *motive* for committing a constituent act that is itself intended to destroy a group; or the intent may be a *further intention* to continue a course of conduct, such as maintaining conditions of life calculated to destroy a group, or to perform independent future acts, such as killing additional members of the group.[28] Finally, the perpetrator of the constituent act may but need not intend to personally destroy the group; it is sufficient to intend that the group be destroyed and that the constituent act contribute to its destruction by oneself or others.

Under customary international law, an act need not occur within any particular context in order to constitute genocide.[29] The Elements of Crimes creates a quasi-contextual element, namely that an act 'took place in the context of a manifest pattern of similar conduct directed against that group *or* was conduct that could itself effect such destruction'.[30] No mental state is required with respect to this new requirement, suggesting that its function may be jurisdictional. However, the most plausible basis for the new requirement is that 'it will be very difficult in practice to provide proof of the genocidal intent of an individual if the crimes committed are not widespread and if the crime charged is not backed by an organisation or a system' unless

---

[27] For example, inflicting conditions of life calculated to physically destroy a group typically involves 'subjecting a group of people to a subsistence diet, systematic expulsion from their homes and deprivation of essential medical supplies below a minimum vital standard'. *Prosecutor v Rutaganda*, Case No ICTR-96-3-T, Judgment, para 52 (6 December 1999). It is hard to imagine how such conduct could occur without the use or threat of force.

[28] *Prosecutor v Jelisic*, Case No IT-95-10-T, Judgment, para 100 n 147 (14 December 1999).

[29] *Prosecutor v Krstić*, Case No IT-98-33-A, Appeals Chamber, Judgment, para 224 (19 April 2004).

[30] Elements of Crimes, art 6(a)(4) (emphasis added). Ibid arts 6(b)(4), 6(c)(5), 6(d)(5), 6(e)(7) (same).

perhaps the perpetrator possesses weapons of mass destruction.[31] More precisely, an individual can *desire* but cannot *intend* to partially or totally destroy a group unless she believes she possesses or can acquire the capacity to do so, either individually or in concert with others. For this reason as well, the focus of this section will be on the distinctive element of the crime of genocide, namely the intent to partially or totally destroy a protected group.

The wrongfulness of genocide may seem too obvious to require an elaborate theoretical explanation. In fact there are two mainstream theories of the wrongfulness of genocide. The first theory, sometimes called 'group pluralism', plausibly holds that the value of a human community is not reducible to the value of its members, and that the partial or total destruction of such a community constitutes a loss of value over and above the death or dispersal of its members. The seriousness of the crime of genocide, it follows, derives from the loss of this relational value when human communities are partially or totally destroyed.[32] This crime is particularly 'of concern' to the international community because the very purpose of the international system is to ensure peaceful coexistence and promote productive cooperation among states characterized by national, ethnic, racial, and religious diversity. No system founded on such a moral and political ideal, and which takes its constitutive values seriously, can fail to condemn the partial or total annihilation of a national, ethnic, racial, or religious group, even when committed within the borders of a single state or against a group with little presence elsewhere in the world.

However, the crime of genocide is not structured as if its function was to protect human communities. The partial or total destruction of social groups can be the result of human action, and if the crime of genocide derives its wrongfulness from this result then the crime should be structured like other result crimes. For instance, criminal law reflects the value of human life primarily by criminalizing as murder culpably causing the death of another human being, secondarily by extending liability to those who attempt or conspire to commit murder, and finally, in a dwindling number of jurisdictions, by separately criminalizing assault with intent to kill. In other words, when wrongfulness derives from results, criminal law starts with the consummate crime of causing that result, continues with the non-consummate crime of attempting or conspiring to cause that result, and in some jurisdictions creates half-consummate offences involving the commission of a lesser wrong with the intent to cause that result.

---

[31] *Jelisic* (n 28 above) para 101.
[32] D. Luban, 'Calling Genocide by Its Rightful Name: Lemkin's Word, Darfur, and the UN Report' (2006) 7 *Chicago Journal of International Law* 303, 310.

Similarly, if international criminal law embraced the group-pluralist theory we should expect it to define a consummate crime of partially or totally destroying a protected group. The commission of such a consummate offence would generally require many co-perpetrators but would still be a plausible potential basis for individual criminal liability. We should also expect to find certain inchoate or non-consummate offences to ensure that those who attempt or conspire to partially or totally destroy a protected group, or incite others to do so, would not escape criminal liability. We might not expect, but would not be surprised to find, separate half-consummate offences involving lesser wrongs committed with the intent to partially or totally destroy the protected group.

As we have seen, international criminal law has taken precisely the opposite approach to defining the crime of genocide. International criminal law defines genocide as killing or harming individual group members with the intent to cause the partial or total destruction of the group as such. It follows that to attempt or conspire to commit genocide is not to attempt or conspire to destroy a protected group but to attempt or conspire to commit a constituent act with the intent to thereby destroy a group. From the perspective of the group-pluralist theory, it is as if international criminal law criminalizes assault with intent to kill but not murder, as well as attempt, conspiracy, and incitement to commit assault with intent to kill but not attempt, conspiracy, or incitement to commit murder.

Additionally, if international criminal law is primarily concerned to prevent the partial or total destruction of groups then it is not clear why genocide should prohibit killing or harming only with the intent to cause this result but not with knowledge that this result will occur or with reckless disregard for the risk that this result might occur.[33] A defendant who acts in order to cause a prohibited result is no doubt more culpable than a defendant who knowingly or recklessly causes a prohibited result for other reasons, but it is not clear why only the former should face international criminal liability. It is of course open to the group pluralist to argue that international criminal law has structured the crime of genocide incorrectly, but this argument will only succeed if no other plausible theory can account for both the wrong and the crime of genocide as currently defined.

Let us turn, then, to the second mainstream theory of the wrongfulness of genocide, sometimes called 'expressivism'. The critical conceptual difference between expressivism and group pluralism is that the group pluralist locates the greater wrongfulness of genocide in that which is intended while the expressivist locates the greater wrongfulness of genocide in the intention

---

[33] Haque (n 18 above) 309–10.

itself. The group pluralist thinks that it is more wrongful to kill or harm with the intent to destroy a group because it would be a more serious wrong to succeed in destroying that group. The expressivist thinks that it is more wrongful to kill or harm with the intent to destroy a group because the perpetrator thereby expresses an incorrect valuation of that group. Now, it is true that the incorrect values expressed by the intent to destroy a group are incorrect in part for the reasons that would make the destruction of that group wrong. The group pluralist values the existence of the targeted group over and above the lives of its members, while the genocidaire incorrectly values the destruction of the group over and above the death of its members. However, the expressivist's position is that the expression of those incorrect values makes an independent contribution to the wrongfulness of their pursuit over and above the wrongfulness of their fulfilment.

There are two ways in which the expressivist position could be developed. First, the incorrect valuations of the wrongdoer may affect the seriousness of the wrong. Alternatively, the incorrect valuations of the wrongdoer may affect his or her own blameworthiness without affecting the seriousness of the wrong. The distinction is of both theoretical and practical importance. First, if genocide is generally a more serious wrong than crimes against humanity then there is generally a stronger moral obligation to prevent genocide than to prevent crimes against humanity. Importantly, military intervention to prevent genocide may be easier to justify than military intervention to prevent crimes against humanity. Second, if perpetrators of genocide are generally more blameworthy than perpetrators of crimes against humanity then there is generally a stronger moral obligation to punish the former than to punish the latter. If so, then international tribunals should prioritize the prosecution of genocide rather than crimes against humanity. This is because the strength of an obligation to prevent a wrong depends on the seriousness of the wrong, including the harmfulness of the wrong, which is unaffected by the blameworthiness of the wrongdoer. By contrast, the strength of an obligation to punish a wrong depends on the blameworthiness of the wrongdoer, which is affected but not determined solely by the seriousness of the wrong.[34] So if genocide is a more serious wrong than

---

[34] For example, we do not have a stronger obligation to prevent intentional murder than to prevent intentional manslaughter committed in the heat of passion, because murder and manslaughter involve the same moral wrong. By contrast, we have a stronger obligation to punish murder than to punish manslaughter, because manslaughter involves the commission of the same wrong under mitigating circumstances. Victor Tadros has suggested in conversation that we have a duty to prevent harms rather than wrongs. However, it seems clear that we have a duty to prevent significant wrongs to others, including wrongs involving degrading treatment, even if those wrongs will not set back their long-term interests.

crimes against humanity then we have stronger obligations to both prevent and punish the former than to prevent and punish the latter. However, if the two wrongs are equally serious but perpetrators of genocide are nevertheless more blameworthy than perpetrators of crimes against humanity then we will have a stronger obligation to punish the former than the latter but equally strong obligations to prevent both.

The question, then, is whether genocide is a more serious wrong than crimes against humanity or whether perpetrators of the former are more blameworthy than perpetrators of the latter for reasons other than the relative seriousness of the two wrongs. As I have argued elsewhere, it is a more serious wrong to kill or harm members of a group with the intent to destroy that group because killing or harming with that intention inflicts an expressive harm over and above the loss of life or injury suffered.[35] An expressive harm, in turn, is inflicted when one person 'is treated according to principles that express negative or inappropriate attitudes toward her'.[36] Typically the infliction of expressive harm compounds other wrongs, so it is important to try to isolate the wrong-making force of expressive harm in particular cases. For example, the maintenance of racially segregated schools in the United States would have seriously wronged black students even if (counterfactually) the schools to which they were assigned did not have fewer resources and inferior facilities than the schools from which they were excluded. The relevant wrong would have consisted in sending black students to different schools than white students because the black students were viewed as inferior and unworthy of sharing social space with whites. Moreover, black students would have been the victims of this wrong, with standing to complain and seek redress, for it would have been they who were being treated with disrespect. Both black and white students could claim to have been treated irrationally or arbitrarily, but only black students could claim to have been wronged.[37]

Similarly, killing or harming with the intent to destroy a protected group expresses the view that members of the protected group are unworthy of sharing the same country, or the same region, or the same world with

---

[35] Haque (n 18 above) 313–15.

[36] E. S. Anderson and R. H. Pildes, 'Expressive Theories of Law: A General Restatement' (2000) 148 *University of Pennsylvania Law Review* 1503, 1527.

[37] It is therefore not strictly correct to say that 'separate is inherently unequal'. *Brown v Bd of Educ*, 347 U.S. 483, 495 (1954). The separation of individuals into materially equivalent facilities based on group membership is only wrongful when that separation expresses a belief that one group is inferior to the other. For example, it is not clear that the maintenance of sex-segregated bathrooms morally wrongs women, while it is clear that the maintenance of race-segregated bathrooms morally wronged black Americans.

members of the perpetrator's group. The intent of the genocidaire is either to leave the group without any members or leave individuals with no distinct group of which to be members. The expression of this attitude inflicts an expressive harm on its victims, compounding the already grave wrongs through which the attitude is expressed. A similar expressive harm is inflicted on the victims of persecution (the deprivation of fundamental rights based on group membership) and apartheid (the commission of inhumane acts in furtherance of the institutionalized oppression of a racial group), both crimes against humanity, since each crime expresses the view that members of the targeted group are unworthy of legal or social equality. Genocidal intent, by contrast, expresses the view that members of the targeted group are unworthy of existence; either they must be destroyed in order to destroy the group or the group must be destroyed as a distinct social entity in order to terminate their membership in the group.

The remaining question, then, is whether the expressive harm inflicted by genocide is substantially greater than the expressive harm inflicted by crimes against humanity committed without the intention to destroy a protected group. After all, every intentional wrong expresses some devaluation of the victim based on some characteristic of the victim. Here is where the group pluralist re-enters the discussion. The attitude expressed by genocidal intent essentially inverts the values of the group pluralist. The group pluralist attributes positive value to the existence of the group as a distinct entity over and above the lives and well-being of its members; indeed, the lives and well-being of group members derive additional value from their incremental contribution to the existence and vitality of the group. The genocidaire attributes positive value to the destruction of the group and to the death and suffering of its members insofar as this incrementally contributes to the destruction of the group. If the group pluralist is correct that the diversity of human communities is a very great value, and one with which international law should particularly concern itself, then it would be reasonable to conclude that an expressive harm constituted by the inversion of this very great value of international concern would be substantially greater than other expressive harms and deserving of greater international condemnation.

Suppose that the preceding expressivist argument does not convincingly demonstrate that genocide is a more serious wrong than crimes against humanity that involve similar constituent acts but that lack the specific intent to destroy a group. Might perpetrators of the former be more blameworthy than perpetrators of the latter, for reasons other than the seriousness of the wrongs they respectively commit? In particular, might this difference in blameworthiness derive from what the intent to destroy a group expresses about the perpetrator, rather than from any expressive harm inflicted on the victim?

Indeed, there is good reason to think that is the case. Start with the familiar proposition that we do not punish actions; rather, we punish people for their actions. What kind of connection must exist between a person and her action for it to be justifiable to punish the former on the basis of the latter? Presumably, the kind of connection sufficient for punishment depends on our conception of the person. Criminal law typically takes persons to be choosing beings and reasoning beings: hence persons may be punished for conduct involving an act or omission they choose to perform (as opposed to an involuntary bodily movement) and which manifests defective reasoning on their part (as opposed to a reasonable mistake of fact).

But persons are also valuing beings and planning beings, and their standing values and temporally extended plans provide a psychologically and morally deeper connection between themselves and their actions than choice or reasoning alone. The connection is psychologically deeper because values and plans influence and structure choice and reasoning over time and across a range of situations; the choices and reasoning in which they result reflect more on the person and less on the circumstances than those which respond to external pressures, sudden impulses, transient moods, lapses of judgement, and unfamiliar situations. The connection is morally deeper because holding incorrect values and harbouring plans involving wrongdoing are themselves morally blameworthy, while wrong choices and defective reasoning can result from a combination of personal traits none of which are themselves morally blameworthy.[38] Presumably, if that which connects a person with an action is itself morally blameworthy then the person is more blameworthy for that action.[39]

It therefore seems plausible to hold that the perpetrator of a wrong whose choices and reasoning involve incorrect values or wicked plans is more blameworthy than the perpetrator of an equally serious wrong whose choices and reasoning have more mundane origins. There is something more and something worse to connect the perpetrator with the wrong. Moreover, it seems plausible to argue that the perpetrator of a wrong that expresses wicked plans is more blameworthy than the perpetrator of an equally serious wrong

---

[38] G. Sher, *In Praise of Blame* (New York: Oxford University Press, 2006) 23–4.

[39] Of course, criminal law already punishes persons on the basis of defective valuing at the moment of action: persons attack correct values by committing purposeful crimes, flout correct values by committing knowing crimes, disregard correct values by committing reckless crimes, and ignore correct values by committing negligent crimes. The question is whether the criminal law should also punish on the basis of holding defective values, that is, defective valuing that endures over time.

that expresses incorrect values. Of course, plans and values differ in a variety of ways: planning is a conscious process, while valuing is often subconscious; plans manifest values while values need not manifest plans; valuing, like believing, seeks to fit the mind to the world, while planning, like desiring, seeks to fit the world to the mind. But the features of values and plans most relevant to moral blameworthiness (and therefore 'deeper' in the sense intended here) concern their structure and their content. Plans shape reasoning and choice by narrowing deliberation, foreclosing reconsideration, and excluding otherwise valid reasons for action. Values, by contrast, are shapeless in the sense that they are not oriented (and do not orient us) toward any particular course of action but rather give rational salience and normative weight to whatever the world throws our way. Moreover, since a wicked plan disposes one to commit a wrong for an inadequate reason, while an incorrect value disposes one to perceive inadequate reasons to be adequate, it seems that plans are morally deeper than values as well. Since it is worse to actually commit a wrong for an inadequate reason than to mistakenly take oneself to have adequate reason to commit the wrong, it seems that it must be worse to be disposed to the former than the latter. Put differently, plans are psychologically and morally deeper than values because they engage with and structure one's will rather than merely one's judgement.

Finally, the blameworthiness of a wrongdoer depends not only on whether the wrong expressed a plan or value but also on the content of that plan or value. Someone who assaults with intent to kill is more blameworthy than someone who assaults with intent to rob, just as someone who thinks their assault is warranted by the ethnicity or religion of their victim is worse than someone who thinks their assault is warranted by the prior wrongdoing of their victim.

It seems to follow that perpetrators of genocide are generally more blameworthy than perpetrators of crimes against humanity because the former are connected to their wrongs by plans whose content is worse than the content of whatever plans the latter may (but need not) have. It also seems to follow that perpetrators of persecution and apartheid can be comparable in blameworthiness to perpetrators of crimes against humanity whose constituent acts involve more serious wrongs (such as murder or rape) because the former are connected to their wrongs by even more defective values.

In conclusion, it seems that there are two viable expressivist explanations of the structure of the crime of genocide as presently defined. The first takes the intent to destroy a group to inflict an expressive harm on the group members who are killed or injured, over and above the loss of life, injury, or material deprivation that they suffer. The second takes the intent to destroy a group to aggravate the blameworthiness of the perpetrator by expressing a wicked plan that provides a psychologically and morally deeper connection between the perpetrator and the killing or harming perpetrated. Both explanations incorporate in different ways the central evaluative claim of the group pluralist, namely that the existence of human communities has value over and above the lives and well-being of their members. The first explanation incorporates the group pluralist claim in order to explain the seriousness of the expressive harm inflicted by wrongs committed with the intention to destroy a group; the second explanation incorporates the group pluralist claim in order to explain the blameworthiness of committing a wrong in furtherance of such a plan. In either case, jurisdiction over the crime of genocide is justified by the expressive rejection of fundamental international values as well as the fact that the intention to partially or totally destroy a group will almost always involve either 'a manifest pattern of similar conduct directed against that group or ... conduct that could itself effect such destruction'.[40]

II. International Crimes in Contrast

The laws and customs of war are designed to guide the conduct of military commanders and soldiers engaged in armed conflict.[41] By contrast, international criminal law is intended to guide the evaluation of past offences by courts. Despite this fundamental difference between the prescriptive function of the laws and customs of war and the evaluative function of international criminal law, the drafters of the Rome Statute chose to closely track the language of the Additional Protocols when defining the corresponding war crimes. As a result, the structure of several important war crimes deviates substantially from the structure of comparable national crimes. Put another way, the Rome Statute not only displays unfamiliar structures (such as contextual elements) but also deploys familiar structures (such as conduct and result elements as well as offence elements and defence elements) in unfamiliar ways. These drafting choices might be thought to manifest an alternative structure, based on a conceptual distinction between attacks and endangerments, but the Rome Statute omits crucial aspects of such a structure and the structure itself may be conceptually unstable.

---

[40] Elements of Crimes, art 6(a)(4). Ibid. arts 6(b)(4), 6(c)(5), 6(d)(5), 6(e)(7) (same).
[41] See part I.A.

A. Conduct and results

The Rome Statute follows the Additional Protocols by declaring it a war crime to '[i]ntentionally direct[] attacks against the civilian population as such or against individual civilians', irrespective of whether the prohibited conduct actually results in loss of civilian life.[42] The Rome Statute also follows the Additional Protocols by declaring it a war crime to:

[i]ntentionally launch[] an attack in the knowledge that such attack will cause incidental loss of life or injury to civilians or damage to civilian objects or wide-spread, long-term and severe damage to the natural environment which would be clearly excessive in relation to the concrete and direct overall military advantage anticipated.[43]

Despite what the wording of the latter offence definition might suggest, the latter war crime does not require that loss of life, injury, or damage occur.[44] Hence, the Elements of Crimes requires only that '[t]he attack was such that it would cause' excessive death, injury, or damage, to clarify that the offence turns on the expected consequences of the conduct, not the actual conse-quences.[45] Like the war crime of Attacking Civilians, the latter offence prohibits launching an attack with certain features rather than bringing about any negative result.

From the deliberative perspective, these offence definitions provide suffi-cient guidance to combatants: if combatants are instructed not to attack civilians then nothing is gained by further instructing them not to kill or harm civilians as the result of such an attack. Similarly, if combatants are instructed not to launch attacks expected to cause excessive incidental harm to civilians then nothing is gained by further instructing them not to cause such harm as a result of such an attack. However, the purpose of criminal law

---

[42] Rome Statute art 8(2)(b)(i). The definition of the offence is adapted from Additional Protocol I, which declares that '[t]he civilian population as such, as well as individual civilians, shall not be the object of attack.' Protocol I, art 51(2). K. Dormann, *Elements of War Crimes Under the Rome Statute of the International Criminal Court: Sources and Commentary* (New York: Cambridge University Press, 2003) 131.

[43] Rome Statute art 8(2)(b)(iv). The definition of the offence is adapted from multiple provi-sions of Additional Protocol I, which prohibit 'an attack which may be expected to cause incidental loss of civilian life, injury to civilians, damage to civilian objects, or a combination thereof, which would be excessive in relation to the concrete and direct military advantage anticipated'. Protocol I, art 51(5)(b). Ibid arts 55(1), 57(2)(a)(3), 57(2)(b), and 85(3)(b).

[44] Dormann (n 42 above) 162 ('In the end, the PrepCom followed the majority view and refused to require that the attack have a particular result').

[45] Elements of Crimes, art 8(2)(b)(iv)(2).

is not merely to guide future conduct but also to inform the evaluation of past conduct. It is because criminal law incorporates the evaluative perspective that it distinguishes between conduct offences and result offences, an important distinction to draw because conduct offences and result offences typically infringe different kinds of values. The wrongfulness of result offences such as murder, battery, and arson lies primarily in the loss of life, injury, or destruction of property they involve. By contrast, the wrongfulness of conduct offences such as rape and blackmail lies primarily in their infringement of abstract values such as autonomy or dignity. By classifying an act as a result offence or as a conduct offence the criminal law indicates which kind of values make the act wrongful and deserving of criminalization.

Evidently, the two war crimes under discussion do not derive their wrongfulness from the infringement of abstract values but from the harm to civilians that they typically cause. The wrongness of attacking civilians and launching attacks that harm civilians derives from the wrongness of killing and harming civilians.[46] By making the derivative wrongs rather than the basic wrongs into war crimes the Rome Statute distorts the moral foundations of international criminal law.

B. Wrongs and justifications

There is a second structural defect in the Rome Statute, namely that it makes it an element of an offence that an attack is expected to cause clearly excessive harm to civilians, rather than make it an element of an affirmative justification defence that the expected harm to civilians is proportionate to the military advantage anticipated. From the deliberative perspective, the Additional Protocols rightly draw no distinction between offences and defences, because both offence elements and justification elements are relevant for guiding behaviour: offence elements reflect reasons against a course of action while justification elements reflect reasons in favour of a course of action.[47] If the reasons against the action are defeated by the reasons in its favour then the action is justifiable. But from the evaluative perspective, the Rome Statute ought to follow national criminal law by sorting wrong-making and wrong-justifying reasons into offences and defences, respectively. The structural distinction between offences and defences tracks the substan-

---

[46] J. Gardner, 'The Wrongdoing that Gets Results' (2004) 18 *Philosophical Perspectives* 53.
[47] K. Campbell, 'Offence and Defence' in I. Dennis (ed), *Criminal Law and Justice* (London: Sweet & Maxwell, 1987) 73.

tive difference between wrongdoing and fault, between having done nothing that calls for justification or excuse and having a justification or excuse for what one has done.[48]

The definition of an offence should contain the minimal elements of a presumptive moral wrong, one whose commission deserves condemnation and punishment unless it can be justified or excused.[49] The Rome Statute declares that intentionally directing an attack against civilians is such a presumptive moral wrong. By contrast, launching an attack against a military objective that is expected to harm civilians only constitutes an offence if the harm to civilians would be clearly excessive. This is a mistake. If a combatant launches an attack that is expected to harm civilians then the combatant has done something that calls for justification or excuse. There is a moral difference between launching an attack expected to harm no civilians and launching an attack expected to harm some civilians, and the way to reflect this difference in the law is by defining the latter as an offence in need of a defence. In this context, the relevant defence would be that the harm to civilians was the unintended side effect of an attack on a legitimate military target; that there was no way to carry out the attack that would have caused less harm to civilians; and that the military advantage the attack would achieve outweighs the harm to civilians. Of course, not every incident in which civilians are harmed should result in a criminal trial; most may be explained to and evaluated by a superior officer charged with monitoring compliance with the law of armed conflict. But, in principle, every combatant who harms a civilian should have to explain herself to someone.

A similar failure to distinguish between offences and defences is displayed by the recent draft amendment to the Rome Statute defining the crime of aggression:

1. For the purpose of this Statute, 'crime of aggression' means the planning, preparation, initiation or execution, by a person in a position effectively to exercise control over or to direct the political or military action of a State, of an act of aggression which, by its character, gravity and scale, constitutes a manifest violation of the Charter of the United Nations.

2. For the purpose of paragraph 1, 'act of aggression' means the use of armed force by a State against the sovereignty, territorial integrity or political independence of another State, or in any other manner inconsistent with the Charter of the United Nations.[50]

---

[48] Duff (n 22 above) 18.

[49] G. P. Fletcher, *Rethinking Criminal Law* (Boston: Little, Brown, 1978) 567–8.

[50] Rev Conf of the Rome Statute, 13th plenary meeting, 11 June 2010, ICC Doc RC/Res. 6 (advance version) (16 June 2010), <http://www.icc-cpi.int/iccdocs/asp_docs/Resolutions/RC-Res.6-ENG.pdf>.

In essence, the Draft Amendment defines aggression as the use of armed force by one state against another state in manifest violation of the U.N. Charter. As a prescriptive rule, the proposed definition is structurally adequate though substantively defective.[51] But as an evaluative rule the Draft Amendment is a structural failure. By making the manifest violation of the U.N. Charter an element of the offence, the Draft Amendment treats the justified use of force and the non-use of force as if they were morally equivalent. Yet if the sovereignty, territorial integrity, and political independence of states are values the infringement of which calls for justification then they should form the basis of the offence definition while conformity with the U.N. Charter should form the basis of an affirmative defence.

Ironically, the U.N. Charter itself contains the correct offence/defence structure. Specifically, article 2(4) of the U.N. Charter lays down a broad prohibition on the use or threat of force:

All Members shall refrain in their international relations from the threat or use of force against the territorial sovereignty or political independence of any state, or in any other manner inconsistent with the Purposes of the United Nations.[52]

Article 51 then recognizes a limited exception to this general prohibition on the use of force:

Nothing in the present Charter shall impair the inherent right of individual or collective self-defence if an armed attack occurs against a Member of the United Nations, until the Security Council has taken the measures necessary to maintain international peace and security.[53]

This is precisely the structure that international criminal law should adopt if it is to capture the relationship between the relevant values of the international system.

C. Attacks and endangerments

Importantly, Antony Duff has recently advocated discarding the traditional conduct/result structure in favour of an attack/endangerment structure that might seem to redeem the Rome Statute.[54] On Duff's account, '[a]n attack is

---

[51] For consideration of the substantive defects of the definition of aggression, see P. H. Robinson and A. A. Haque, 'Justice and Deterrence in International Law' (manuscript on file with author).

[52] Charter of the United Nations art 2(4).

[53] Ibid art 51.

[54] Duff (n 22 above) 158 (arguing that 'every justified criminal offense must either consist in an attack on or an endangerment of a legally protected value, or must be suitably related to such an attack or endangerment').

an action or omission that is intended to injure some value or interest',[55] while 'I endanger another if I create a significant risk that he will be harmed'.[56] As Duff explains, attacks manifest hostility to the value or interest attacked, while endangerments manifest indifference to the value or interest endangered; furthermore, attacks involve 'being guided by wrong reasons' while endangerments involve 'not being guided by right reasons'.[57] Duff argues that the attack/endangerment structure reflects the fact that certain 'kinds of criminal harm (such as those suffered by victims of murder, rape, or burglary) [] are partly constituted by the actions that generate them'[58] while within the conduct/result structure 'crimes are defined in terms of the causation (or creation of a risk) of independently identifiable harms that the criminal law seeks to prevent'.[59]

However, there are at least three reasons why Duff's account cannot vindicate the structure of the Rome Statute. First, the Rome Statute does not distinguish between successful and unsuccessful attacks, and this would be a major structural defect even on Duff's view. For Duff argues that the law should criminalize successful attacks as primary offences and should criminalize unsuccessful attacks under 'a narrow law of attempts' that applies only to a defendant who is '"in the process of committing" the crime that would complete the attack'.[60] When such an attempt fails, Duff writes that 'we have reason to be relieved, and to qualify our condemnation . . . but not to refrain from condemnation altogether'.[61] Duff then leaves open whether a broader law of attempts, exemplified in the Model Penal Code, should criminalize mere preparation to attack.[62] By contrast, the Rome Statute adopts the broader law of attempts that Duff finds dubious but fails to make the distinction between successful and unsuccessful attacks that Duff thinks crucial.[63] In other words, the Rome Statute contains only two crimes—Attacking Civilians (either successfully or unsuccessfully) and attempt (in the broad sense)—when even on Duff's view at least three are required—successfully attacking civilians, unsuccessfully attacking civilians (or attempting to attack civilians in the narrow sense), and preparing to attack civilians (or attempting to attack civilians in the broad sense). Duff writes that 'attempts are attacks that fail', which would seem to imply that attempting to attack civilians just is unsuccessfully attacking civilians.[64] But this would be incorrect: attempts to cause harm are attacks that fail; attempts to attack

[55] Ibid 149.   [56] Ibid 151.   [57] Ibid 151.   [58] Ibid 155.
[59] Ibid 153.   [60] Ibid 159.   [61] Ibid 159.   [62] Ibid 159–60.
[63] Rome Statute art 25(3)(f) (imposing liability for '[a]ttempts to commit [an international] crime by taking action that commences its execution by means of a substantial step, but the crime does not occur because of circumstances independent of the person's intentions').
[64] Duff (n 22 above) 148.

are not attacks at all. The Rome Statute distinguishes between attacks and attempts to attack, but not between successful and unsuccessful attacks.

Second, the Rome Statute does not distinguish between consummated and unconsummated endangerments. As Duff observes, under national criminal law consummated endangerments are generally punished when the perpetrator is reckless or even negligent with respect to the resulting harm. However, unconsummated endangerments are only selectively criminalized, typically when they involve specific conduct such as driving.[65] By contrast, the Rome Statute criminalizes knowingly endangering civilians irrespective of whether harm results. Once again, Duff's attack/endangerment structure cannot vindicate the Rome Statute because Duff recognizes the moral significance of resulting harm while the provisions under discussion do not.

Finally, upon close inspection the attack/endangerment distinction appears to depend upon the conduct/result distinction it is designed to displace. Recall that Duff defines an attack as an act or omission intended to injure some value or interest. Yet this definition equivocates between two senses of injuring. One injures an interest by setting back that interest as a result of one's action, while one injures a value by engaging in conduct that fails to respect that value. An attack therefore necessarily involves the intent to bring about results that set back interests or to engage in conduct that disrespects values. Indeed, the distinction between successful and unsuccessful attacks that Duff endorses seems to just be the distinction between successful and unsuccessful attempts to bring about certain results or engage in certain conduct. Similarly, Duff acknowledges that the wrongfulness of endangerments is a function of the result caused or risked and the perpetrator's mental state.[66]

To be sure, the attack/endangerment distinction tracks two other distinctions that are of the utmost importance on any non-consequentialist moral view. If it is a more serious wrong, all else being equal, to kill someone than to allow someone to die then this is probably because the seriousness of the two wrongs is a function not only of the 'independently identifiable harm[]' of death but also of 'the actions that generate' that harm. Similarly, if it is a more serious wrong, all else being equal, to kill intentionally than to kill recklessly then this is probably because the seriousness of the two wrongs is partly a function of 'the intentional structure of the agent's action' as well as 'the practical attitudes displayed in and part[ly]-constituted by those actions'.[67] However, there is no obvious reason why one cannot incorporate both the doing/allowing distinction and the intention/foresight distinction into a conduct/result structure. One can maintain that the most seriously wrongful

---

[65] Ibid.   [66] Ibid 156.   [67] Ibid 154.

form of murder involves causing death by intentionally killing as opposed to by recklessly killing or by intentionally letting die yet still maintain that it is the causing of death that does most of the wrong-making work. Murder might not be quite so bad were it not for the killing, but it would be far less bad were it not for the dying.

III. Conclusion

The purpose of this chapter has been to further our understanding of the structure of international crimes by analyzing the contextual elements that distinguish international from national crimes as well as the decision to structure certain international crimes in terms of conduct rather than result and to make acting without justification an element of certain offences rather than making acting with justification an element of an affirmative defence. In the process, the chapter has discussed the displacement function of the laws of war, the group dynamics of crimes against humanity, the destructive and expressive aspects of genocide, and the viability of an attack/endangerment structure for criminal wrongdoing. Just as the concepts and methods of criminal law theory can illuminate the structure of international crimes, so too can investigation of the structure of international crimes broaden and deepen the concepts and methods of criminal law theory.

7

Legal Form and Moral Judgement:
Euthanasia and Assisted Suicide

Alan Norrie

I. Introduction

In this chapter, I consider the way in which categories of legal responsibility in the criminal law's general part are used to finesse broader moral conflicts around questions of euthanasia. Euthanasia and its close cousin assisted dying represent extremely problematic areas for the criminal law, as the recent formulation of prosecutorial guidelines for assisted suicide testify.[1] The effect of the guidelines is to make no formal change in the law, which continues to prohibit assisted suicide. They make it clear as a matter of official practice, however, that where the law on its face has been broken, there will be no prosecution if the defendant was motivated by good moral reasons.[2] This is a form of criminal regulation that operates by juxtaposing legal rule and administrative discretion. The effect is to balance conflicting social, political, and moral claims in a society where there is no consensus as to the rights and wrongs of helping someone to die. In this way, a pragmatic compromise is able to reflect a moral impasse in a way that appears to give something to everyone. Thus the 'pro-life' lobby can at least say that the law has not changed and no symbolic succour has been given to the pro-euthanasia view, that a line has not been crossed. Those in favour of assisted suicide can claim to have made headway in chipping away at the monolithic view that assisting death is impermissible, and exposing the law's 'hypocrisy', while still having to accept that it has not formally changed.

---

[1] <http://www.cps.gov.uk/publications/prosecution/assisted_suicide_policy.html>.

[2] For example, with regard to whether a person stood to gain from a death, it is stated (para 44) that 'The critical element is the motive behind the suspect's act. If it is shown that compassion was the only driving force behind his or her actions, the fact that the suspect may have gained some benefit will not usually be treated as a factor tending in favour of prosecution.'

On the surface, this appears to be little more than the kind of balancing act that occurs when a legal rule is maintained in a situation where social mores have changed or are in irreconcilable conflict.[3] Underneath, however, the issue of assisted suicide, together with that of euthanasia, tells us something more general about the nature of criminal law regulation, and the role of the formalistic conception of responsibility that lies at its core. In addition to the moral complexity surrounding euthanasia, there is a complexity in the criminal law form itself that enables the moral problems to be finessed. A deeper view of the relationship between law and morals would be to say that the moral complexity in euthanasia and assisted suicide is mediated by the peculiar complex of form and substance in the legal categories of responsibility. This enables a deeply conflicted moral issue to be managed, temporarily at least, through the legal structure, the 'architectonic', of the criminal law's general part. It is such a complex vision of the criminal law's general principles of responsibility that I wish to develop here, in order to apply it generally to questions surrounding euthanasia.

In thinking about the criminal law's architectonic, I will be bringing to bear my previous analysis of the role of formalization on the categories of criminal law, a development that begins to occur in the early nineteenth century, and which sets up a tension in the law between formal and substantive approaches to criminal responsibility.[4] In thinking about euthanasia, I will be examining two different situations: those of active killing, in the sense of actually bringing about or contributing to a person's death;[5] and of supporting or assisting a person to commit suicide. In both cases, I will be looking at how the law finesses the moral problem by permitting some forms of active killing or assisted suicide despite both being officially prohibited. The chapter has four sections. In the next, I elaborate an argument on the nature of legal form in the criminal law, considering three different

---

[3] Surveys reveal that around 80 per cent of the British public are in favour of euthanasia for persons suffering painful, incurable disease (N. Lacey, C. Wells, and O. Quick, *Reconstructing Criminal Law* (Cambridge: CUP, 2010), 619), and there have been a number of cases sympathetically highlighted of assisted suicide in recent years. At the same time, there is powerful opposition from religious groups against changing the law. On recent attempts at law reform on assisted suicide in England and Wales, see ibid 637. The position argued for below is that, from a non-religious moral perspective, both sides have a point.

[4] A. Norrie, *Punishment, Responsibility and Justice* (Oxford: OUP, 2000); *Crime, Reason and History* (Cambridge: CUP, 2001), chs 2–3; *Law and the Beautiful Soul* (Abingdon: Routledge, 2005) ch 4.

[5] Euthanasia may be voluntary (requested or consented to), non-voluntary (where it is not possible for the person to consent), or involuntary (where death is contrary to a person's wish, or consent was not sought). It may also be active (killing) or passive (letting die). See J. McMahan, *The Ethics of Killing* (New York: OUP, 2002) 457. Here I focus on the active, voluntary or non-voluntary, forms of euthanasia.

approaches, the moral, the political, and the critical, to the idea of legal responsibility, and arguing for a critical understanding of a dynamic of form and substance at its heart. In the following section, I consider the nature of the moral impasse on euthanasia, arguing that there are 'principled' moral reasons for accepting some forms of euthanasia or assisted suicide, and 'practical' moral reasons for refusing them. Then, in two final sections, I consider how the law operates with regard to voluntary and non-voluntary active euthanasia and assisted suicide, in light of the law's formal structure and the moral issues.

II. Legal Form: 'Moral', 'Political', and 'Critical' Approaches

In order to understand how the law works in this area, it is necessary to understand the legal forms of responsibility that make up the criminal law architectonic in a different way than is normally the case in liberal criminal law scholarship. I will state this assertively, while realizing that the claim I make may require to be tailored differently for different theorists in the tradition.[6] Nonetheless, at the core of the liberal approach in recent years has been a sense of a homology between moral rules and legal rules, so that, for example, the legal conception of intention shadows and is given its validity by a moral conception of intention. As Antony Duff has succinctly put it, 'As with morality, so with law'.[7] Such a conception may be open to quite different interpretations. For example, a Kantian individualist will shape the concept of intention differently from a communitarian of either a Hegelian or Aristotelian bent. Nonetheless, the underlying sense is that a moral account of responsibility holds the key to an adequate legal understanding. This is not to say that a moral approach does not recognize that legal concepts are also importantly political and institutional, or that rules elaborated by a state may be different from rules elaborated by a moral philosopher. For example, in moral philosophy, there is the possibility of fine-grained tuning of judgement which is not possible in law. Equally, other political or institutional considerations may come into play in law that are not there in philosophy. But if that is the case, I think the position adopted tends to

---

[6] See the recent discussion of the different approaches sailing under the 'moral' flag in A. Brudner, *Punishment and Freedom* (New York: OUP, 2009) 17. For the differences between individualist and communitarian moral approaches, discussing the work of Michael Moore and Antony Duff, see A. Norrie, *Punishment, Responsibility and Justice* (n 4 above) chs 5–6.

[7] R. A. Duff, *Intention, Agency and Criminal Liability* (Oxford: Blackwell, 1990), 102.

be that the 'other things that come into play' are post-hoc considerations which may temper, or even befoul, an otherwise adequate moral understanding,[8] yet still be accepted as necessary in a process of moral-to-legal translation. Then the question becomes one of monitoring or controlling the extraneous post-hoc considerations in favour of underlying moral-legal principles.

The moral approach to legal responsibility, however, is not the only way that liberal theory can go. Alan Brudner has recently developed an alternative approach that he calls 'political'.[9] If we follow this a little, we will be able to draw out the nature of the legal architectonic at the core of law. Brudner argues against the moral view just described that principles of responsibility, and therefore the general structure of criminal law, are founded on the classical liberal view of principles of *political* authority to be found in Kant, and then developed by Hegel. From Kant, Brudner takes the retributive idea of punishment as the coercion of the criminal's freedom, which is given in return for the initial coercion of freedom that was present in a crime. This provides a universal basis for political and legal obligation founded on the idea of formal freedom, that is, the simple claim that all human agents are in principle capable of acting on the basis of making choices, regardless of what those choices may substantively be. It is important to see that this is an abstract, formal, as its name indicates, account of freedom, which is quite removed from the actual needs or desires of choosing agents. It is the simple ability to make choices, the agent as a 'choosing mechanism' one might say, that is relevant. Now, as Brudner indicates, this is a very limited, indeed a dehumanizing, conception of human agency in that it says nothing of the choices people actually make, or the contexts in which they make them.[10] It requires accordingly to be supplemented by richer conceptions of freedom, including a positive freedom to act in conditions which permit one to choose according to one's real interests ('real autonomy'), and a freedom to draw upon and find expression for one's life in a community ('communal wellbeing').[11]

From my point of view, the important thing to note is that to this tripartite and developing vision of the forms of freedom, there correspond specific distinctions in the general structure of the criminal law. The realm of formal freedom is reflected in the law of *mens rea* and *actus reus*, while real autonomy

[8] See eg the role that 'policy' arguments play in A. Ashworth, *Principles of Criminal Law* 6th edn (Oxford: OUP, 2009) ch 3.

[9] *Op cit*, n 6.

[10] *Op cit*, n 6, 297–300.

[11] It is in the move from the second to the third form of freedom that the influence of Hegel is seen in Brudner's argument.

issues are reflected in regulatory or welfare offences, and some of the defences are justified by the sense of what a community feels about wrongdoing in the light of excuses that a defendant might make for a crime. What is the value of this tripartite, structural scheme for our purposes here? It is not my intention to argue that Brudner's political approach is correct and the moral approach wrong. My own view, from a critical standpoint, is that both positions tell part of the story, while misrepresenting the whole in which both play their part.[12] I do think, however, that it is helpful in that it affirms something of the normative structure of the criminal law that moral approaches tend to ignore, and that is the sense of an overall architectonic of the law. Brudner is able to argue that different forms of normative argument concerning different forms of freedom are located in the overall structure of the criminal law differently. In particular, his argument points to the formalism that lies at the law's core, in its principles of *mens rea* and *actus reus*. In going back to Kant, and in placing Kant alongside Hegel,[13] Brudner indicates that there is something in the abstract Kantian principles that is intrinsic to a politically formulated architectonic of the criminal law. Political or institutional design is not separate from and additional to moral considerations but rather lies at the normative core of the law, in a formalistic account of the abstractly free individual who makes choices whatever the substantive ends or values may be that he or she endorses. Broader moral considerations, such as those identified in the moral approach are not thereby removed from the law, but are allocated their place in it according to its overall politico-normative structure.

I highlight Brudner's approach because its insistence on a political structure to the law founded on the normative principle of abstract, individual freedom also reflects my own position, albeit I approach it from a critical and sociological standpoint. My view too is that there is a formal structure allocating normative issues differentially in the criminal law, but I see the resulting layout of issues of responsibility as unsuccessfully synthesized and as essentially contradictory. The argument focuses, like Brudner's, on the realm of formal freedom at the core of the law, but departs from him in that I argue, first, that formal freedom or a 'morality of form' is the historical product of a particular kind of society in which abstract, formal legal subjectivity complemented marketization, or the exchange of commodities, as central to the organization of social relations; and second, that the formal freedom adequate to the market and instantiated in the legal subject existed in contradiction with and within a world that denied agents the context in which to

---

[12] See discussion in A. Norrie, 'Alan Brudner and the Dialectics of Criminal Law' (2011) 14 *New Criminal Law Review*, 449.

[13] This is not necessarily how Brudner sees it: see discussion in *op cit*, previous note.

translate their formal freedom into a realm of 'real freedom' or 'free community', in the terms of Brudner's tripartite schema.[14] The critical view, accordingly, agrees with the political view that modern social life can be represented in terms of a progressive grading of forms of freedom. It sees these forms of freedom, however, as existing in contradiction to, not as completing, each other under modern social conditions.

Focusing on criminal law, the argument is that social, political, and historical considerations structure the abstract nature of legal form, providing criminal law with its architectonic of offence (*mens rea* plus *actus reus*) and defence. Modern law expresses a notion of human freedom that is abstract, universal, and formalistic, and in its abstraction and universality, one that is important but also importantly limited. It is important because it articulates a general sense of individual political freedom, one that is associated with a basic idea of agential freedom. It is importantly limited because it operates by way of a formalization of ethical categories that excludes substantive moral concerns that pertain in different social contexts. It works essentially by establishing a form/substance dichotomy at the heart of criminal responsibility, which means that criminal law forms are expressed in formal, neutral, factual, psychologistic terms. Why such terms? 'Formal' because of the account of freedom that lies at the core; 'neutral' because the abstract freedom of the legal subject is the same for all; 'factual' and 'psychologistic' because it expresses responsibility in cognitive terms of intention, foresight, and voluntariness— terms that at least appear neutral because they are shorn of moral substance.

This is a prevalent and continuing way of doing criminal responsibility, and is seen for example in the 'orthodox subjectivism' of the textbook tradition in England and Wales.[15] It should be noted, however, that its consequence is that a formalistic way of doing responsibility is always subject to criticism from positions that adopt a more morally substantive approach to issues,[16] so that a form/substance dichotomy, albeit one with form in the driving seat, is generally to be observed in the criminal law itself. Thus it is that legal categories always tend to 'hunt in pairs': intention and motive, subjective and objective, offence and defence being three main ones.[17] The

---

[14] A. Norrie, *Crime, Reason and History, op cit*, n 4, ch 2.

[15] A tradition emphasizing the subjective, psychological, autonomy of the criminal that includes the work of Glanville Williams and Smith and Hogan, and more recently Andrew Ashworth, though the last argues for a 'welfare principle' alongside an 'autonomy principle' as lying at the core of the criminal law.

[16] This is why the moral approach operates as an effective critique of orthodox subjectivist positions in the law.

[17] The first term in each opposition is developed in factual, psychological terms as central to legal responsibility, and the second is then the locus of additional, morally substantive, information.

general point is that a formalistic conception of legal freedom is achieved by excluding substantive moral concerns, but these return to trouble the law. For example, the division of motive from intention is a classic piece of formalism, but issues concerning motive return to trouble legal doctrine.[18]

That is the general argument. What, however, is specific and interesting in the case of euthanasia and assisted suicide is that it is this very dichotomizing procedure, the law's failure to achieve a synthesis in Brudnerian terms, that seems to help it out. Many of the oppositions set out above are central to how the law handles different kinds of euthanasia: the distinction between motive and intention is central to permitting certain kinds of active killing, as is the distinction between offence and defence; in the case of assisted suicide, it is motive, which plays no part in the legal definition of the crime of assisting a suicide, which animates the discretionary decision not to prosecute. In such cases, there is often the appearance that legal categories are functioning normally in the euthanasia context as they do elsewhere, but there is a surreptitious play on those categories which permits outcomes that should not really be permitted on a standard interpretation.

The issue is complicated. At one level, one can only be struck by the law's moral ineptitude in its dealings with euthanasia. The abstract formalism of its categories fails to carry necessary and appropriate moral distinctions. For example, the contract killer and the mercy killer are on the face of the law both culpable, and equally so, under the general definition of the crime of murder. An illustration is the case of the doctors in the conjoined twins case, *Re A (children)*.[19] In intending to separate the twins, knowing that one is virtually certain to die, the doctors satisfy the *Woollin*[20] test for the *mens rea* of murder. The definition of the offence having been satisfied, doctors are murderers who require a defence, but do we think of doctors in such a situation as murderers?[21] At a second level, however, this abstract legal formalism gives the law a certain backhanded ethical facility, in its ability to manoeuvre under cover of form, and thereby to finesse social and moral conflicts around a contentious moral subject.[22] Officially, it appears to uphold a general prohibition against killing, the 'sanctity of life' position, while permitting 'quality of life' and choice issues to have their effect surreptitiously. Thus, *Re A* notwithstanding, the law of *mens rea* proves

---

[18] A. Norrie, *Crime, Reason and History, op cit*, n 4, 36–46.

[19] [2000] 4 All ER 961.

[20] *R v Woollin* [1998] 3 WLR 382.

[21] If it is said that doctors are not murderers because a murderer is one who commits the offence of homicide without a valid defence, this does not avoid the moral problem, for we do not think of doctors as having committed any offence for which they might need a defence.

[22] As we shall see, it does not work quite so well with assisted suicide.

flexible enough, and perhaps self-consciously so, to permit the issue of mercy killing to be dealt with as a question falling under the general rules of *mens rea*. This allows some mercy killing cases to be filtered out and treated differently from the normal run of cases, while it appears as though the general rules of *mens rea* are applied in such cases as in all others. The formal legal categories resolve the matter, without any public commitment or substantive declaration that mercy killing is permitted. The ensuing benign hypocrisy operates through formal law, and allows society to have its moral cake and eat it.

III. Underlying Moral Issues

Before coming to the law itself, I want to discuss the moral issues concerning euthanasia. As already stated, there is no agreement in modern British society, or indeed in many other western societies, on this matter.[23] Disagreement expresses itself as a conflict between the 'sanctity of life' on the one hand and the 'quality of life' or 'right to choose death' views on the other. The former is associated with religious views, but also works as a shorthand for the moral claim that human life is paramount and has intrinsic value,[24] and the latter is the view that quality of life issues may be equally or more important in some situations, and that a person may choose to die where such issues exist. In this section, I simply wish to elaborate a moral view that identifies something of the main positions and indicate what I take to be the difficulty in formulating a clear-cut position one way or the other. I begin by comparing sanctity and quality of life positions, and proposing that even if there is a good argument in principle in favour of sometimes admitting the latter, society might not want in practice to admit it in law.

If we start with a sanctity of life position, this affirms the value of human life in a way that trumps even claims to self-determination. Human life just is a morally foundational good, and is never to be attacked.[25] The best to be said for euthanasia is that it may be permitted in its passive form ('letting die')

---

[23] Though compare the situation in Holland: P. Lewis, *Assisted Dying and Legal Change* (Oxford: OUP, 2007).

[24] See eg J. Glover, *Causing Death and Saving Lives* (London: Pelican, 1977). See also G. Dworkin, R. G. Frey, and S. Bok, *Euthanasia and Physician-Assisted Suicide* (Cambridge: CUP, 1998), and J. McMahan, *The Ethics of Killing* (n 5 above) ch 5. For an excellent overview of the area, see N. Lacey, C. Wells, and O. Quick, *Reconstructing Criminal Law* (n 3 above) 618–42.

[25] Though, as Jeff McMahan notes, *op cit*, n 5, 466–7, those who argue for the sanctity of life often do so inconsistently, in that they do allow certain instances where a 'non-innocent' person can be killed, such as in self-defence, in war, or as punishment.

where a person is dying and life surrenders itself up to a 'natural' process.[26] In one form of the argument, there is a straightforward ethical validation of individual human life; in another, it is human being *qua* species or relational being that is valued. The latter is the view that there is an important sense in which a person's life is not just her own, but has value beyond what the individual perceives it to be. There seems to me to be something fundamentally important in both claims, and with them a general ground for safeguarding life from attack. At the same time, however, such an approach can have morally problematic results: people who suffer from terminal or degenerative illness, for example, who want to die must remain alive in great pain or discomfort until death comes 'naturally' to them.[27] Similarly, people who suffer from long-term disability or paralysis which grossly diminishes their capacities for life and who cannot take their own lives, are not permitted to die. In such circumstances, the argument for sanctity of life may seem somewhat sanctimonious to the person who is not allowed the assistance to end their own life. There have been cases in the media in recent years where the moral difficulty in insisting on the sanctity of life in such situations has been made clear.[28] Though such cases will not disturb the position of she who believes fundamentally in the sanctity of life, they do lead others to accept that there may be exceptional cases where sanctity gives way to quality of life issues.

In an indirect form, the sanctity of life argument draws strength from what one can call the possibility of dystopian futures. There is a concern that once we move away from sanctity of life claims, we open the door to various dangerous possibilities. If life loses its sanctity for the terminally ill or the physically paralyzed, it may also lose it for other groups where their quality of life might be regarded as diminished, such as the long-term depressed, the mentally and physically handicapped, and so on. There may then be a 'slippery slope' as between different degrees of quality of life,[29] and then,

---

[26] Though any death involves a natural, biological, process whereby life closes down, what it means for nature 'to take its course' is debatable in social situations involving, for example, hospital care. Passive euthanasia relies on the problematic distinction between acts and omissions, a distinction that lawyers acknowledge is hard to sustain. See A. Norrie, *Crime, Reason and History*, *op cit*, n 4, 123–4.

[27] Though their death may in law be hastened by medical treatments administered for other purposes such as to alleviate pain: see the discussion in the next section below.

[28] See eg the case of Daniel James who was paralyzed in a rugby accident and was assisted to travel to Dignitas by his parents, where the Crown Prosecution Service determined it would not be in the public interest to prosecute (<http://www.cps.gov.uk/news/press_releases/179_08/>), or those of two mothers charged with the murder or attempted murder of their disabled adult children, Frances Inglis and Kay Gilderdale, discussed below.

[29] Where the line should be drawn between for example the terminally and degeneratively ill, the paralyzed or badly disabled but physiologically stable, and the long-term mentally ill or depressed is an important question.

further, between voluntary and involuntary forms of euthanasia.[30] Against this, those supporting the quality of life stance will say that where freedom of choice pertains, there is a check on a drift to authoritarian forms of euthanasia, but much would then depend on what is meant by freedom of choice and how it is ascertained. Such a view is reflected in concerns that people may be pressured by those around them to 'choose' to die, and that, where assisted suicide is permitted in law, it will be the poor and unwanted who will make that 'choice', for their life chances as elderly or infirm will be much less than those of the wealthy with similar conditions.

I return to this point shortly. Suffice it to say for now that while there are good moral reasons of either a direct (that human life should be generally valued as of intrinsic worth) or an indirect (that allowing exceptions would lead to a slippery slope) kind for supporting a sanctity of life view in the case of the terminally ill and ancillary cases, there are also good moral reasons for allowing exceptions to it. The latter stem from a quality of life view and, linked to that, the possibility of choosing the time and place of one's own death.[31] The possibility of agency as a central element in what it means to be human is premised on the notion of human freedom, and freedom implies a number of different elements. These include a simple freedom to be left alone with one's life, as well as a positive freedom to become what we have it within ourselves to be. Such freedom then entails further conceptions of autonomy, emancipation, and flourishing, insofar as human life reflects the potentialities in human being. The ability to choose one's own death reflects many of these aspects of human freedom, from the simple sense that one should be left alone to do what one likes with one's life to the more complex sense that an autonomous life would include amongst its components control over one's death, and then on to the sense—that is surely there in the term 'euthanasia' (a 'good death')—that a flourishing life is one in which one is genuinely able to register the time to go. These are moral arguments placing choice and quality of life ahead of sanctity of life, and therefore for the validity of suicide and assisted suicide, and the killing of a person who is unable to take their own life but who wants to die. A good life means a good death too, and it is this kind of argument that leads one to think that a categorical prohibition on voluntary euthanasia or assisted suicide is problematic.

---

[30] For recent discussions of the 'slippery slope', see P. Lewis, *op cit*, n 23, who argues there is no evidence for its existence and K. Greasley, '*R(DPP) v Purdy* and the Case for Wilful Blindness' (2010) *Oxford Journal of Legal Studies* 1.

[31] It can be argued, as does Ronald Dworkin, that the ability to choose the time of one's own death is so central to the nature of human life as to be crucial to a sanctity of life position, R. Dworkin, *Life's Dominion* (London: Harper Collins, 1993) 215–17. But there may be more to the intrinsic value of life than this, even if it is a central feature.

Thus far, it might be thought that for anyone who does not have a fundamental commitment to the sanctity of life on, for example, religious grounds, a balancing of sanctity and quality of life issues will lead to the conclusion that euthanasia and assisted suicide should be available in certain circumstances, and this should be publically declared as such. Whilst in principle, such a position seems right, in practice I hesitate to take this route for a reason briefly mentioned above. This concerns the problem of the differential social impact that such a position would have on the poor and the well-to-do,[32] and because of the possibility that, in the future, a society with a population that is ageing and impoverished might be inclined to convert the permissive 'can' into the persuasive 'ought' (and then the required 'should'?). To talk of the freedom to choose one's death is not to talk of the specific conditions under which differently situated people will make their choices. The strongest arguments for a balancing of sanctity and quality of life arguments so as to permit some kinds of good deaths identify specific situations where the balance works in favour of honouring the choice of death over life. If we say that freedom of choice to die should be upheld in certain circumstances, we are saying that situations of free choice are available. It could be said, however, that such possibilities for freedom of choice are not available in the here and now, certainly not for all people. Wealth, poverty, and class structure have a profound effect on the choices people make.

In practice, there may be a tension between what should ideally happen and what might actually happen if various forms of euthanasia were legalized. In the case of assisted suicide, consider the deaths of individuals with terminal illnesses who have chosen to die, who plan their deaths, and who are able to pay to travel to the Dignitas clinic in Zurich with their close family. Everything has a measured, respectful character. This kind of death is, however, only likely to be for a few, and should be contrasted with the concern that legalizing assisted suicide would mean that many people who are poor, who are leading lives in straightened circumstances, and who feel themselves to be a burden on their families would then be pressured directly or indirectly to 'choose' to die.[33] Nor in a society in which dystopian and authoritarian features are already present can one rule out the possibility that the circumstances of choice will be worse in the future. Accordingly, in these circumstances, one might say that even if each human being has the real potential to live a good life and die a good death, that does not lead to the conclusion that the law should be changed to permit this to happen. A door

---

[32] See the argument by Sissela Bok in Dworkin, Frey, and Bok, *op cit*, n 24.

[33] This is not to deny that the wealthy may also be pressured to choose to die by relatives anxious for their wealth, but I do not take this to be a structural condition on the possession of wealth.

that was once opened would be hard to close. Just as one has to balance different arguments around sanctity and quality of life, so one has to measure different practical outcomes in the real world. At bottom, there is a question about how 'good death' works in society as a whole, specifically about the relationship between individual and collective human flourishing with regard to it. Thinking about the balance between the two may lead one to favour the sanctity of life position overall, even if one accepts there are good arguments for a limited quality of life exception.

Put shortly, it may be argued that the moral balance is in favour of saying that the better off should not be allowed a good death until everyone is able to have the same. This is, however, a deeply problematic conclusion. I am suggesting that there is a practical moral sense in arguing that the moral flourishing of some with regard to a good death may have to be checked in favour of the protection of the lives of others from bad deaths in a divided society. This means that we cannot individually be allowed to flourish until such time as we all are able to do so. But if this is so, it seems to be a conclusion that is both cogent and unacceptable. There is also surely a moral conviction that those who really can decide to die at a time of their choosing in the here and now should be allowed to do so, should not have to undergo pain and suffering for the general social good. There is therefore a major premise, that the moral risks of permitting assisted suicide and voluntary euthanasia may be too great under modern social conditions to permit legalization; and also a minor premise, that people should be allowed where possible to seek a good death under conditions that genuinely enable it. The problem is that the major and minor premises are in conflict. How to deal with this? Optimally, we should move to a society where social justice is taken seriously; until then, what is the answer? A second best solution might be to think about whether it is possible to maintain both premises: at the institutional level, a prohibition on the pursuit of good deaths coupled with, at the individual level, their informal acceptance through, somehow, the turning of a blind eye. This would inevitably be a complicated and messy way of trying to deal with a difficult moral problem, and one wonders how it could be achieved. What, it might further be asked, could this possibly have to do with a system of bright lines regulation such as that provided by the criminal law?

IV. Legal Form and Moral Substance: Active Euthanasia

The argument I began to outline in the first main section was that the formalism of legal categories of responsibility initially makes the criminal

law inhospitable to moral nuance. However, that very inhospitability generates a legal praxis that requires and enables lawyers subtly to negotiate moral
problems under cover of inflexible law and legal form. There is an intricate
interplay between what the law formally says, and how it reflects substantive
moral issues in practice. In this section, I look at this interplay with regard to
the law of intention, and the relationship between moral and legal argument.
I also consider why the defence of necessity is a problematic alternative, and
conclude by considering recent cases of mercy killing not involving doctors.

As regards intention, an early flavour of the way in which criminal law
categories are maintained but also finessed is seen in *Dr Adams's case*, where
it was held that a doctor may do 'all that is proper and necessary to relieve
pain ... , even if the measure ... may incidentally shorten life'.[34] But under
the law of contributory cause, *any* shortening of life or hastening of death
counts towards criminal causation. To avoid the problem, Lord Devlin had
resort to what he termed a 'common sense' view of causation. Underlying the
invocation of common sense, however, was a supervening moral distinction
that has become crucial in this area: between medical intervention aimed to
relieve pain which incidentally shortens life, and an intervention which is
aimed to shorten life.[35] Here, we are in the realm of intention. In the later
case of *Dr Cox*, a distinction was drawn between a doctor's 'primary' and
'secondary' purpose in administering treatment. As against the incidental
hastening of death (a 'secondary' purpose) pursuant to a course of treatment
with the primary purpose of easing suffering, it was stated that '[W]hat can
never be lawful is the use of drugs with the *primary purpose* of hastening the
moment of death'.[36]

This analysis of primary and secondary purpose, however, is challenged by
the approach to intention in *Woollin*,[37] where any secondary purpose that has
consequences that are foreseen as virtually certain to occur is promoted to the
same position and status as a primary purpose. That was the background to
the judge's direction to the jury in *Dr Moor's case*.[38] There, the instruction
was that the jury consider, first, whether the doctor's purpose had not been to
give treatment to relieve pain. If it had not been, then the jury had to be sure
that he intended to kill his patient, and intention meant purpose. If Dr Moor
thought it only highly probable death would follow the injection, there
would be no intention. The jury was offered an 'out' and took it, finding
Dr Moor not guilty, but this direction failed to relay to the jury the essence of
Woollin, that if the doctor thought it virtually certain death would follow, he

[34] N. Lacey, C. Wells, and O. Quick, *op cit*, n 3, 705.   [35] *Ibid*, 705.
[36] *Ibid*, 706 (emphasis added).   [37] *R v Woollin* [1998] 3 WLR 382.
[38] A. Arlidge, 'The trial of Dr David Moor' (2000) *Criminal Law Review* 31.

would have the intention to kill.[39] The direction was to put it mildly highly favourable to the defendant. It led to a subsequent proposal suggested by Senior Counsel in the case that intention may be found 'if death was a virtually certain result (barring an unforeseen intervention) and his primary intention was not purely to relieve pain and suffering but to cause death'.[40]

This is an attempt to splice together the *Woollin* direction and the primary purpose rule, but it is not clear that it would work, for the two parts of the test come from different moral backgrounds. One is the idea that a foreseen virtually certain consequence is ipso facto so tied to a direct purpose that it is a consequence that is owned by the actor. The other is that one's purpose is circumscribed by one's moral commitments, and one only owns those actions to which one is morally committed. In this second view, one may accept consequences which are not intrinsic to one's moral commitment, where those consequences are themselves means to the end of that commitment but, importantly, only where they are not significantly at moral odds with it. Doctors who inject a patient to ease pain and suffering are arguably in that category, for easing pain is a necessary and sufficient part of their work and commitment as doctors even if it hastens death. But, if that is the case, then one does not need the additional test of foresight of virtually certain consequences to resolve the matter: the purpose analysis will do all the work anyway. On the other hand, if one goes with the foresight of virtual certainty rule, then the question of purpose is in principle irrelevant.

As already intimated, there is a problem with the universalism and formalism of the law of intention here, but there is also a possible 'informal' solution to it, within the law. The problem with the law's formalism lies in the foresight of virtual certainty analysis, which lacks an adequate moral grasp of what is substantively at stake in cases like mercy killing. The problem with its universalism is that rules should apply in all cases. From a morally substantive or contextual point of view, however, things are different. Thinking in terms of the moral content of the conduct that occurs, a person only morally endorses those virtually certain consequences which are not at significant moral odds with what it is one seeks to do. This is the analysis of a 'moral threshold'.[41] The simple view that one accepts the virtually certain

---

[39] Subject to the potential proviso in *Woollin* concerning what a jury is 'entitled to find' discussed below.

[40] *Op cit*, n 38.

[41] The term 'moral threshold' may be mine (*A. Norrie, Crime, Reason and History*, n 4, 56–8), but reflects an original argument by Duff. See eg R. A. Duff, *op cit*, n 7, 84, where an example is the examiner who fails a student knowing it will upset her. Despite the upset being virtually certain, the examiner does not intend it. For discussion of Duff's position and its limits, see A. Norrie, *Law and the Beautiful Soul*, n 4, 62–9.

consequences of one's actions regardless of their moral implications threatens to be over-inclusive. *Woollin* reflects the problem, but it also has a possible way out of it, in the stipulation that a jury is 'entitled to find' an intention to kill where it nonetheless finds that D foresaw a consequence as virtually certain. If it is 'entitled to find', then this is arguably permissive rather than obligatory, so it can also choose *not* to find an intention where it finds foresight of virtual certainty. This seems to be the logic of entitlement, and it is seen in the analysis of *Matthews and Alleyne*,[42] which argues that *Woollin* did not produce a law of intention, only a rule of evidence.

Of course, it is bizarre to argue that the law has no definition of intention, both because it seems fairly clear that it does have a definition, albeit one that is too broad, and because, more generally, it is just strange that a central concept in the criminal law should remain undefined. But the claim may be an important one. It may do important moral work in cases where a jury does not wish to find intention. Note, however, that the judges in *Re A*[43] declined to go down this route, preferring to claim that *Woollin* intention was satisfied in the case of the doctors in that case. This decision stands in contrast to the more flexible, 'evidential', reading of intention permitted by *Matthews and Alleyne*. What one sees in *Woollin* is a tension between a formalistic statement of the law of intention in factual, psychologistic terms (what did D foresee as a virtually certain outcome?), and a hidden, morally substantive, informal invitation to go another way (what virtually certain foreseen outcomes did D morally endorse through her actions?). This tension is indicative of an underlying ethical-legal relation that is unresolved but always present.[44]

The law on intention reflects underlying moral issues in the euthanasia cases. These operate as a 'shadow' on it, but the signal fact in relation to all of them is that they are not part of the law. There is, first, the doctrine of double effect. This is the claim that '[O]ne may permit the evil effect of his act only if this is not intended in itself but is indirect and justified by a commensurate reason'.[45] This is drawn on in some medical cases,[46] but it is essentially problematic for the law because it in effect permits a citizen or group of citizens (such as doctors) to second-guess what the law is. It is a requirement of legal form that it apply universally in society, that it be clear as to the forms of conduct to which it applies, and that it brook no challenge from any other source in its sovereign territory. Double effect challenges this because it

---

[42] [2003] 2 Cr App R 30.   [43] [2000] 4 All ER 961.

[44] G. Fletcher, *Rethinking the Criminal Law* (Oxford: OUP, 1975) 400–1.

[45] D. Price, 'Euthanasia, Pain Relief and Double Effect' (1997) 17 *Legal Studies* 323.

[46] *Airedale NHS Trust v Bland* [1993] 2 WLR 316, 370; *Re A (children)* [2000] 4 All ER 961, 1012.

permits an alternative evaluation of law to compete with the official definition. Nonetheless, I think it plainly underpins the moral calculations that go
into practical decision-making in this area of the law. The same is true of the
idea of a moral threshold, mentioned above. A good example is the case of
Gillick,[47] where the doctors' intention to treat under-age girls by prescribing
contraceptive pills was held to be an answer to any offence of aiding and
abetting unlawful sexual intercourse. It could hardly be denied that prescrip-
tion would enable sex, but it was not part of a doctor's role to do anything
other than protect her patients' health. Such an open endorsement of a moral
threshold position would be quite problematic if it were to be extended more
broadly, but somehow, it is permitted in the case of doctors.

One specifically legal analysis that can reflect the moral threshold or
double effect arguments concerns necessity as a justificatory defence. The
doctors in these cases, it may be said, are caught between conflicting duties, in
that they must treat their patients even if treating them would bring them
into collision with the law. They must negotiate a balance of evils, and
hastening the death of a patient (or prescribing the pill) may involve such a
balance.[48] Against this, however, it should be noted that any general balancing of a doctor's duty to treat a patient when compared with the duty not to
kill would be hard to resolve in favour of the doctor's duty to treat. If the duty
not to take life is, as the law claims, one of the most fundamental obligations
imposed on citizens, then it is hard to see that a doctor's duty to treat a
patient can be weighed in the balance against it.

Furthermore, the law of necessity makes it clear that this is a defence of
very limited application, and not in cases of killing. It is true that *Re A*
muddies the waters here, but it is very clear that the judges' intention in that
case was not to extend necessity to cover situations of doctors causing the
deaths of their patients, but was limited to the very precise circumstances of
the conjoined twins. The general problem with the necessity defence is
reflected in the judges' discomfort in *Re A* in formulating it: a declaration
that the law of necessity goes beyond the precise facts of that case would be
too open a statement that the law does permit the taking of life in situations
such as that of mercy killing. Extending the law of necessity beyond *Re A*'s
precise facts would establish the morally substantive proposition that mercy
killing is allowed, but it is just that morally substantive conclusion that the
law cannot draw, for it cannot go against the official position that states that
killing is wrong. As I have said above, there are both real-political and

---

[47] *Gillick v West Norfolk and Wisbech Area Health Authority* [1986] AC 112.
[48] A. Ashworth 'Criminal Liability in a Medical Context: the Treatment of Good Intentions' in
Simester and Smith (eds), *Harm and Culpability* (Oxford: OUP, 1996).

institutional conditions that make it impossible to move forward and under-lying moral-political reasons why this may be no bad thing. In a situation of real-political blockage and moral-political concern, the use of a morally substantive defence such as necessity is unacceptable and, arguably, undesir-able. Better perhaps to stay with the formal account of *mens rea* and smuggle in the morally substantive position in the interstices of that law.

Turning now to recent euthanasia cases not involving doctors, we see that the issue that hoves into view is the distinction between motive and intention, for motive is the 'home' of moral substance alongside the formalism of intention in the standard form/substance dichotomy at the core of the law. Of course the 'first rule' of criminal law is that the two should be kept apart.[49] Here we are back on the familiar terrain of comparing mercy and contract killers, and affirming their equal guilt. Nonetheless it is clear that even if this is so, it is motive that makes the difference in practice in mercy killing cases. The recent conflicting decisions in the cases of two mothers, Frances Inglis and Kay Gilderdale, who both killed their disabled adult children suggest that it is how a defendant comes across in terms of their overall character and the precise moral circumstances in which they act, where these reveal their motives, that is relevant. Frances Inglis stated that she had killed her severely brain damaged son 'with love in her heart', yet she was convicted of murder and found by the judge to have undertaken a 'calculated and consistent course of criminal conduct' and to have 'intended to do a terrible thing'.[50] Kay Gilderdale in contrast was found not guilty of attempted murder with the judge describing her as a 'caring and loving mother', and openly ques-tioning why she had been prosecuted for attempted murder, when she had pleaded guilty to aiding and abetting suicide.[51] The CPS were left to assert that 'the intent was clear on our evidence',[52] and they were probably right in so thinking. What went wrong for Frances Inglis? It is likely that she came

---

[49] Is this just an obscure slogan? I think not: it is there for a purpose, which is to separate out a factual and a moral understanding of legal responsibility. It has significant effects in cases, eg *Chandler v DPP* [1964] AC 763. It is certainly a very problematic separation, so it does lead to 'obscurity' in the law, but it is a *necessary* obscurity based upon the formal structuring of the legal architectonic. The 'moral' approaches discussed in the first section have difficulty in grasping this because they do not see that law has a formal structure allocating moral issues in a distinctive non-moral way, based upon what Brudner calls 'political' grounds. The 'critical' approach which I advocate latches onto the failure of the political approach to organize the law in an overall rational manner, but it accepts that the political approach grasps something about the structure of the law. See A. Norrie, *Punishment, Responsibility and Justice* (n 4 above) on the idea that the criminal law form involves 'false but necessary' distinctions.

[50] *Guardian* 21 January 2010.

[51] For which offence she was given a suspended sentence.

[52] *Guardian* 26 January 2010.

across as a person too caught up in her own emotional concerns to act fully in terms of what was right for her son. He had been unable to express a wish in the matter. This is borne out by the ground of her appeal that the defence of provocation in a situation of severe emotional stress should have been left to the jury. In dismissing this argument, the Court of Appeal noted that the defendant was in complete control of herself, was obsessive in her conviction that her son should die, had acted without regard for the views of other family members, and bore some responsibility for her son's condition due to an earlier unsuccessful attempt to kill him. She might have been better placed had she claimed diminished responsibility, but had not done so because she wanted all the facts to come out.[53]

Finally, the hidden moral issue of motive, expressed through the formal language of intention, is seen quite clearly in another case from a few years ago, that of Barbara Salisbury.[54] Salisbury was a nurse on a geriatric ward in Crewe, who was convicted of the attempted murder of two patients and acquitted with regard to two more. The general evidence was that she was obsessed with unblocking beds in the ward. She was described at trial as having a bad attitude, as upsetting and offending people, as brusque and as callous. Sentencing her for the crimes for which she was convicted, the judge stated that she had broken her duty of care and abused her position of trust 'by attempting to hasten death'. This was contrasted by the prosecution with 'easing the passing', which is permissible, but it is a fine line between the two. The knife edge is seen in one of the deaths for which she was acquitted. There, she was involved in administering diamorphine to a patient and allegedly saying to him, 'Give in, it's time to go' as she did so. Her evidence was that her words were, 'It's ok to go now'. Did it matter which words precisely she had used and which tone she had used them in? I think it did. Administering a pain-killing drug which will hasten death is acceptable if done in the right spirit, and the words that she spoke could have been said in a kindly or a callous way. If they were found to have been said in a kind way, it would have been a comforting, compassionate, assistance to the patient not aimed at hastening death but easing the passing. If they had been said in a callous way, the same words, and accompanying deeds, could be interpreted as aimed directly at pushing the patient toward his death. A decision of guilt and innocence as to intention in such a case surely depends on the attitude or

---

[53] *R v Inglis* [2010] EWCA Crim 2637. On appeal the sentence was reduced from nine to five years on the mitigating grounds that she believed this to be an act of mercy, and suffered mental disorder as provided under the Criminal Justice Act 2003, s 269 and Sch 21.

[54] *Guardian* 29 April 2004.

the motive with which deeds are done or words said. It's not what you say, but the way that you say it.

V. Legal Form and Moral Substance: Assisting Suicide

The same kind of interplay between formal law and underlying ethics is also at play in the area of assisted suicide, though the nature of assisted suicide entails a different arrangement for legal practice. It may however be helpful first to summarize what I have said in the previous section. With active euthanasia, the main work is done by the distinction between primary and secondary purpose, though this has to be read in the light of the distinction between direct and indirect intent. The extension of intention to include primary and secondary purposes in the line of cases leading to *Woollin* presents a problem. It is negotiated in active euthanasia cases by the moral, motive-based assertion that, though a killing may have been intended, the fact that it was carried out with a 'good heart' or other accepted moral or professional intention deflects the focus from the intention to kill or to commit a criminal act to an easing of suffering. The position is slightly different as between the doctors cases and the case of a parent such as Kay Gilderdale. With doctors, it is possible to claim that treating the patient represents the primary purpose, or the moral focus of their intentional agency, or an alternative moral effect to death. With a case such as that of Mrs Gilderdale, what is the distinct primary purpose or focus of her agency that can be taken as the alternative to the intention to kill? It can only be a loving commitment to bring an end to suffering, but the problem here is that this is essentially a euphemistic way of speaking about what Mrs Gilderdale in fact did, that she killed her daughter. There is no doctor's obligation or practice to fall back on as the 'narrow horizon' for action which blocks the criminal goal from view. Ending suffering just is killing the daughter. These are in law hard cases to decide in favour of the defendant and involve a fuller quotient of jury equity than the doctors cases, where a distinct medical purpose can be ascribed. Juries just have to 'feel' their way to a decision without the prop of an alternative distinct intention to rely upon.

How does it work with assisted suicide? It is also hard to see such cases as involving an alternative purpose under which what then becomes the second-ary purpose of assisting another's dying can nestle. If a spouse helps his or her partner to travel to Zurich, or to take a dose of drugs *that will kill*, there is no possible alternative purpose such as alleviating pain, just as there is no plausible argument that travelling to Zurich will broaden the deceased's horizons. The irreducible intention to assist the suicide is all too clearly visible. Presumably, if prosecutions were brought, it would be open to the defendant simply to argue the moral issue in the open of the courtroom and say that she acted from the best of intentions, and with love in her heart. The criminal law, however, could only take so many of such cases, which presumably are more numerous than those where a parent actively kills a loved one, before a disparity between the law and the outcomes of such cases, or the scandal of the difference in outcomes between individual cases, brought the law into disrepute. These are hard cases for the law to deal with because it is too clear that defendants intentionally break it, without an alternative purpose to hang on to,[55] and defendants have themselves got the message that this is so: hence their resort to the Dignitas clinic in Switzerland, which means that the main activities around the suicide take place in a foreign jurisdiction. Yet, this hardly lets the law, or the defendant, off the hook. Assisting a terminally ill sufferer to travel abroad to their death is a form of aiding and abetting in its own right, yet even before the new CPS guidelines, no one had been prosecuted for so doing.

Before the new guidelines were issued by the DPP, the way in which the problem of assisted suicide was dealt with was by means of a discretion to prosecute, the grounds of which remained undisclosed. After the guidelines, of course, the discretionary basis is disclosed. In the draft guidelines, two sets of factors were regarded as germane to the decision to prosecute. One set concerned the condition of the 'victim', the other the position and motives of the defendant. In their revised form, the condition of the 'victim' has been removed from the criteria, leaving the motives of the defendant as the main factor. This was as a result of arguments that identifying certain conditions as being likely to lead to suicide would place a degree of pressure on those suffering from such conditions to think of themselves as potential suicides. In that way, it raised the morally substantive concern that some lives were of less value than others.[56] It is the argument of this chapter that one way of dealing with the problem of euthanasia is not to treat it in a way that confronts actual moral concerns about the value of life. Better instead to treat it as a matter of individual choice for 'victims' (but without reference made to their actual conditions),[57] and as a matter of individual attitude on

---

[55] An alternative route here has historically been available through the partial defence of diminished responsibility. Whether this route has been closed off by recent reform of the Homicide Act 1957, s2 remains to be seen. See R. Mackay, 'The New Diminished Responsibility Plea' (2010) *Crim LR* 290.

[56] An argument prosecuted in K. Greasley, *op cit*, n 30.

[57] <http://www.cps.gov.uk/publications/prosecution/assisted_suicide_policy.html>. Of 16 factors in favour of prosecution, the first five concern the ability of the deceased to make a sound choice. These

behalf of defendants acting out of care and love and without self-interest in relation to a person to whom they are personally connected.[58] Dropping reference to the quality of specific kinds of lives is another means of finessing the substantive issues by focusing on intentions, and here the intention to assist suicide is buttressed, in the guidelines but not in the law, by heavy reliance on motive.

Hence the resort to motive as the main consideration in deciding to prosecute leaves the law of assisted suicide in much the same place as the law of active euthanasia with regard to doctors and others who hasten death: it is ultimately a question of motive, regarded as a means for qualifying their otherwise clearly criminal intentions. The principal difference concerns where and how the supplementing of the law of intention with motive occurs. In the medical euthanasia cases, it primarily occurs informally in individual decisions not to prosecute, while in the parental mercy killings, it is a matter of jury equity (or perversity). In assisted suicide it now occurs at the prosecutorial stage through a formal structuring of the discretionary process that stands in uncomfortable juxtaposition to the law that denies it. Whether the kind of balance this provides represents a long-term solution to the problems of moral principle and practice described above, only time will tell. The mere publicization of the terms of discretion may in itself promote the practice with ramifications that are not yet known.[59] In suggesting that such a balancing exists and has been enabled by the formalism of the legal architectonic, I have not argued for anything other than an ad hoc, and therefore possibly a temporary, solution to the problem society faces. The underlying issue, especially in the case of assisted suicide at present, concerns the possibility of good deaths in a morally bad—economically unequal, structurally unjust—

include: that the victim was under 18; did not have the capacity to reach an informed decision; had not reached a voluntary, clear, settled, and informed decision; had not clearly and unequivocally communicated a decision to commit suicide to the suspect; and did not seek the encouragement or assistance of the suspect personally or on his or her own initiative.

[58] Factors relevant to prosecution concerning the suspect include that he was not wholly motivated by compassion, for example, he stood to gain from the death of the victim; that he pressured the victim; or did not take reasonable steps to ensure that any other person had not pressured the victim; that he had a history of violence or abuse against the victim; that the victim was physically able to undertake the act that constituted the assistance him or herself; that the suspect was unknown to the victim and encouraged or assisted the victim by providing information via a website or publication; that he gave encouragement or assistance to more than one victim; that he was paid for his or her assistance; that he was acting in his or her capacity as a medical doctor or other professional carer, or as a person in authority, where the victim was in their care; that he was aware that the victim intended to commit suicide in a public place; that he was acting in his or her capacity as a person involved in an organization or group, a purpose of which is to provide a physical environment in which to allow another to commit suicide.

[59] K. Greasley, *op cit*, n 30.

society, and *that* problem lies beyond the power of the cunning of law and legal form to resolve.

VI. Conclusion

In this chapter, I have considered how a critical analysis of criminal law can be brought to bear on the problems of euthanasia and assisted suicide. In part II, I contrasted 'moral', 'political' and 'critical' approaches to criminal law. Put briefly, a 'moral' approach to criminal law considers how a social practice ought to be treated normatively, and then how this should be reflected in the law. A 'political' approach, such as Brudner's, sees the law as possessing a formal quality, which reflects in a structured way how freedom and a person's belonging in a community are internally related within an ethical-legal totality. Against 'moral' approaches, it argues that the study of criminal law is not simply an exercise in applied moral theory. By itself, the 'moral' approach fails to grasp law's *differentia specifica* as a form of political morality. A 'critical' approach also acknowledges the formal structuring of law, espe-cially around abstract ideas of freedom. This gives rise to the idea that law's formal structure of 'general' (offence and defence, etc) and 'special' parts constitutes a specifically *legal* architectonic. But it also argues against the 'political' approach that the broader synthesis of freedom and community envisaged there is not possible in a socially contradictory and structurally unequal society. Law's formal conception of freedom, in an 'unsynthesisable' social whole, is from an overall ethical point of view a source of weakness, not strength. That is the case, and this is the main argument here, *except* insofar as it becomes indirectly or obliquely a useful resource in negotiating moral conflicts such as those we see in regard to euthanasia and assisted suicide.

The abstract formalism of law's architectonic emphasizes legal form over moral substance, psychological intention over moral purpose (or motive), and a formal definition of the offence alongside a limited set of exceptional moral defences. This makes the law morally inflexible at one level, but oddly useful at another, when it comes to finessing practical, morally and politically contentious, issues such as euthanasia and assisted suicide. A society such as ours finds it impossible to reach a consensus, or escape an impasse here, but is still able to accommodate its conflicts under the cover of formal law. This is seen especially in the way the law of intention plays out. At the formal level, it operates as a law that is not a law, or one with a built-in capacity to self-cancel. With regard specifically to medical euthanasia, it is a law that slips in *sotto voce* an exceptional interpretation ('primary purpose') for just such cases.

In other euthanasia situations, it is the basis for prosecutorial, judicial, and jury-based discretion in particular cases. The greatest difficulty emerges in cases of assisted suicide, where there are no actors with a special status (ie doctors), or a 'primary purpose' that is (in a limited sense) distinguishable from directly helping to bring about death. This makes the informal finesse harder to achieve, and is evidenced in the recent emergence of a *formal* contradiction between a law prohibiting assistance and lawful guidelines enabling it.

That, however, is not how things usually work, and the best way to explain the tensions within the law, and how these tensions are productive for social order, is through a 'critical' approach. Only with such an approach can the oblique or indirect relation between the moral, political, and juridical aspects of criminal responsibility be sustained.

8

Abnormal Law: Teratology as a Logic of Criminalization

MR McGuire

It comes as no great insight to remind ourselves that criminalization processes sometimes display an ambiguous relationship between their (internal) rationales and more general principles of rationality. Work on the rationales of criminalization has been a neglected area of scholarship[1] perhaps because, as Nicola Lacey has recently argued, 'the field has hardly moved on from the nineteenth century'.[2] But one, perhaps overdue, observation is the way that the development of criminal law has often been equally motivated by elements of the *irrational* as by the coherent, evidence-based, thinking we might expect to find. On the assumption that criminalization functions as much as a social as a legal practice, I intend, in this chapter, to consider how certain ostensibly irrational components within social praxis contribute towards the formation of law. That is, rather than viewing criminalization in more usual terms—as a response to norm violations—I want instead to consider how it may, on occasions, be influenced by our confrontations with what I will term the *abnormal*. Prima facie, this contrast appears to be questionable—no doubt because the difference between a 'deviation from a norm' and an abnormality is not immediately obvious. There are, however, signs that this prejudice has begun to shift in recent years, with criminologists in particular engaging with some of the more substantive effects of abnormalities upon criminal justice.[3] Confrontations with what David Garland characterized as the 'other'[4] have begun to be taken more seriously, whilst

---

[1] See Mill (1859), Feinberg (1984–8), Schonsheck (1994), and Husak (2007), for some more and less well known endeavours of this kind.

[2] Lacey (2009, p 937).

[3] See eg Garland (1996), Melossi (2000), Ericson (2007).

[4] Garland (2001).

Foucault's under-explored account of the abnormal other in terms of what he called the 'human monster'—which argued that it be read as a juridical as well as a conceptual category—has been re-examined in Andrew Sharpe's useful study[5] of the 'legal monster' within English law. Such thinking parallels other developments within social science—in particular economics—where there has been an increasing realization that effective modelling of social actors' behaviours also requires the inclusion of (seemingly) irrational motivations.[6] In this chapter I want to test some of these developing insights by suggesting that a focus upon the abnormal does not just offer a useful 'filling out' of any normative theory of criminalization, in particular its wider (ir)rationales. It also provides an essential tool for tracing long-established and recurring patterns within it. Evidence of what I will call a 'teratology', or rationale of the abnormal, underlying these patterns suggests that contemporary criminal justice practice continues to be shaped in its image as much as any pre-modern jurisdiction ever was. For at the root of many of the current concerns about the direction law is taking in the face of competing demands from security, globalization, and new technologies is the threat of law's subjection to a process of what René Girard once termed 'monstrous doubling'—the point at which the influence of our teratologies so undermines the functioning of law that it, like the monster, begins to become an 'anomalous' thing.[7]

I. Norms, the Abnormal, and the Irrational

Why, as I argue, can an abnormality be taken to generate responses that are both substantive and yet distinct from a mere deviation from a norm? The powerful instinctual impacts of abnormalities upon our attitudes (repulsion, dread, anger, and so on)—impacts which seem to go far beyond the effects of norm violations—might constitute one immediate reason for granting this. In addition, certain conceptual (and ontological) discontinuities also lend support to the idea that abnormality cannot be exhaustively analyzed in terms of norm violation. The observation that, like a rule, norms indicate relation-ships *between* states of affairs, but are not themselves states of affairs contrasts usefully with the way that abnormality appears to be something which *can*

---

[5] Sharpe (2009 and 2010).
[6] See Lunn (2009) or Parisi and Smith (2005) for a general account here. Psychologists have also begun to analyze the influence of a number of 'basic biases' which (systematically) cause us to behave in ways describable as irrational. See Kahneman and Tversky's (1979) for a groundbreaking attempt to unify psychological and economic insights about irrational behaviour.
[7] Girard (2005, p 170).

be thought of in this way. For example, whilst a biological defect might be recognized as a substantive property of something, driving on the wrong side of the road seems unlikely to be seen in this way. Similarly, whilst an abnormality might be regarded as explanatorily prior to a norm deviation (ie she drove on the wrong side of the road *because* she was mentally ill, cognitively impaired by alcohol, emotionally unstable, and so on), the converse is less clear. A second argument follows from these reflections on properties—in particular the ways in which certain properties are held to be *ontologically* coherent. For if abnormalities were simply negations of norms then they would be instances of negative properties, and there have been good philosophical reasons for supposing that negative properties cannot be genuine properties. For example, if causal efficacy is seen as the basis for distinguishing real properties from the ersatz ones,[8] then abnormality cannot be a negative property since it *can*, as we have just seen, induce causal outcomes. Given the linguistic resources at our disposal it has perhaps been all too easy simply to assimilate abnormalities and norm violations. A better distinction might perhaps be made between *negated*-norms (which do involve norm violations) and *non*-norms (substantive, causally efficacious states of affairs which 'go beyond' the normal), and it is something like this distinction that I will have in mind in what follows.

In turn, positing legal responses to abnormality as *irrational* responses raises difficult questions about the relationship between these concepts. Indeed we might ask whether the rationality or irrationality of the law is relevant here at all given that it may be just as possible to have *rational* responses towards the abnormal (ie to run away) as it is to have irrational responses to *normal* circumstances (eg to attack someone who has just helped you).[9] Whilst an account of rationality per se is clearly beyond the scope of this chapter, it is worth saying a little more about what the claim that legal responses to abnormality can sometimes be irrational ones might mean. For the assumption that the familiar trope of the 'reasonable person' within legal discourse is a synonym for a rational one is certainly not self-evident.[10]

Rorty, who dismissed the idea that rationality possessed any intrinsic nature, argued that calling a piece of reasoning 'rational' simply means that

---

[8] See Shoemaker (1980, 1998) for a version of the causal efficacy argument. Armstrong (1989, pp 82–4) develops this line on properties.

[9] Thanks to Lindsay Farmer for pressing this point. One response to it might be to accept that abnormalities do not *always* produce irrational responses—without that lessening the interest of when they do. Alternatively it might be countered that what *appears* to be a rational response turns out later to have strong irrational components—for example in ignoring or deliberately excluding important evidence from legal judgments.

[10] See Sibley (1953) for an early exposition of this argument.

it conforms to certain standards held by communities.[11] On this line irrationality would emerge simply where we do not behave in accordance with those
standards. But Rorty's response would again blur the requisite distinction by
making norm violations and abnormality similar in virtue of failing to conform
to certain community standards. Fortunately there is no need to relativize
rationality in this way in order to make the point. At the very minimum,
rationality appears to require good reasons, where 'goodness' can be associated
with the *internal* coherence of a set of beliefs of statements, or *external* factors
such as credible evidence or principles of justice such as 'fairness'. Law functions rationally then, where it adheres to internal logical rules such as non-
contradiction, bases judgments on evidence rather than subjective imaginings,
and operates in accord with widely held normative standards. It is where there
is a failure to conform to these standards (and not just in virtue of omission—
since it is not irrational to make a mistake) that I will take evidence of
irrationality to have emerged. For example, a judgment resulting in an individual being found guilty of some crime might be viewed as an irrational one if it
involved certain internal contradictions or if it were influenced by external
factors irrelevant to the case (such as the defendant's ethnicity).

In what follows I will therefore distinguish the abnormal from the irrational by viewing the former in terms of (ostensibly) substantive social formations and the latter in terms of the effect upon our responses such formations
may induce. And I will argue that irrationality may arise within these
responses where, as Girard suggests, the abnormal 'disproportions' them.
For science, as we will see, this has often meant a disproportionate obsession
with finding a material basis for abnormalities more properly located within
the realm of sociological explanation. In criminal law it has meant the
production of legislation disproportioned by the subjective influences of
popular prejudice, rather than objective evidence of harm or offence. And
it is in this way that law's encounter with abnormality all too often transforms
the 'reasonable' person into one driven by less transparent forces.

II. Abnormality and Criminalization (I): Lombroso, Science, and Abnormality

The idea that abnormalities might be substantive (ie causally efficacious)
properties of things finds a perfect illustration in the Lombrosian project
of essentializing criminal types. Lombroso's notorious reflections on the

---

[11] See Rorty (1991).

criminal set out a position where features perceived as 'abnormal' become legitimized as objective, scientifically determinable predictors of criminal behaviour (and by extension legitimators for criminalization processes). For Lombroso, there were certain abnormalities that were so basic to nature that, not only did they mark out criminals as 'biological freaks',[12] but they could even indicate criminality in life forms other than humans. On this basis even plants could be said to display a primitive criminality in that '... premeditation, ambush, killing for greed ... are derived completely from histology or the micro-state of organic tissue—and not from an alleged will'.[13] It is in his theory of atavism where we find the clearest typologization of abnormality— as a form of evolutionary regression.[14] However, criminals are not just abnormal individuals in virtue of their possessing the instincts and mental capacities of 'primitives', but because (in a unique form of biological entropy) they are actively degenerating:

> The criminal is an atavistic being, a relic of a vanished race ... Atavism, the reversion to a former state, is the first feeble indication of the reaction opposed by nature to the perturbing causes which seek to alter her delicate mechanism. ...
>
> The ætiology of crime, therefore, mingles with that of all kinds of degeneration: rickets, deafness, monstrosity, hairiness, and cretinism, of which crime is only a variation.[15]

The explanatory power Lombroso granted to abnormality was controversial enough at the time and has long been dismissed as 'bizarre' or an 'unfortunate episode in the history of criminology'.[16] But the primordial appeal of Lombrosian thought cannot be discounted quite so easily. Not because we believe it to be correct, but because its essentialism remains so instinctively compulsive. In this way, the influence of Lombrosian thinking upon rationales of criminalization, far from being relegated to absurdity, has merely taken on newer, more socially acceptable forms.

As we will see, the key aspect of the Lombrosian approach was not its particular taxonomy of abnormalities, but the assumption that in 'scientizing' them objective indicators of criminality could be discerned. Law-making in the totalitarian states of the 1930s constituted an immediate and well-

---

[12] The description is Savitz' in the reprint edition of Lombroso-Ferrero (p xxix).

[13] 1984, p168.

[14] His theory was considerably changed and expanded over time, but in *L'Uomo Criminale* several abnormal types are identified as a basis for criminality—for example the epileptic and morally insane which he groups under the common class of 'lunatics'.

[15] G. Lombroso-Ferrero (1911).

[16] See Goring (1913). The quotes, respectively, are from Jupp (1989, p 2) and Smart (1976, p 32) (see Mooney, 2000 for more).

discussed manifestation of this assumption. For example, Nazi science pioneered the proclivity for locating the 'defects' of homosexuality within medical, rather than political discourses. Amendments to existing anti-gay laws in Germany during the 1930s allowed for a range of medical interventions to 'cure' this supposed defect, including castration and the notorious 'Vaernet Cure'—the attempt to reverse homosexuality by implanting artificial glands which released testosterone.[17] In the USSR, the perceived abnormalities of homosexuality were read slightly differently—as a kind of predictor for more general disorder and the most corrosive form of deviance (from the socialist perspective) of fascism. This assumption—that from abnormality, further abnormalities follow—is one that I will return to later.[18]

Appeals to abnormality as a rationale for criminalization were certainly not restricted to totalitarian regimes,[19] and even there new laws often simply extended existing prejudices and controls. Nazi fixations with identifying criminality as biological abnormality drew upon existing programmes in the (democratic) Weimar Republic, where the criminal justice system was firmly under the influence of works like Kretschmer's *Physique and Character* (1921), and where almost all criminological research was already controlled by doctors and psychiatrists. We see similar prejudices in respectable academic journals of the 1920s and 1930s where papers asserting definitive scientific links between abnormality and criminality were a regular feature. Good's (1932) study of abnormality and crime was typical, claiming to have shown how 'mental defectives are more prone to criminal conduct than other types of abnormalities...(and) the group designated moral imbeciles supplies a large number of criminals'.[20] Such claims were particularly well received in the USA where Henry Goddard's assertion that 'feeble-mindedness' was hereditary, or William Sheldon's concept of 'constitutional psychology' became important influences upon theories and practices of criminalization. Sheldon linked body-type to personality, identifying a class he called 'mesomorphs'—(muscular and hard body types) who were 'more likely' to be criminal than other body-types.[21] Judge Olsen, Chief Justice of the municipal court of Chicago, typified the readiness of the legal profession to defer to the scientists' views on this, arguing that:

---

[17] See Hackett (1995).

[18] Seen in Gorky's famous rallying cry of 1934, 'Destroy the homosexuals – Fascism will disappear': Healey (2007, p 227).

[19] The hormone operations in Nazi Germany were, for example, very similar to those imposed by the British criminal justice system upon Alan Turing and which later resulted in his suicide.

[20] There are many other similar examples. See eg Jennings (1930).

[21] Sheldon's work remains popular amongst many criminal justice practitioners and theorists in the USA. See eg Cortés and Gatti (1972).

crime is a social defect based on mental defect... the accumulated records show that it runs in family stocks and is subject to the laws of genetics like other characteristics.[22]

The scientific legitimization of correlations between criminality and abnormality resulted in tangible criminalization processes. By the 1920s a number of US states had passed forcible sterilization laws and, whilst the number of individuals subjected to these was low at first, the rate of sterilizations rose dramatically after the Supreme Court legitimized the practice in *Buck v Bell* in 1927.[23] The director of the US Eugenics Record Office, Harry Laughlin, even set out a 'Model Eugenical Sterilization Law', which called for a general sterilization of the 'socially inadequate' (defined as consisting of the 'feebleminded, insane and criminalistic').[24] Though this never made it onto the Federal statute books, widespread sterilizations of criminals were conducted and it was not until 1942, when *Skinner v Oklahoma* established that these must be applied 'equally' (ie to white collar, as well as working class criminals), that any sort of legal challenge began to surface.[25] Even by 1956, 27 US states retained sterilization laws—with the last forced sterilization taking place as late as 1981.[26] Similar laws had been passed in jurisdictions as varied as Sweden, Australia, Switzerland, Norway, and Canada amongst many others.[27]

The re-evaluations of scientific authority in determining criminality after 1945 tempered some of its more extreme (biological) reductionist tendencies. But more recent scientific techniques—in particular DNA analysis and neural imaging—have provided new legitimations for using abnormality as an indicator of criminality. Charles Murray's notorious attempt to associate supposed cognitive abnormalities such as low IQ with race may have been widely questioned,[28] but elsewhere the work of criminologists like James Q. Wilson or cognitive scientists like Adrian Raine represent examples of thriving research programmes into the 'biological criminal'.[29] Elsewhere the increasing role of psychological profiling within criminal justice or the

---

[22] Cited in Laughlin (1936).

[23] 274 U.S. 200 (1927).

[24] Laughlin (1922, ch XV, s 2(b)).

[25] 316 U.S. 535 (1942).

[26] This took place in Oregon, where its 'Board of Eugenics' (later euphemized as the 'Board of Social Protection') continued to practise until 1983.

[27] Whilst the UK never ratified any such laws, it was not for want of trying. Churchill for example attempted to introduce a clause in the 1913 Mental Deficiency Act which permitted forced sterilization of the 'feeble-minded', though this was eventually rejected (see MacNichol, 1989).

[28] See Herrnstein and Murray (1994).

[29] See Wilson (1985) and Raine (2002) for some trends here. Walby and Carrier (2010) offer a more recent perspective.

use of medication to sedate, or to sufficiently 'normalize' mentally disturbed prisoners so as to make it legal to execute them—emphasize how science is again central to the project of identifying abnormalities considered 'predictive' of criminality.

III. Theorizing Abnormality and Criminalization

Whilst criminal law scholarship has tended to focus on the role of norms rather than abnormalities, criminological and anthropological literatures have displayed a greater readiness to engage with the latter.[30] One set of associations has centred on the way that certain abnormalities generate irrational fears and panics which legitimate new programmes of legislation or social control.[31] Young people have been especially prominent recent subjects of such moral panics in that they seem to:

mark the possibility of the next problem—being abnormally abnormal or pathological. It is in this space—the relationship between normal abnormality and the abnormal abnormalities—that the youth problem is constructed.[32]

The resulting legal (and extra-legal) responses to the 'abnormality' of youth—covert surveillance, dispersion zones; curfews, injunctions, use of sonic repulsion devices, and even prohibitions against certain forms of attire—hardly seem to represent legal responses commensurate with the level of threat they present. What they do suggest is a key effect of abnormality hinted at earlier, namely its power to amplify perceptions of an initial irregularity into a sense of *generalized* disorder or chaos. This is something which Agamben has referred to as a '*iustitium*', or 'state of exception', a point that I will return to in more detail later.

A second variety of analysis has focused more upon the *kinds of things* which constitute abnormality. Garland, for example, distinguishes between two differing (criminological) frameworks centred, respectively, upon normality and abnormality—the *criminology of the self*, and the *criminology of the other*.[33] Within the former, criminals are not abnormal but are rather like us (or at least what we are supposed to be like). They are rational consumers,

---

[30] The anthropology of law has been particularly rich in this regard—see eg Nader (1965), Rafter (1997), and Schneider and Schneider (2008).

[31] See Cohen's classic work on moral panics (1972). See also Young (1968) and more recent work by Ditton and Farrall (2000) and Walklate (2004).

[32] Clarke (2008).

[33] Garland (1996). See eg Hallsworth (2000), Aas (2007).

who make choices in the market, guided by free will and an informed weighing of options. They are also the subjects of criminological theories which are preferred and sponsored by the state, such as rational choice theory, situational crime prevention, and routine activities theory. As 'rational' members of society—albeit ones who play fast and loose with the rules—this type of criminal seems to constitute a risk which can be managed by the solid, calculative principles of science and mathematics and which can be accommodated within target-based approaches that demonstrate (at least within the state's fantasy of crime control) the 'effectiveness' of criminal justice policies.

The criminology of the other, by contrast, is concerned precisely with the less manageable threats presented by the abnormal. Garland is a little vague about what constitutes 'others' but he does recognize that generalized categories of abnormality can serve to 'demonise the criminal, to act out popular fears and resentments and to promote support for State punishment'.[34] However he never arrives at any more developed taxonomy, nor does he identify why 'the other' has this kind of normative effect upon criminalization—perhaps because he simply accepts their 'otherness' as an unanalyzable property of 'opaquely monstrous creatures beyond or beneath our knowing'.[35] This omission seems to ignore good evidence for the existence of structure, regularity, and consistency within the category of 'the other'—not least in its historical longevity and cross-cultural aspects. Thus, whilst criminology has established a plausible case for the role of 'othering' within criminalization processes, it has been less successful in identifying the specific effects of abnormality upon them. To begin to better understand this we need to turn to a more detailed account of its primal force.

IV. Abnormality and Criminalization (II): Foucault's Monsters

In a seminal series of lectures at the Collège de France, Foucault confronted the effects of abnormality upon law more directly.[36] As elsewhere in his work, his primary concern here was with defining a genealogy, in this case how techniques for managing and disciplining abnormality (legally or otherwise) shifted during the nineteenth century. Foucault realized that 'the abnormal' is not only a space which *can* be mapped, legally or otherwise, but also that a defining coordinate point within that legal space is what he called 'the human monster'. As he argues:

[34] (2001) p 137.   [35] Ibid 184.   [36] Foucault (1974).

the notion of the monster is essentially a legal notion...(for) what defines the monster is the fact that its existence is not only a violation of the norms of society but also a violation of the laws of nature. The field in which the monster appears can thus be called a juridical-biological domain.

A second crucial aspect of Foucault's account for the argument here is his realization that something happens to legal process when confronted by 'the monster' for this:

traps the law while breaching it. When the monster violates the law by breaching it, it *triggers the response of something quite different from the law itself.* It provokes either violence, the will for pure and simple repression or medical care and pity.[37]

By associating the (implied) disorders of the monster with disorders within the law, Foucault thereby anticipates both Girard's and Agamben's ideas about the effects of abnormality upon rational/legal process.

Foucault's account, though central to any examination of the legal force of the abnormal, still leaves us with some major explanatory gaps. First, his identification of the monster as a disciplinary subject peculiar to the emergence of nineteenth-century science overlooks both the deeper historical roots and the ongoing influence of the phenomenon. Second, his stress upon the phenomenal and biological aspects of the monstrous obscures some of the important ways in which wider perceptions of abnormality have served to motivate regulation. This presumption is shared by Sharpe, in his otherwise very useful historical account of the way that 'offences against nature' in the juridico-biological sense can be correlated with specific interventions within English law. Whilst two-headed babies, hermaphrodites, or other biological deviations offer useful insights into the way that abnormality has been received and controlled, my argument is that these constitute only a kind of *terra ultima* within a much wider, and more significant field of encounters. That is, the category of the monster is really only a kind of a special case—a 'limit point'—within the more general continuum of responses provoked by our sense of the abnormal.[38]

Foucault also leaves open the vital question of what this 'something different from the law' might be and how it might be relevant to the study of criminalization. Trying to work out some of the details of this relationship will be the primary concern of the rest of the rest of this chapter. But to get to this point, a better sense of the way particular varieties of abnormality sometimes destabilize law production is required. This will emphasize how

---

[37] Both the previous quotes are from Foucault (1974, p 56).

[38] Tarde's 'zero of monstrosity' (cf Sharpe, 2010, p 48) anticipates this scalar approach.

contemporary attempts to scientize abnormality simply reproduce a more general set of cultural and historical assumptions. In addition, by systematizing the abnormal more completely within a teratological framework, its normative impacts upon criminalization begin to become clearer.

V. 'If a Monster. . . . ': Teratology and Systematizing the Abnormal

The idea alluded to earlier, that abnormality does not just constitute a form of risk but that it can act as a predictor for *further* abnormality, has been a recurring historical control fantasy. The actuarial approaches now prevalent within most criminal justice systems not only arguably manifest this philosophy, but also constitute specific instances of the attempt to systematize abnormalities for the purposes of social control. The roots of this predilection go very deep, for it was as common an assumption in the pre-modern world as it now seems to be within the post-modern. An extraordinary text from Ancient Babylon called the *Summa Izbu* provides one historical precedent for this tendency. The *Summa Izbu* functioned as one of a variety of predictive tools for politicians and lawmakers of the time, and sought to correlate anomalies in birth (animal or human) with impending anomalies in the legal and political sphere.[39] Its predictions came in the form of a series of *if. . . then* propositions of the following kind:

If a monster/abnormal birth has two heads, and the second one is above its right shoulder - then there will be pestilence in the land and revolt against the king...

If a monster has two heads and the second one is on his chest, then the crown prince will seize the throne.[40]

This sense that, from abnormality further abnormality can be inferred, continued into the medieval period and beyond. In 1512 for example, Europe was convulsed by reports from Ravenna of a child born with a horn on its forehead, a 'devil's hoof' on one leg and a eye in the middle of another leg: a child so monstrous that 'never in memory of man has there been anything like this'.[41] Most commentators of the time interpreted the subsequent sacking of Ravenna by the French as the sad but inevitable outcome of what this deviation from nature had presaged. As one put it, 'it was evident what evil the monster had meant for them. It seems as if some

---

[39] Izbu is often translated as 'monster' but can also simply mean 'malformed'.

[40] Tablet 8, lines 33–44. See Rochberg (2004).

[41] Niccoli (1990, p 35).

great misfortune always befalls the city where such things are born.'[42] The conclusion, in other words, was clear. The failure of the Ravennan authorities to protect their city could be directly attributed to their failure to take abnormal action in the face of abnormality.

Social responses to the abnormal have therefore often been associated with projects of systematicity: the attempt to manage it more effectively by taxonomizing its various manifestations. It is fascinating to note how often such attempts have corresponded to the kind of knowledge considered legitimate at a particular time, so that Francis Bacon's call for 'a particular natural history of . . . monstrous births of nature' signalled the emergence of a new and now familiar project: the shift away from identifying 'merely fabulous' things towards their comprehensive scientific taxonomization.[43] But early endeavours of this kind remained firmly attached to the phenomenal-biological aspects of the abnormal. In his *Systemae Naturae* for example, Linnaeus' influential system of botanic categories was supplemented by a less plausible categorization of the human species, one which included two special classes: '*Homo ferus*' (wild men) and '*Homo monstrosus*' (monsters). De Buffon's opposition to Linnaean categories did not extend to rejecting monstrosity as a feature of nature, and his system remained similarly attached to its physical aspects. Thus, he defined three classes of monster, arranged in terms of a normative-mereological system of 'appropriate or inappropriate' body parts:[44]

(a) those with excessive parts;
(b) those lacking parts;
(c) those with inappropriate, or reversed positioning of parts.

Though de Buffon's scheme was not, of course, supported by any properly derived evidence, its attempt at systematicity is further evidence for the growing belief that abnormality, at least in its physical sense, *could* be mapped in some more coherent way. This project of systematization, which was to finally replace the notion of monstrousness with abnormality, was seen in many other similar taxonomies advanced between the late eighteenth and early nineteenth centuries. Some even anticipated the contemporary taste for finding abnormality in *social* as well as purely physical facts. Morel, for example, who had made a careful study of de Buffon's work, advanced a theory of 'degeneration'[45] which anticipated Lombrosian atavism

---

[42] Ibid 50.
[43] See Deutch and Nussbaum (2000, p 106).
[44] Cf Tremain (2005, p 183).
[45] (1857). See also Tremain (ibid 176).

in arguing that certain humans—especially the criminal, or 'dangerous classes'—were literally 'degenerating' back into subhuman forms.

This project of a teratology—the systematic mapping of the abnormal—was to be most completely realized within medical science, from whence its name originates.[46] Malebranche's idea that abnormal births were caused by a pregnant woman's imagination,[47] had been supplanted by the work of Etienne St Hilaire who, for the first time, used comparative anatomical studies to demonstrate that it was interruptions in the development of the foetus which was the decisive causal factor.[48] The new science of teratology became a flourishing branch of contemporary obstetrics and seemed, at first, to have exposed the fallacies of using monstrosity as a category of nature or as a predictor for other (social) abnormalities like criminality. In this new climate of scientific certainty Mary Shelley's *Frankenstein* (which had been published in 1818) sounded one of the few discordant notes. For rather than serving to displace the monster as a salient category of nature, she seemed to suggest that science simply functions as a force for generating *new* kinds of abnormality. The emergence of the Lombrosian criminal monster was just one amongst many scientific reifications of abnormality the new century was to bring.

VI. Teratology as Crime Science?
Profiling the New Monsters

Whatever its primordial (and populist) appeal, the more recent 'teratological' order of control, seen in projects like crime profiling or risk management, remains legally contentious. In US courts, psychological profiles have been admitted as 'expert' evidence on only around 17 occasions (and were subsequently rejected on appeal), whilst police profiles have often been regarded as unreliable.[49] In the UK, profiling has been met with similar scepticism and has figured only twice as evidence in the courtroom—evidence eventually ruled as inadmissible in both cases.[50] But the crucial qualification here is of course 'in the courtroom'. Elsewhere in the criminal justice system and

---

[46] From teras = monster. The term 'teratology' was first used by Etienne St Hilaire's son Isidore, who continued his father's work on monstrosity and foetal abnormalities—see St Hilaire, I. (1857).

[47] Where any shock or trauma experienced by the mother was 'communicated' to the foetus: Malebranche (1753).

[48] St Hilaire (1822).

[49] Cf Alison et al (2002).

[50] *R v Stagg* (1994) 9 *Arch News* 4 and *R v Gilfoyle* [1996] Crim LR 198. See Meyer (2007) for more details on this and for a series of useful examples of attempts to use profiling in US case law.

beyond, determining criminal risk on the basis of measurable abnormalities is now an obsession—irrespective of any scientific doubts or legal controversies around it.

To engage effectively with assumptions like these and their specific impacts upon criminalization I argue that we need to engage more effectively with *how* our teratologies are structured. This requires more than merely psychological accounts of fear or insecurity, for whilst psychology may offer insights into the cognitive basis for our perceptions of abnormality, it tells us nothing about their social construction. In much the same way as gender does not reduce to biological facts, our perceptions and social responses to the abnormal are not just a matter of brain states or conditioning. Rather they are rooted in the ways social order and disorder is normatively judged and institutionally managed. Thus the teratology I argue we need is a criminological tool, one shaped by *hermeneutic* considerations, which serves to highlight recurring responses within socio-legal praxis to the abnormal.

In this context at least three key patterns in the way abnormality is perceived seem to be identifiable. As hermeneutic constructs these, of course, function more like ideal types than fixed particulars so that across distinct cultures and contexts, teratologies may be differently composed. But no matter how varied each culture's monsters may be, I argue that there are sufficient commonalities for certain recurring templates to be discernible and it is by way of these that law's transformation into 'something quite different from law' can begin to be more profitably traced.[51]

A. *De re* abnormality

A first patterning is most clearly linked to traditional conceptions of abnormality *as* monstrosity, in that it is predominantly characterized by responses to phenomenal or biological conditions. Perceived in this way, abnormality has much to do with older taxonomies such as de Buffon's, originating (for example) in apparent excess or lack of physical parts, in inappropriate mixing of parts (as in human-animal hybrids), or in more general phenomenal discordances. The effects of *de re* abnormality upon legal outcomes have

See Hicks and Sales (2006) and Kocsis and Palermo (2007) for a wider discussion about some of the issues and problems around profiling.

[51] Elements of the structure which follows are found in previous discussions of the monstrous, though these are usually historically based and focused mostly upon what I term its *de re,* or phenomenal/biological aspects (see eg Graham, 2002). Sharpe displays a similar proclivity, though he does acknowledge that 'if the abnormal individual is a contemporary monster, this cannot follow merely from an analysis of the body' (2010, p 51).

been clear enough. For example, the thirteenth-century common law texts of Bracton and Britton indicate how careful attention was paid to the number of body parts an individual possessed, since excess or lack could form a legal boundary between personhood (which conferred legal rights) and monstrosity (which removed them).[52] Thus, whilst a child with six fingers, or with four *was* counted amongst the class of children, a child with three hands or feet was not and was thereby deprived of many basic rights, notably those of inheritance. A lack of, or disproportion in parts as a basis for monstrosity in medieval law was further supplemented by 'hybridity', most obviously in the legally ambiguous figure of the hermaphrodite (where a mingling of body parts, rather than disproportion amongst them formed the criterion for abnormality). Though English law did not specifically criminalize hermaphrodites, it is certainly clear that their *de re* abnormality shaped other regulatory responses, most obviously the denial of certain basic rights. Hermaphrodites were forbidden, for example, to enter holy orders, whilst prohibitions against them serving as judges emphasize the fundamental sense in which they were seen to be 'outside' of the law.[53]

The influence of *de re* abnormality within contemporary teratologies and its resulting impacts upon law remains surprisingly strong. Biological factors are probably now more influential than purely phenomenal ones—for example searches for the criminal 'gene' or the emergence of what has been called the 'genetically at risk' individual have been striking instances of the revived influence of physical abnormalities upon social control.[54] Significantly, sanctions are often extra-judicial: those with long-term genetic illnesses face increasing controls from the insurance industry in obtaining basic rights to healthcare, employment, and so on.[55] A particularly interesting set of examples here centre upon the legalities of disease, especially HIV and its transmission. As many HIV advocates have pointed out, of all the many equally deadly or infectious diseases, it is only (conscious) transmission of HIV which has been criminalized.[56] Whilst it is true that other contagions may also be socially stigmatized there is no legal basis to this, so that it is hard to avoid the conclusion that the reasons for this highly targeted programme of

---

[52] See Sharpe (2009, p 5ff) for more details here.

[53] Ibid 73.

[54] See Rose (2000).

[55] For a discussion of these issues within European jurisdictions see Godard et al (2002). A more general overview is contained in Rothstein (2004). Genetic discrimination has itself been criminalized in certain jurisdictions, for example in the US Genetic Information Nondiscrimination Act (GINA) of 2008, though its protections are limited (see Goldgar, 2010).

[56] See eg HIV in Europe (2010), THT (2009).

criminalization arise from something peculiar to the HIV carrier—the taint of *de re* abnormality their disease carries.

Whilst the veneer of scientific legitimacy has tended to highlight biological abnormality as a predictor for disorder, phenomenal conditions also continue to generate socio-legal responses to *de re* abnormality. A notorious feature of Lombrosian preconditions for criminality were specifically phenomenal characteristics like tattoos, the width of an eyebrow, or sloping foreheads, and whilst the teratological force of these particulars may have declined, other kinds of phenomenal abnormalities remain or have replaced them. Some are familiar enough—skin colour, body shape, and even gender continue to combine with underlying biological facts in influencing a variety of more or less severe criminalizations.[57] Indeed, even 'pure' (ie non physically based) phenomenal facts may, on occasion, still possess sufficient teratological weight to combine with other prejudices in the creation of new offences. Historical examples of 'sumptuary laws' such as the Roman Aurelian dictat which criminalized the wearing of shoes that were red, yellow, green, or white,[58] or new offences in England from the early 1300s which criminalized certain ways of dressing were not just about enforcing a particular social hierarchy, but were expressions of a fundamental disgust with attire 'unnatural' to certain sections of society.[59] More recent prohibitions, against the wearing of a hood, or civil ordinances against baggy trousers,[60] maintain these traditions by reading appearance in terms of the kind of *de re* abnormalities which require legal constraint.

B. *De more* abnormality

It seems equally obvious that what the body *does*, as much as what the body looks like can also be read in terms of abnormality. As Simmel's seminal work on the power of the (social) boundary suggested, it is not just that the mores of the day set conditions for the kind of boundary violations more usually associated with norm negations.[61] Rather, as Simmel suggests, in this context

---

[57] Discriminatory criminalization of women within the Islamic world is an obvious example—see WFAFI (2005) for some instances here. See Banyard (2010) for a discussion of legal anomalies around gender in the West. Segregation laws, legal support for slavery, or judicial sterilizations of ethnic minorities constitute a few of the more obvious ways in which the *de re* abnormalities around skin colour have also generated law.

[58] Payne (1965).

[59] For example, agricultural labourers could only wear woollen garments, whilst buttons were banned for all but the very privileged (cf Ribeiro, 2003).

[60] See Newton (2009).

[61] See Simmel (1997).

the boundary constitutes 'a sharply demarcated *existential* space [which] coincides with the intensity of social relationships'.[62] Standard *de more* constructions such as 'the heretic' or 'the Jew' illustrate how it is the very existential conditions of their being, rather than a failure to conform per se, which may so intensify reactions that offences are constructed around them. In the *Siete Partidas* (a code passed by Alfonso the Wise in 1348), for example, criminal offences directed at Jewishness included 'being served' by a Christian or bathing in the presence of a Christian'.[63] Similarly, as the fourth Lateran Council of 1215 warned, if criminal law was not used to 'cleanse their lands of heretics' secular authorities would also be declared 'heretic'.[64] The Heresy Acts of 1401 and 1414, which permitted bishops to arrest anyone suspected of heresy were one typical outcome.[65]

A second modality in the effects of *de more* abnormality upon law can be seen in responses to what might be called 'functional' abnormalities: varieties of behaviour also perceived as existentially abnormal. One useful set of examples here cluster around the traditional figure of the vagabond, an individual who engaged in movements and journeys alien to the (largely static) life of the medieval village. For Deleuze the abnormality of a nomad or vagabond arises precisely because their existential state is one of anomaly.[66] The primordial illegality of the vagabond was noted by Hobbes who associated it with their lack of any, 'subjection to laws, (or) ... coercive power to tie their hands'.[67] The ineluctable use of law against them this entailed would, argued Hobbes, mean that 'fewer acts of violence, robberies, (or) murders will be committed'.[68] In Europe the criminalization of the vagabond originates from at least the fourteenth century with the scope and severity of laws gradually increasing, usually in ways totally disproportionate to the behaviour in question. From 1536, vagabonds could be whipped for a first offence, have part of their ear removed for a second, and might be executed for a third.[69]

Contemporary attitudes towards homelessness, vagrancy, and poverty indicate the recurring teratological force of *de more* constructions like the vagabond in structuring law, where 'deficient socialization'[70] has often been sufficient justification for criminalization. Again our teratologies exhibit a striking continuity over time in this regard. What has been called the 'criminalization of poverty' has been noted by various commentators who

---

[62] Frisby (1992, p 105).　　[63] cf Halsall (2006).
[64] See Forrest (2005, p 31).　　[65] See Tanner (1951, p 95).
[66] Deleuze and Guattari (1984).　　[67] cited in Beier (1987, p 6).
[68] Ibid.　　[69] See Hanawalt and Wallace (1998).
[70] The term is Hirshi's (cf Gottfredson and Hirschi, 1990)—a sure sign that the criminological literature has often contributed to the construction of *de more* abnormality as well as illuminating it.

have suggested that the recent expansion in laws directed at the less well off are not just aimed at offences 'typical of the poor' (ie shoplifting, welfare offences, and so on), but at the deeper *de more* abnormality of poverty itself.[71] In its 2009 report, the US National Law Center on Homelessness and Poverty[72] found that the number of ordinances against the poor had been consistently rising since 2006, and that US cities were increasingly using:

the criminal justice system to punish people living on the street for doing things that they need to do to survive. Such measures often prohibit activities such as sleeping/ camping, eating, sitting, and/or begging in public spaces and include criminal penalties for violation of these laws.[73]

New legal powers in the UK (such as the ASBO) can be argued to have performed similar functions. Legitimized by the need to control anti-social behaviour, or the construct of a 'Broken Britain', such law is just as plausibly seen as a way of exerting control over the *de more* abnormalities of poverty.

A third modality here arises from behavioural factors rooted in more overt irregularities in demeanour, especially mental illness. In pre-modern society the mad were often viewed as harmless.[74] But as madness was increasingly transformed into a form of *de more* abnormality it began to assume the now familiar role of a predictor for other kinds of disorder. Thus the plagues and wars which had disrupted the pre-modern world eventually 'proved' that madness was linked 'to the powerful tragic forces that controlled the world'.[75] Madness was not just evidence for the presence of evil (such as demonic possession), but the spread of something far more corrosive, a 'senseless unreason'.[76] The result was an increasing equation of mental illness with criminality, one which culminated in the mentally ill being placed in prisons or forced labour in the workhouse.[77] A series of new laws across Europe in the late eighteenth and early nineteenth centuries which began to shift the insane into hospitals indicate the new influence of science upon the legal construction of *de more* abnormality, one which set the scene for the coercive management of the mentally ill under the facade of 'treatment'. This was now, in effect, 'a gigantic moral imprisonment, a microcosm of the bourgeois

---

[71] See eg Gans (1995), Mandell (1991), Reiman (2008), Waqaunt (2009).
[72] NLCHP (2009).
[73] Ibid 9. See Papke (2009) for more examples of this kind.
[74] Erasmus' *In Praise of Folly* (1511) celebrated the deranged individual as a source of divine inspiration.
[75] Foucault (2005, p 22).
[76] Ibid.
[77] Porter (2002).

society and its values'[78] which was not meant to normalize the abnormal (an impossibility) but to regulate it through various institutions, only one of which was law. The legalized brutalities of frontal lobe lobotomies or electroshock therapy which characterized early twentieth-century forms of treatment indicate the paucity of rights or formal protection for the mentally ill, a position maintained in the shift towards mass medication which has followed. In turn, the new justifications for sedating criminals and prisoners and an expansion of new mental 'illnesses' like bi-polarity or ADHD (with the accompanying necessity for drug interventions) reproduces a criminal-psychotic continuum which legitimates control without even the need for criminalization. In a telling contemporary reversion to the pre-modern order around 16 per cent of all US prisoners (approximately 250,000 individuals) are diagnosed as having psychiatric disorders, making prisons once again the largest *de facto* mental institutions.[79] Around 30 per cent of mentally disturbed prisoners are being held with no charges having been made against them.[80]

C. *De ignote* abnormality

The previous two patterns of teratological responses at least exhibit a definitive presence, a concretization of the 'what-it-is' which requires control, whether through criminalization or more informal mechanisms. However, a third, deeper teratological patterning goes beyond even that. For this is an abnormality which seems to lie outside the realm of determinate objects or their properties, one casting the more sinister shadow—of the '*ignotus*' or the unknown. There seems to be a strong sense in which this constitutes a master category of any teratology, one which feeds the more immediate constructions of *de re* and *de more* abnormality. For abnormality here finds its most extreme form as pure anomaly, a null state of the unknowably disordered which not only inverts '*scientia*' but which, in its ontic form (as 'non-life') brings with it our ultimate dread: death itself. Adorno was well aware of the transcendent force the unknown may carry, recognizing how the merest suggestion of it can induce terror:

---

[78] Foucault (2005, p 507).

[79] USDOJ (1999).

[80] NAMI (1992). Prisoners were held for reasons such as awaiting evaluation, or transportation to other institutions. Of those who were incarcerated most were for relatively minor offences such as trespass.

The gasp of surprise which accompanies the experience of the unusual becomes its name. It fixes the transcendence of the unknown in relation to the known, and therefore terror as sacredness.[81]

This 'gasp of surprise'—sanctified all too easily in the notorious Rumsfeldian taxonomies of 'known' or 'unknown' 'unknowns'—has been key to many significant recent criminalizations legitimized by (supposed) security imperatives, along with swathes of new extra-legal regulatory responses. Together these have now transformed terror from an emotion into a construct of control.

At least three permutations of *de ignote* abnormality can be discerned. One is the fundamental teratological constant of unknown *spaces* which were at the heart of many dark pre-modern imaginings. Sometimes these were close at hand—the dark forest, or the empty heath at the edge of the village, which all needed special care or supernatural intervention to be rendered harmless. But beyond these more immediate spatial unknowns were places literally beyond the edge of the map, the unknown spaces which mapmakers instinctively identified with *de ignote* abnormality by populating them with monsters. *Prima facie*, there seems to be no obvious influence of these spatial unknowns upon contemporary criminal law, for surely our maps and satellite navigation systems have diminished their force and with that any need to legislate against them? In fact there is good evidence for the continuing power of the (spatial) unknown, in the form of one of the most prolific programmes of criminalization in recent times. The emergence of the internet and the 'cyberspace' thought to come with it has served to generate a new set of inspirations for the teratological imagination. We see this in the oft repeated claims that online communication involves a 'new frontier', or a 'wild zone' where reality becomes 'virtual'. The *de ignote* abnormality this invokes inevitably becomes threatening, for it has quickly become a space which creates 'unprecedented opportunities for crime' and 'infinitely new possibilities for the deviant imagination'.[82] Law is here rendered more powerless than in the face of other abnormalities, since the 'vacuum of a lawless space' the internet is supposed to represent,[83] is seen as something inherently 'unregulatable'.[84] The system of control which has emerged bears no relation to any quantifiable level of threat posed by online communication and is unprecedented in technological history. There is no definitive count of the new laws related to communications technologies, but it is clear that in the 15 or so years since it

---

[81] 1989 (p 15).
[82] Grabosky and Smith (2001, p 29) and Jewkes (2002, p 2).
[83] Espiner (2008).
[84] Post (1995).

has been widely accessed, the internet has generated more legislation than the entire 150 years of electronic communication which preceded it.[85]

Legal outcomes of *de ignote* abnormalities can also be generated by what might be called 'unknown beings'. At a deeper, more metaphysical level such entities have sometimes taken the form of the implacable ancestor, or demons with unspeakable powers. The (ever present) threat of unknown invaders from across the sea presents an alternative more concrete pre-modern *de ignote* constant. Again, it is not hard to find their contemporary counterparts. For the contemporary imagination *de ignote* abnormalities of this kind are regularly generated by figures such as the 'immigrant', the 'migrant', or the 'asylum seeker', which all come with an almost automatic sense of legal anomaly.[86]

The regulation of new information communication technologies—where the *de ignote* abnormalities of 'cyberspace' have been further augmented by those of the creatures imagined to populate it—again provides a fertile set of examples. Once subsumed under the primordial influence of *de ignote* abnormality, cyberspace quickly turned from a 'magical' into an unknown space, one populated by both *de re* and *de more* monsters. Entities like the 'cyberstalker', the 'groomer', or the 'cyberterrorist' may have been given names, but the relentless flow of legislation they have generated also under-lines the sense that we cannot ultimately know who they are. The supposed anonymity of online communication and the hyperspatial 'always on' acces-sibility it offers, augments the sense of their intangible malevolence with an order of threat now capable of reaching out to us at any time, from any-where.[87] But worse, 'cyberspace' has also seemed to generate altogether new varieties of unknown entity, creatures now spawned, Frankenstein-like, from science itself. A new language of infection and viral spread begins to augment traditional fears of entities that are 'organized' in ways we cannot understand (from the insect world to the crime syndicate or the street gang). This permeates our experience of online communication as, in an implicit mirror-ing of the (biological) threats presented by bacteria, a parallel micro-world of electronic infection emerges. This threat of parasitical electronic life is complemented by new kinds of primordial monster, now spawned out of inhuman digital anatomies. Thus, the emergence of entities like the 'botnet' is about far more than the development of new tools for criminals to use in

---

[85] See my (2007) for a more detailed comparison of historical communications legislation.

[86] See Welch and Schuster (2005).

[87] The compelling horrors of the internet cannibal and his willing victim, or the symbioses between other 'deviants' (sexual or otherwise)—whose communions are facilitated by extended communica-tion—present another perspective upon the abnormal beings to be found 'in cyberspace'.

their usual business of theft and fraud.[88] Instead the botnet also becomes a 'presence', an unknown entity which threatens us as much with its alien, inhuman qualities as with its impact upon property crime.

A third permutation of the way that *de ignote* abnormalities can be manifested is worth mentioning in conclusion. As well as spaces or entities, there may also be encounters with unknown events, or forces of nature/ society. For the pre-modern world encounters with such forces were of course varied and regular—the flash of marsh-gas, or a rumble of thunder were anomalies needing special interventions to diminish their threat. Yet our everyday world remains just as subject to the influence of inexplicable forces. The backfiring car in the night that might be 'a gunshot' or the distant shout which could be 'an attack' continue to populate our teratologies with un-certainties only new criminalizations sometimes seem able to address. Here again science has all too often served to generate as many new abnormalities as it was supposed to have explained away. Thus, the series of catastrophes which now confront us, from global warming to asteroid impacts, may be understandable in terms of the physical laws which govern them, but these merely serve to confirm that they are 'unknowns' of an even greater order. For, of course, to experience them would be to be destroyed by them.

VII. 'Something Quite Different from the Law Itself'—Abnormal Law

At the very least then, it seems plausible that our teratologies exhibit enough of a definable structure for our theories of criminalization to extend beyond mere recognition of 'othering'. But it is also clear that their referents are rarely of the kind that merit the attention of objective scientific inquiry. This is not to say that our teratologies are groundless. Indeed, part of their force derives from the fact that our worst nightmares may, on very rare occasions, turn out to be realities. But whilst our dread of the monstrous may be argued to originate in what 'really is' monstrous, most of the time it does not. More often it is simply the primal force of *de ignote* abnormalities which is at work, transforming our fear of the unknown into the more tangible *de re* and *de more* forms which constitute 'others' at particular times and in particular places. Thus, in tracing the peculiar effects of abnormality upon the development of law it is in

---

[88] A botnet is an array of computers programmed to act 'independently' as agents for DoS attacks on networks, for the purpose of closing them down, or gathering information of interest (such as passwords), see Berinato (2006).

the irreducible nullity of this anomalous realm where its effects can be most profitably discerned. In closing, it is worth noting two impacts of this kind.

A first involves the phenomenon of *disproportioning*: ie ways in which teratologies distort, exaggerate, or malform the production of criminal law. On the one hand this may be seen in legal processes which manifest Girard's notion of 'monstrous doubling' alluded to earlier. These are processes which exhibit an almost geometric kind of transformational symmetry, translating our perceptions of something as 'distorted' into a legal counterpart. The result is law which is itself 'disproportionate', where the appropriate balance between offence and sanction we expect of due legal process is lost. Disproportionate sentencing is one permutation, whilst unfocused sanctions might count as another.[89]

This disproportioning effect may also have an 'infective' as well as a geometric character. Here law becomes literally 'diseased' by manifesting deformed or superfluous legal parts. A clear instance of this has involved the well-documented phenomenon of 'overcriminalization' and the role of our teratologies in provoking what Husak called 'too much law'.[90] Such effects may also be manifested in a more literal growing of superfluous legal parts, overproductions of law where adequate sanctions already exist. Take, for example, the legislative excesses around online stalking or bullying unleashed in the US in the wake of cases such as the recent Lori Drew prosecution.[91] Whilst around 45 US states already possessed adequate stalking laws (laws which already replicated many sanctions available within earlier legislation), the furore around the Drew case pushed many of these states to replicate existing provisions by creating still more new 'cyber' bullying laws. And if that were not enough a new federal 'cyberbullying' law was also set in motion, one which also included unfocused sanctions threatening to criminalize behaviours with no real connection to the original offence.[92]

A second class of effects our teratologies produce upon law can be seen in a more wholesale lurch into anomaly, where law is used to *undermine* law or to

---

[89] For example the threats to withdraw all internet connections for downloaders (thereby also removing internet access for those within a household who share the connection) that was contained in the proposed UK Digital Economy Bill. A similar law was recently declared unconstitutional by French courts (Wray, 2009).

[90] 2007, p 3.

[91] Drew was implicated in the suicide of a 13-year-old girl called Megan Meier who she insulted using a fake online persona (Zetter, 2008).

[92] For example, one of the clauses in this (so-called) 'Megan Meier' bill (H.R. 6123) would criminalize 'any communication . . . with the intent to coerce, intimidate, harass, or cause substantial emotional distress to a person, using electronic means to support severe, repeated, and hostile behaviour'. This would also criminalize many kinds of perfectly legitimate critical comments made online if they were judged to be 'severe' or 'repeated' (cf Volokh, 2009).

legitimate other (non-legal) forms of regulation. As we have seen, there is recurring evidence that our teratologies may, on occasions, identify an abnormality as so 'anomalous' that a sense that law is inadequate to deal with it also emerges. This may result in what Richard Ericson has called 'criminalization through counterlaw': varieties of legal response where 'malicious demons are identified, resentment of them deemed virtuous and relief found through a culture of blame'.[93] The 'laws against law' which result manifest a response to the abnormal that was alluded to earlier: the belief that the 'law must be broken in order to save the social order'.[94] It is here where the anomalousness at the heart of any teratology is at its most powerful, one also seen in notions such as Agamben's *iustititia* or state of exception, where due process or the rule of law is seen as so inadequate that it must be replaced by emergency powers. There is, in fact, a plausible sense in which law can be said to originate from such encounters, for inherent to its functioning is always the attempt to leave such primal chaos behind. As Agamben put this:

The exception does not subtract itself from the rule; rather, the rule, suspending itself, gives rise to the exception and, maintaining itself in relation to the exception, first constitutes itself *as* a rule.[95]

In these senses abnormal law might be seen as something more than a mere response to abnormality in its various forms. Rather, its anomalies also serve as a *precondition* for law itself, forming a primal regulatory state to which law reverts all too easily when confronted by 'too much' abnormality.

It is in these kinds of responses to the abnormal that we begin to see more clearly what Foucault might have meant when he said that the abnormal may produce something quite different from the law itself. For if the abnormal is, in one sense, our window into the anomalous then it should not be so surprising that a common effect of encounters with it has been a reversion to legal anomaly: abnormal responses have often seemed to be the only responses capable of managing abnormality. No less surprising should be the fact that the impact of the abnormal may sometimes distort other (ostensibly) rational institutions, in particular science, which undermines its core mission by trying to systematize what may not just be necessarily unsystemic, but which may not even exist in any measurable sense at all.

How then might the recognition that our teratologies are as much a part of any 'logic' of criminalization as more rational responses to harms or offences impact usefully upon a normative theory of the practice? If it is accepted (as it surely must be), that criminalization is a process which is rooted in the social,

---

[93] 2007, p 24.   [94] (p 26, p 23).   [95] (1998, p 18).

the conclusion that our impulse to criminalize is not always about establishing a rule of law seems unavoidable. For it may have just as much to do with attempts to shelter us from our longstanding dread of the kind of anomalies the abnormal seems to threaten. Indeed, this may be the very basis upon which criminalization as a social practice ultimately rests. Thus, in a world with a growing sense of unknown risks, coming from a range of unknown unknowns, beings, or events, any reminder that the construction of law is often based as much upon fantasy as genuine threat comes as a timely warning. And in this way, a clarification—or at least its recognition—of the teratological may not just enrich a normative approach to criminalization, but provide a resource for maintaining and respecting legal authority in the face of threats which appear to demonstrate its redundancy.

References

Aas, K., 'Analysing a World in Motion: Global Flows Meet "Criminology of the Other"' (2007) 11 *Theoretical Criminology* 283

Adorno T. and Horkheimer, M., *Dialectic of Enlightenment* (trans John Cumming) (London: Verso, 1989)

Agamben G., *Homo Sacer: Sovereign Power and Bare Life* (Standford, CA: Stanford University Press, 1998)

Alison, L., Bennell, C., and Mokros, A., 'The Personality Paradox in Offender Profiling' (2002) 8(1) *Psychology, Public Policy, and Law* 115–35

Ariely, D., *Predictably Irrational* (New York: HarperCollins, 2008)

Armstrong, D., *Universals: An Opinionated Introduction* (Boulder, CO: Westview Press, 1989)

Banyard, K., *The Equality Illusion* (London: Faber and Faber, 2010)

Beier, A., *Masterless Men: The Vagrancy Problem in England, 1560–1640* (London: Methuen, 1987)

Berinato, S., 'Attack of the Bots' *Wired* 14.11.

Clarke, J., 'What's the Problem? Precarious Youth: Marginalisation, Criminalisation and Racialisation' (2008) 6 *Social Work & Society* 2

Cohen, S., *Folk Devils and Moral Panics* (London: MacGibbon and Kee, 1972)

Cortés, J. and Gatti, F., *Delinquency and Crime: A Biopsychological Approach* (New York: Seminar Press, 1972)

Deleuze, G. and Guattari, F., *A Thousand Plateaus* (trans Brian Massumi) (London and New York: Continuum, 2004)

Deutsch, H. and Nussbaum, F., *Defects: Engendering the Modern Body* (Ann Arbor: University of Michigan Press, 2000)

Ditton, J. and Farrall, S. (eds), *The Fear of Crime* (Aldershot: Ashgate, 2000)

Earle, A., *Customs and Fashions in Old New England,* (New York: Charles Scribner & Sons, 1893)

Ericson, R., *Crime in an Insecure World* (Cambridge: Polity Press, 2007)

Espiner, T., 'Ashdown: Internet is a "lawless space"' (27 November 2008) *ZdNet*

Forrest, I., *The Detection of Heresy in Late Medieval England* (Oxford: Clarendon Press, 2005)

Foucault, M., *Abnormal: Lectures at the Collège de France, 1974–1975* (ed. Valerio Marchetti and Antonella Salomoni, trans. Graham Burchell) (New York: Picador, 2004)

—— *History of Madness* (London: Routledge, 2005)

Frisby, D., 'Social Space, the City and the Metropolis' in *Simmel and Since: Essays on Georg Simmel's Social Theory* (New York: Routledge, 1992)

Gale, S., 'The Impact of Information Technology Upon Civil Practice and Procedure' in Edwards, L. and Waelde, C. (eds), *Law and the Internet: Regulating Cyberspace* (Oxford: Hart, 1997)

Gans, H., *The War Against the Poor: the Underclass and Anti-Poverty Policy* (New York: Basic Books, 1995)

Garland, D., *The Culture of Control: Crime and Social Order in Contemporary Society* (Oxford: Clarendon, 2001)

—— 'The Limits of the Sovereign State' (1996) 36 *British Journal of Criminology* 445–71

Girard, R., *Violence and the Sacred* (New York: Continuum, 2005)

Godard, B. et al, *Genetic Information and Testing in Insurance and Employment: Technical, Social and Ethical Issues*, EUROGAPPP Project, European Society of Human Genetics, Public and Professional Policy Committee, 2002)

Goldgar, C., 'The Genetic Information Nondiscrimination Act (GINA): How PAs Can Protect Patients and Their Families' (July 2010) *Journal of American Physician Assistants*

Good, T. S., 'Crime and Abnormality' (1932) *Howard Journal* (vol iii) 57–65

Goring, C., *The English Convict* (HMSO, printed by Darling and Son Ltd, 1913)

Gottfredson, M. and Hirschi, T., *A General Theory of Crime* (Stanford: Stanford University Press, 1990)

Gould, S. J., 'Measuring Bodies: Two Case Studies on the Apishness of Undesirables' in Gould, S. J., *The Mismeasure of Man* (New York: W.W. Norton, 1981) 113–45

Graham, E., *Representations of the Post-Human: Monsters, Aliens and Others in Popular Culture* (New Brunswick, NJ: Rutgers University Press, 2002)

Hackett, D., *The Buchenwald Report* (Boulder, San Francisco: Westview Press, 1995)

Hallsworth, S., 'Rethinking the Punitive Turn. Economies of Excess and the Criminology of the Other' (2000) 2(2) *Punishment & Society* 145–60

Halsall, P., 'Las Siete Partidas: Laws on Jews, 1265' *Internet Medieval Sourcebook*, Fordham University Center for Medieval Studies

Hanawalt, B. and Wallace, D., *Medieval Crime and Social Control* (Minneapolis: University of Minnesota Press, 1998)

Healey, D., *Homosexual Desire in Revolutionary Russia* (Chicago: University of Chicago Press, 2001)

Herrnstein, R. J. and Murray, C., *The Bell Curve* (New York: The Free Press, 1994)

Hicks, S. and Sales, B., *Criminal Profiling: Developing an Effective Science and Practice* (Washington: APA Books, 2006)

HIV in Europe 2009, 'The Criminalisation of HIV in the European Region', see: <http://www.hiveurope.eu/Projects/Criminalisation/tabid/75/Default.aspx>

Husak, D., *Overcriminalization: The Limits of the Criminal Law* (New York: OUP, 2007)

Jennings, H., *The Biological Basis of Human Nature* (New York: W.W. Norton, 1930)

Jupp, V., *Methods of Criminological Research* (London: Routledge, 1989)

Kahneman D. and Tversky, A., 'Prospect Theory: An Analysis of Decision under Risk (1979) 47(2) *Econometrica* 263–92

Kocsis, R. and Palermo, G., 'Contemporary Problems in Criminal Profiling' in Kocsis, R. (ed), *Criminal Profiling: Principles and Practice* (Totowa, NJ: Humana Press, 2007)

Lacey, N., 'Historicising Criminalisation: Conceptual and Empirical Issues' (2009) 72(6) *Modern Law Review* 936–60

Laughlin, H., *Eugenical Sterilization in the United States* (Psychopathic Laboratory of the Municipal Court of Chicago, 1922)

—— 'The Biological Aspects of Crime', pamphlet in the Harry Laughlin papers (Pickler Memorial Library, Trusman State Univerity Kijksville, MO, 1936)

Lombroso, C., *Criminal Man* (trans. Gibson, M. and Rafter, N.) (Durham, NC: Duke University Press, 1984)

Lombroso, G., *Criminal Man: According to the Classification of Cesare Lombroso* (Montclair, NJ: Patterson Smith, 1911/72)

Long, K., *Hermaphrodites in Renaissance Europe* (Aldershot: Ashgate, 2006)

Lunn, P., *Basic Instincts: Human Nature and the New Economics* (London: Marshall Cavendish, 2009)

MacNichol, J., 'Eugenics and the Campaign for Voluntary Sterilization in Britain Between the Wars' (1989) 2(2) *Social History of Medicine* 147–69

Malebranche, N., *Tractatus de inquisitione veritatis* (Geneva: Fratres De Tournes, 1753)

Mandell, B., 'The War Against the Poor' (2001) 8 *New Politics* 2

McGuire, M., *Hypercrime: the New Geometry of Harm* (Abingdon, Oxford: Routledge, 2007)

Melossi, D., 'Changing Representations of the Criminal' in Garland, D. and Sparks, R., *Criminology & Social Theory* (Oxford: Clarendon, 2000) 149–82

Meyer, C., 'Criminal Profiling as Expert Evidence? An International Case Law Perspective' in Kocsis, R. (ed), *Criminal Profiling: Principles and Practice* (Totowa, NJ: Humana Press, 2007)

Mooney, J., *Gender, Violence and the Social Order* (New York: Palgrave MacMillan, 2000)

Morel B., *Traité des Degenerescences Physiques, Intellectuelles et Morales de l' espece Humaine* (Paris: Masson, 1857)

Nader, L., 'The Anthropological Study of Law' in *The Ethnography of Law*, a special publication of *American Anthropologist* (1965) 67 (6, part 2) 3–32

NAMI, 'Criminalizing the Seriously Mentally Ill: The Abuse of Jails as Mental Hospitals' (National Alliance for the Mentally Ill, 1992)

Newton, E., 'Ban on Drooping Drawers Faces Legal Challenge' *New York Times* (12 April 2009)

Niccoli, O., *Prophecy and People in Renaissance Italy* (Princeton, NJ: Princeton University Press, 1990)

NLCHP, *Homes Not Handcuffs: The Criminalization of Homelessness in U.S. Cities* (The National Law Center on Homelessness & Poverty Report, July 2009)

Parisi, F. and Smith, V. (eds), *The Law and Economics of Irrational Behavior*, (Stanford, CA: Stanford University Press, 2005)

Papke, D., 'Law, Legal Institutions, and the Criminalization of the Underclass', (Marquette University Law School Legal Studies Research Paper Series, No: 09-27, 2009)

Payne, B., *History of Costume from the Ancient Egyptians to the Twentieth Century*, (New York: Harper & Row, 1965)

Post, D., 'Anarchy State and the Internet' (1995) *Journal of Online Law*, Article 3, Available at SSRN: <http://ssrn.com/abstract=943456>

Rafter, N., 'The Anthropological Born Criminal' in Rafter, N. (ed), *Creating Born Criminals* (Urbana and Chicago: University of Illinois Press, 1997) 110–32

Raine, A., 'The Biological Basis of Crime' in Wilson, J. and Petersilia, J. (eds), *Crime: Public Policies for Crime Control* (Oakland, CA: ICS Press, 2002) 43–74

Reiman J., 'The Bonus of Bias: Jeffrey Reiman Discusses the Criminalization of the Poor' (2008) 74(1) *Criminal Justice Matters* 20–21

Rochberg, F., *The Heavenly Writing: Divination, Horoscopy, and Astronomy in Mesopotamian Culture* (Cambridge: CUP, 2004)

Rorty, R., *Objectivity, Relativism and Truth*, (Cambridge: CUP, 1991)

Rose, N., 'The Biology of Culpability: Pathological Identity and Crime Control in a Biological Culture' (2000) 4(1) *Theoretical Criminology* 5–34

Rothstein, M. *Genetics and Life Insurance: Medical Underwriting and Social Policy* (Cambridge, Mass: MIT Press, 2004)

Saint-Hilaire, E., *Philosophie anatomique. Des Monstruosités humaines, ouvrage contenant une classification des monstres*... (Paris: Auteur, 1822)

Saint Hilaire, I., *Histoire générale et particulière des anomalies de l'organisation chez l'homme et les animaux* (Paris: J.B. Baillière, 1857)

Schneider, J. and Schneider, P., 'The Anthropology of Crime and Criminalization' (2008) *Annual Review of Anthropology* Vol 37, 351–73

Schonsheck, J., *On Criminalization: An Essay in the Philosophy of the Criminal Law* (Dordrecht: Kluwer Academic Publishers, 1994)

Sharpe, A., 'England's Legal Monsters' (2009) 5(1) *Law, Culture and the Humanities* 100–30

—— *Foucault's Monsters and the Challenge of Law* (Abingdon, Oxford: Routledge, 2010)

Sheldon W., *The Varieties of Human Physique: An Introduction to Constitutional Psychology* (New York: Harper, 1940)

Shoemaker, Sydney, 'Causal and Metaphysical Necessity' (1998) 79(1) *Pacific Philosophical Quarterly* 59–77

——'Causality and Properties', reprinted in *Identity, Cause and Mind* (Cambridge: CUP, 1980)

Sibley, W., 'The Rational and the Reasonable' (1953) 62 *Philosophical Review* 554

Simmel G., 'The Sociology of Space' in Frisby, D., and Featherstone, M. (eds), *Simmel on Culture* (London: Sage, 1997) 137–70

Smart, C., *Women, Crime and Criminology: A Feminist Critique* (London: Routledge and Kegan Paul, 1976)

Tanner, J., *Tudor Constitutional Documents, A.D. 1485–1603: With an Historical Commentary* (Cambridge: CUP, 1951)

THT, 'Criminalisation of HIV Transmission in Europe' (Terrence Higgins Trust, 2009) see <http://www.gnpplus.net/criminalisation/results1.shtml>

Tosi, A., 'Homelessness and the Control of Public Space – Criminalising the Poor (2007) *European Journal of Homelessness* Vol 1, 224–36

USDOJ, 'Mental Health and Treatment of Inmates and Probationers' (US Department of Justice Report, 2009) NCJ 174463

Volokh, E., 'Federal Felony To Use Blogs, the Web, Etc. To Cause Substantial Emotional Distress Through "Severe, Repeated, and Hostile" Speech?', *Volokh Conspiracy* (2009), see: <http://www.volokh.com/posts/chain_1241740320.shtml>

Wacquant, L., *Punishing the Poor: The Neoliberal Government of Social Insecurity* (Durham, NC: Duke University Press, 2009)

Walby, K. and Carrier, N., 'The Rise of Biocriminology: Capturing Observable Bodily Economies of "Criminal Man"' (2010) 10(3) *Criminology and Criminal Justice* 261–85

Walklate, S., *Gender, Crime, and Criminal Justice,* (Cullompton: Willan, 2004)

Welch, M. and Schuster, L., 'Detention of Asylum Seekers in the UK and USA: Deciphering Noisy and Quiet Constructions' (2005) 7(4) *Punishment and Society* 397–417

Wetzell, R., 'Criminology in Weimar and Nazi Germany' in Becker, P. and Wetzell, R. (eds), *Criminals and their Scientists: The History of Criminology in International Perspective* (Cambridge: CUP, 2006) 401–24

WFAFI, 'Official Laws against Women in Iran' (2005) see: <http://www.wfafi.org/laws.pdf>

Wray, R., 'Internet cut-off threat for illegal downloaders' *Guardian* (25 August 2009)

Young, J., 'The Role of the Police as Amplifiers of Deviance, Negotiators of Reality and Translators of Phantasy', *NDC 1st Symposium* (November 1968)

9

Criminalization Tensions: Empirical Desert, Changing Norms, and Rape Reform

Paul H Robinson[1]

This chapter is part of the organizers' larger Criminalization Project, which seeks, among other things, to develop theories for how criminalization decisions should be made. The argument presented here is that there is both instrumentalist and deontological value in having criminalization decisions that generally track the community's judgements about what is sufficiently condemnable to be criminal, but that there also are good reasons to deviate from community views. Interestingly, those in the business of social reform may be the ones who have the greatest stake in normally tracking community views, in avoiding community perceptions of the criminal law as regularly and intentionally doing injustice. It is the social reformer who may have the most to gain by building the criminal law's moral credibility so that those hard-earned 'credibility chips' can be used to have criminal law lead rather than follow community views when the reformer seeks to use law to help change existing norms.

Let me begin by putting this discussion in the context of the larger Criminalization Project of which it is part. That Project considers how criminalization decisions should be made. One aspect of that question is: Should criminalization decisions be guided by what the community holds to be morally condemnable? There are at least two separate issues here: Should criminalization be limited to what is morally condemnable? And should condemnability be measured by the community's views?

There is an enormous literature on the first issue, of course, including such debates as: Should the criminal law permit strict liability offences? Should the

[1] The author thanks the participants of the September 2009, Glasgow Conference on the Criminalization Project, for their comments and suggestions.

criminal law be used to punish regulatory violations that do not rise to the level of morally condemnable conduct? My own view, shared by many desert advocates, would be to set condemnability as a prerequisite for criminal liability.[2] In this paper, I want to focus primarily on the second question: Should the criminalization decision be guided by community views of what is condemnable conduct (rather than the views of moral philosophers, for example)?

The issue of the advisability of constraining criminalization by moral condemnability has moved from an academic to a practical issue in the United States. Two years ago, the American Law Institute amended its Model Penal Code for the first time in the 47 years since its promulgation. The amendment shifted the Code's distributive principle for punishment from the traditional 'laundry list' of alternative mechanisms of coercive crime control—deterrence, incapacitation of the dangerous, rehabilitation—to a distributive principle that set moral desert as the dominant and inviolable first principle.[3]

The Model Code does not address the issue of whether desert as a distributive principle should be based upon a moral philosophy conception of desert, what might be called 'deontological desert', or based upon the community's shared lay intuitions of justice, what has been called 'empirical desert'.[4] On the other hand, it has been argued that in practice the latter is more likely to control than the former, if for no other reason than because of the notorious level of disagreement among moral philosophers about a wide range of, if not all, desert issues, which makes it difficult to operationalize a notion of deontological desert. In contrast, empirical desert can be authoritatively determined simply by doing the empirical studies. More on this in section II below.

Even if it is empirical desert, rather than deontological desert, that comes to be the distributive principle for punishment under codes based upon the Model Penal Code, the deontologists might well be quite happy. It may well be that empirical desert is the closest approximation of deontological desert that they are ever likely to have adopted in a working criminal justice system.

---

[2] Aspects of this requirement at times have been formalized. See eg MPC §2.12(2) (permits a defence if 'the defendant's conduct [caused or threatened the offense harm or evil] to an extent too trivial to warrant the condemnation of conviction').

[3] Compare MPC §1.02 (Official Draft 1962) to §1.02 (Amendment 2007). The latter requires the court: 'to render punishment within a range of severity proportionate to the gravity of offenses, the harms done to crime victims, and the blameworthiness of offenders'.

[4] Paul H. Robinson, 'Competing Conceptions of Modern Desert: Vengeful, Deontological, and Empirical' (2008) 67 *Cambridge Law Journal* 145 [hereinafter 'Competing Conceptions'].

(And there are some deontologists who would define desert in such a way as to suggest that empirical desert *is* deontological desert.[5])

I. The Attraction of Empirical Desert as a Distributive Principle for Criminal Liability and Punishment

Some of us have argued that empirical desert is an attractive distributive principle for punishment because such a distribution of liability and punishment in accord with the community's shared intuitions of justice builds the moral credibility of the criminal justice system and thereby promotes co-operation and acquiescence, harnesses the powerful social influences of stigmatization and condemnation, and increases criminal law's ability to shape societal and internalized norms. (Others have argued that empirical desert is an attractive distributive principle because it promotes democratic ideals.[6]) To summarize briefly the 'utility of desert' arguments:[7]

First, some of the system's power to control conduct derives from its potential to stigmatize violators—with some potential offenders this is a more powerful, yet essentially cost-free, control mechanism when compared to imprisonment. Yet the system's ability to stigmatize depends upon it having moral credibility with the community. That is, for a conviction to trigger community stigmatization, the law must have earned a reputation for following the community's view on what does and does not deserve moral condemnation. Liability and punishment rules that deviate from a community's shared intuitions of justice undermine this reputation.

Second, the effective operation of the criminal justice system depends upon the cooperation, or at least the acquiescence, of those involved in it—offenders, judges, jurors, witnesses, prosecutors, police, and others. To the

---

[5] See Paul H. Robinson, 'The Role of Moral Philosophers in the Competition Between Philosophical and Empirical Desert', Symposium Issue, (2007) 48 *William & Mary Law Review* 1831, 1839–1842.

[6] See eg Andrew E. Taslitz, 'Empirical Desert: The Yin and Yang of Criminal Justice' in Paul H. Robinson, Steve P. Garvey, and Kimberly Kessler Ferzan, *Criminal Law Conversations* (Oxford: OUP, 2009) 56; Adil Ahmad Haque, 'Legitimacy as Strategy', id 57.

[7] For a fuller account, see Paul H. Robinson and John M. Darley, 'Intuitions of Justice: Implications for Criminal Law and Justice Policy' (2007) 81 *Southern California Law Review* 1–67 [hereinafter 'Implications']; Paul H. Robinson, *Distributive Principles of Criminal Law: Who Should Be Punished How Much?* (Oxford: OUP, 2008)[hereinafter 'Distributive Principles'] chs 8 and 12; Paul H. Robinson, 'Empirical Desert' in Robinson, Garvey and Ferzan (eds), *Criminal Law Conversations* (n 6 above) 29–39; Paul H. Robinson, Geoff Goodwin, and Michael Reisig, 'The Disutility of Injustice', (2010) 85 *New York University Law Review* 1940–2033 [hereinafter 'Disutility'].

extent that people see the system as unjust—as in conflict with their intuitions about justice—that acquiescence and cooperation is likely to fade and be replaced with subversion and resistance. Vigilantism may be the most dramatic reaction to a perceived failure of justice, but a host of other less dramatic (but more common) forms of resistance and subversion have shown themselves. Jurors may disregard their jury instructions. Police officers, prosecutors, and judges may make up their own rules. Witnesses may lose an incentive to offer their information or testimony. And offenders may be inspired to fight the adjudication and correctional processes rather than participating and acquiescing in them.

Criminal law also can have effect in gaining compliance with its commands through another mechanism: if it earns a reputation as a reliable statement of what the community perceives as condemnable, people are more likely to defer to its commands as morally authoritative and as appropriate to follow in those borderline cases in which the propriety of certain conduct is unsettled or ambiguous in the mind of the actor. The importance of this role should not be underestimated; in a society with the complex interdependencies that characterize ours, a seemingly harmless action can have destructive consequences. When the action is criminalized by the legal system, one would want the citizen to respect the law in such an instance, even though he or she does not immediately intuit why that action is banned. Such deference will be facilitated if citizens believe that the law is an accurate guide to appropriate prudential and moral behaviour.

Perhaps the greatest utility of empirical desert comes through a more subtle but potentially more influential mechanism. The real power to gain compliance with society's rules of prescribed conduct lies not in the threat of official criminal sanction, but in the influence of the intertwined forces of social and individual moral control. The networks of interpersonal relationships in which people find themselves, the social norms and prohibitions shared among those relationships and transmitted through those social networks, and the internalized representations of those norms and moral precepts control people's conduct. The law is not irrelevant to these social and personal forces. Criminal law, in particular, plays a central role in creating and maintaining the social consensus necessary for sustaining moral norms. In fact, in a society as diverse as ours, the criminal law may be the only society-wide mechanism that transcends cultural and ethnic differences. Thus, the criminal law's most important real-world effect may be its ability to assist in the building, shaping, and maintaining of these norms and moral principles. It can contribute to and harness the compliance-producing power of interpersonal relationships and personal morality, but will only be effective in doing so if it has sufficient credibility.

The extent of the criminal law's effectiveness in all these respects—in bringing the power of stigmatization to bear, in avoiding resistance and subversion to a system perceived as unjust, in gaining compliance in borderline cases through deference to its moral authority, and in facilitating, communicating, and maintaining societal consensus on what is and is not condemnable—is to a great extent dependent on the degree to which the criminal law has gained moral credibility in the minds of the citizens governed by it. Thus, the criminal law's moral credibility is essential to effective crime control, and is enhanced if the distribution of criminal liability is perceived as 'doing justice'—that is, if it assigns liability and punishment in ways that the community perceives as consistent with its shared intuitions of justice. Conversely, the system's moral credibility, and therefore its crime control effectiveness, is undermined by a distribution of liability that conflicts with community perceptions of just desert.

Confirming the findings of previous studies,[8] the most recent set of studies show that many modern crime control doctrines seriously conflict with the community's shared intuitions of justice, that this conflict does indeed undermine the criminal law's moral credibility, and that this loss does indeed have practical consequences that undermine the criminal justice system's crime-fighting effectiveness.[9]

II. Objections to Empirical Desert

A variety of criticisms have been offered against distributing criminal liability and punishment according to principles that track the community's shared intuitions of justice.[10]

A. Notions of desert as hopelessly vague

A common objection to empirical desert as a distributive principle is its supposed vagueness. Some writers may be willing to concede that desert is not a hopelessly vague concept, that it has some meaning, but would make a related but slightly different criticism: desert cannot specify a *particular amount* of punishment that *should* be imposed; it can only identify a *range*

---

[8] See Disutility (n 7 above) Part V.F.

[9] See Disutility (n 7 above) Parts V and VI.

[10] For authorities relating to the claims within this section, see Robinson and Darley, Implications (n 7 above) 31–45.

of punishments that *should not* be imposed because such punishment would be seriously disproportionate.

These complaints are based in part on a failure to appreciate the specific demands of desert and of people's intuitions about it. The confusion arises in part from the failure to distinguish two distinct judgements: setting the endpoint of the punishment continuum and, once that endpoint has been set, ordinally ranking cases along that continuum. Every society must decide what punishment it will allow for its most egregious case, be it the death penalty or life imprisonment or 15 years. Once that endpoint is set, the distributive challenge that desert must guide is to determine who should be punished how much. That process requires only an ordinal ranking of offenders according to their relative blameworthiness. The result is a specific amount of punishment for a particular offence, but that amount of punishment is not the product of some magical connection between that violator's offence and the corresponding amount of punishment. Rather, it is the specific amount of punishment needed to *set the offender's violation at its appropriate ordinal rank* according to blameworthiness, relative to all other offences. If the endpoint were changed, the appropriate punishment for each offender would change accordingly.

Those who complain that empirical desert is vague seem incorrectly to assume that it must provide a universal, absolute amount of punishment as deserved for a given offence no matter the time or jurisdiction. Instead, however, the content of empirical desert is to ensure that offenders of different blameworthiness are given different amounts of punishment, each to receive an amount that reflects his blameworthiness relative to that of others. Uncertainty about deserved punishment arises not from vagueness in the ordinal ranking of offences according to offender blameworthiness but rather from differences in the endpoint that different societies adopt or that different people would want their society to adopt. Once that endpoint is set, the *distribution* of punishment to offenders according to empirical desert suffers no vagueness problem.

But this does not fully settle the vagueness complaints. Some writers argue that even ordinal ranking is something that can be done only in the vaguest terms; establishing specific rankings is impossible. The claim is that ranking offences according to blameworthiness is beyond the ability of people's intuitions of justice. People can roughly distinguish between 'serious' and 'not serious' cases but cannot provide the nuance needed to do more.

The claim is empirical and empirically it is false. The evidence from a wide variety of studies is quite clear: subjects display a good deal of nuance in their judgements of blameworthiness. Small changes in facts produce large and predictable changes in punishment.[11] The empirical evidence suggests that people take account of a wide variety of factors and often give them quite different effect in different situations. Alexis Durham offers this summary: 'Virtually without exception, citizens seem able to assign highly specific sentences for highly specific events.'[12] People's intuitions of justice are not vague or simplistic, but rather sophisticated and complex.

B. Hopeless disagreement as to notions of desert

Another common objection to using empirical desert as a distributive principle is that, even if individuals may have a clear and specific notion of what desert demands, people disagree among themselves. Again, this common wisdom simply does not match the empirical reality. The studies show broadly shared intuitions that serious wrongdoing should be punished and broadly shared intuitions about the relative blameworthiness of different cases, especially of the most common kinds of offences.

In one study that illustrates the striking extent of the agreement,[13] subjects were asked to rank order 24 crime scenario descriptions according to the amount of punishment deserved. Despite the complex and subjective nature of the judgements, the researchers found that the subjects had little difficulty performing the task and displayed an astounding level of agreement in their ordinal ranking. A statistical measure of concordance is found in Kendall's W coefficient of concordance, in which 1.0 indicates perfect agreement and 0.0 indicates no agreement. In the study, the Kendall's W was .95 (with p < .001), an astounding result. (One might expect to get a Kendall's W of this magnitude if subjects were asked to judge an easy and objective task, such as judging the relative brightness of different groupings of spots. When asked to perform more subjective or complex comparisons, such as asking travel magazine readers to rank eight different travel destinations according to their level of safety, one gets a Kendall's W of .52. When asking economists to rank the top 20 economics journals according to quality, one gets a Kendall's W of .095.) Even more compelling, the astounding level of agreement cuts across all demographics. People from very different backgrounds, situations, and perspectives all agreed upon the relative blameworthiness of the 24 offenders.

---

[11] See eg the impressive nuance repeatedly shown by subjects in the 18 studies reported in Paul H. Robinson and John M. Darley, *Justice, Liability and Blame: Community Views and the Criminal Law* (Boulder: Westview Press, 1995).

[12] Alexis M. Durham III, 'Public Opinion Regarding Sentences for Crime: Does it Exist?' (1993) 21 *Journal of Criminal Justice* 1, 2.

[13] Paul H. Robinson and Robert Kurzban, 'Concordance & Conflict in Intuitions of Justice' (2007) 91 *Minnesota Law Review* 1829–1907 (2007) [hereinafter 'Concordance'].

Similar conclusions are found in cross-cultural studies.[14] The level of agreement is strongest for those core wrongs with which criminal law primarily concerns itself—physical aggression, taking property, and deception in exchanges—and becomes less pronounced as the nature of the offence moves farther from the core of wrongdoing. However, the data overwhelmingly refutes the common perception that there is never agreement as to intuitions of justice.

Disagreements among people's intuitions of justice do exist. People obviously disagree about many things relating to crime and punishment, as the endless public debates make clear. But some appearances of disagreement are simply misleading. Poor testing methods will predictably underestimate the extent of agreement. When a test scenario is written ambiguously so that different test participants perceive the facts differently, the existence of shared nuanced intuitions of justice itself will predict different judgements among the participants. So too, when a case in the headlines has social or political implications, its relevant facts commonly will be perceived differently by different people. What one makes of the police testimony in the O.J. Simpson case or the Rodney King case may depend upon how one has come to view police officers from one's daily life experiences. If people draw different conclusions from the testimony, they are likely to have different views of the relevant facts, which predictably results in different views on the liability and punishment deserved.

One may wonder how the extent of agreement among people about intuitions of justice, sometimes at astonishing high levels, could have been missed for so many years. How could the common wisdom have gotten it so wrong? Part of the answer is the above-mentioned failure to distinguish between issues of absolute severity and ordinal ranking. People's disagreement about the proper endpoint for the punishment continuum tends to obscure the existing agreement on the ranking of offences along that continuum. Also as noted, our frequent disagreement with others about cases in the news creates a false impression that we disagree about principles of justice when in fact we only disagree about the case facts.

Because some disagreement does exist, especially as the issue moves out from the core of wrongdoing, it is inevitable that any rule the criminal law adopts will deviate from some people's views. In these situations, advancing

---

[14] See Graeme Newman, *Comparative Deviance: Perception and Law in Six Cultures* (New York: Elsevier, 1976) 141–3; Julian V. Roberts and Loretta J. Stalans, 'Crime, Criminal Justice, and Public Opinion' in Michael H. Tonry (ed), *The Handbook of Crime & Punishment* (New York: OUP, 1998) 42–3 ('there is a significant degree of agreement across countries in terms of the relative seriousness of crimes. Many studies have replicated the relative ranking of crimes across a number of countries, including Canada, Denmark, Finland, Great Britain, Holland, Kuwait, Norway, Puerto Rico, and the United States').

the law's crime control effectiveness means adopting the rule that will least undermine its moral credibility. That commonly will mean adopting the rule that reflects the majority view, but not always. If advancing the criminal law's overall moral credibility with the community is the goal, one would want to take account of the strength of feeling of each of the opposing views.

One might wonder why core intuitions of justice are so widely shared. Whether due to some evolutionarily developed mechanism or to shared social learning, or some combination of the two,[15] it is clear that the source of these intuitions is beyond even the powerful influences of culture or demographics. Because one does not see such differences with respect to core intuitions, it follows that they must be somehow fixed, and therefore will be resistant to attempts by social engineers to manipulate them, at least using the kinds of intrusions on personal autonomy that a liberal democracy would permit. The point here is not to say that our existing intuitions are good, or bad. Rather, they are the reality of what it means to be human, and effective social engineers must deal with the world as it exists, not as they wished it were. More on the implications for social reformers in Sections IV and V below.

C. People's natural judgements about punishment are based on deterrence or incapacitation, not desert

Another criticism levelled against using empirical desert as the basis for distributing criminal liability and punishment is that people's punishment judgements are not really based on desert but rather on factors relating to effective deterrence or incapacitation. That is, when people ostensibly decide what punishment an offender should get, they are really deciding how much punishment is needed to deter or incapacitate. Again, however, the view does not match the available data. Studies examining the criteria on which people rely when making punishment judgements have found it to be desert; people's punishment judgements typically ignore deterrence or incapacitation concerns.

For example, one such study exploring whether desert or incapacitation was the driving force gave participants 10 short descriptions of criminal cases, which were generated by combining five levels of case seriousness (theft of a CD, theft of a valuable object, assault, homicide, and assassination) with two levels of criminal history (no prior history, history of actions consistent with

---

[15] See Paul H. Robinson, Robert Kurzban, and Owen Jones, 'The Origins of Shared Intuitions of Justice' (2007) 60 *Vanderbilt Law Review* 1633–88. [hereinafter 'Origins']

the crime committed). Participants were asked to assign a proper punishment to each case without any indication as to what the decision should be based upon, using a 7-point scale of punishment severity and a 13-point scale of criminal liability grades. Participants were thereafter asked to reconsider the scenarios and assign punishments from a just deserts perspective and from an incapacitation perspective.

Punishment assignments based on just deserts were closely aligned with the original intuitive decisions, while punishments assigned using the incapacitation model were not. 'What this suggests is that the default perspective of sentencing is indistinguishable from the just deserts perspective, but that both [default and explicit desert] are significantly different from the incapacitation perspective.'[16] Other studies, which also pitted justice against deterrence, reinforce this conclusion. People's intuitive default for assigning criminal liability and punishment is just deserts. While participants explicitly endorse deterrence justifications for punishment, they actually meted out sentences 'from a strictly deservingness-based stance'.[17]

D. Empirical desert as inevitably draconian

Some resistance to relying on empirical desert as a basis to distribute liability and punishment comes from a challenge not to its empirical foundation but rather to its expected results. The line of reasoning goes something like this: (1) I don't like many of the modern crime control reforms—such as 'three strikes' habitual offender statutes, lowering the age of prosecution as an adult, strict liability, high penalties for drug offences, and criminalizing what had previously been regulatory offences; (2) these reforms are the product of recent democratic legislative action that reflects the community's views; (3) therefore, giving explicit deference to empirical desert will only increase the influence of the public's apparent preference for draconian measures.

Such reasoning both misconceives the nature of empirical desert and mistakenly assumes that modern crime politics produces results that track people's intuitions of justice. In fact, empirical desert has little to do with, and indeed dramatically conflicts with, the modern crime control programmes like those listed. Indeed, as noted above, recent research confirms that these

[16] John M. Darley, Kevin M. Carlsmith, and Paul H. Robinson, 'Incapacitation and Just Deserts as Motives for Punishment' (2000) 24 *Law and Human Behavior* 659, 667.

[17] Kevin M. Carlsmith, John M. Darley, and Paul H. Robinson, *Why Do We Punish? Deterrence and Just Deserts as Motives for Punishment* (2002) 83 *Journal of Personality and Social Psychology* 284, 295.

modern crime control doctrines seriously conflict with the community's shared intuitions of justice.[18]

There is a substantial difference between the principles that people intuitively use in assessing relative blameworthiness and the political crime control programmes that their politicians support. The former can be reliably determined only through social science research that manipulates case scenarios and sees what effects the manipulations have on people's liability assessments. The researchers do not even ask subjects what rules they prefer but rather construct for themselves the liability rules that they see the subjects in fact using as they intuitively assess blameworthiness. The latter, political action on crime legislation, is a product of the well-known distortions of the political process generally and the special distortions of crime politics in particular. Media hype and misleading polling produce a fear of crime that politicians take to require harsher crime legislation on pain of political death. The results have little connection with the community's shared intuitions of justice.[19]

What the above arguments for the utility of desert suggest is that the criminal law's long-term crime control effectiveness will be hurt by these kinds of modern reforms that conflict with the community's intuitions of justice. While people may be happy to see their politicians 'get tough on crime', it will nonetheless happen over time that, as the deviations from people's intuitions of justice accumulate, people will come to see criminal conviction and punishment as lacking in moral authority and that loss of moral credibility will weaken the law's ability to harness the power of social influence and the other mechanisms by which the law's moral credibility promotes compliance.

E. Empirical desert as potentially immoral

While empirical desert has an easy answer to most of the criticisms noted above, it is vulnerable to one important criticism: it is potentially unjust. While a community may collectively believe that certain conduct is moral or certain punishment is just, those beliefs may be false. Witness the case of slave holders in the pre-Civil War South. Empirical desert can only tell us what people think is just. It cannot tell us what actually is just. In other words, it cannot tell us what an actor 'deontologically deserves'.

---

[18] See eg Robinson, Goodwin, and Reisig, Disutility (n 7 above) (reporting results of empirical studies testing people's intuitions of justice on cases under modern crime control programmes); Robinson and Darley (n 11) 139–47 (Study 13), 189–97 (Study 18).

[19] See Disutility (n 7 above) Part IV.

Of course, this potentially immoral objection applies to the use of *any* instrumentalist crime control principle for the distribution of liability and punishment, and among such principles, empirical desert may be the least objectionable, for it may best approximate a distribution according to true (deontological) moral blameworthiness. Nonetheless, empirical desert is conceptually and practically distinct from deontological desert, and as such can be fairly criticized for this.

On the other hand, while it may be tempting to prefer reliance upon 'deontological desert', this option is simply not available in the real world. How is one to decide that a shared community view in fact conflicts with true desert? And who is to be relied upon to make this decision? Which moral philosophers are to be preferred over others when they disagree, as they commonly do?

The fact is that every generation must live within a certain zone of ignorance. In a hundred years, the community may believe, as some now urge, that animals should have the same rights as humans. We will seem maddeningly ignorant and foolish to these people. Why could we not see something that is so obvious to them. (Is this not what we think of people of only a few decades ago when we think of the treatment of women? For many of us, it is within our own lifetime, yet we may wonder: What were we thinking?)

The difficulty, of course, is that we cannot know what today will be obvious to others in the future. In our present time and circumstances, we can only act in responsible good faith to try to do what we think is right in judging what is and is not sufficiently condemnable to deserve criminal conviction. We cannot defer to every person who has a conflicting moral view. In the next century, human rights for dogs may seem right and obvious, or it may seem as silly then as it seems to (most of) us today. We need not and ought not defer to everyone who claims to have some special moral insight.

It is consistent with our democratic ideals that those who disagree with the rest of the community should have to persuade us of the rightness of their view of what is condemnable. In other words, deontological reasoning ought to be encouraged and cherished by those who seek to shape community views, but, at least in the criminal law context, the system is better served by generally tracking the community views as they exist, not as some minority would want them to exist. However, as the next section discusses, there are sometimes good reasons for deviating from desert, and one of those may be to let social reformers see if they can successfully make their case to the community.

III. Justifying Deviations from Desert to Change Societal Norms

With this introduction to empirical desert, the remainder of the chapter addresses some of the issues, including complications, that can arise when one adopts empirical desert as one's distributive principle. Specifically, one can imagine a number of situations in which one might want to deviate from empirical desert. There are difficulties with justifying deviations from desert for coercive crime control purposes because such deviations undermine the crime control goal sought to be achieved,[20] but there are other interests, such as legality or control of police and prosecutors, that might justify some deviation from desert.[21] Doing justice and controlling crime are important interests to a society, but they are not the only interests. As I have discussed elsewhere, some of the present deviations are more justifiable than others.[22]

In this chapter I address a different sort of justification for deviating from desert: using law to help change existing societal norms. If law always tracks shared community views, then it becomes difficult, if not impossible, for social reformers to use criminal law to change existing moral norms.[23] Drunk driving and domestic violence, for example, are instances in which community views have changed over the past several decades, in part because criminal law got out in front of community views rather than strictly following them.

However, the point I want to make here is that the social reformers' decision on whether to urge deviating from community views is not always an easy one. The deviation can have serious costs to a planned reform programme, even as it can have benefits. Let me use as a case study the situation of rape law reformers. Assume you are a reformer who believes that men do not take sufficiently seriously the importance of ensuring clear and free consent before having intercourse. You might view current law, and community views, as problematic because they seem to accept in some ways the attitude of today's typical young man, who you think is insufficiently sensitive to the importance of clear and free consent. You might easily conclude that the criminal law's traditionally demanding culpability

---

[20] See generally Robinson, *Distributive Principles* (n 7 above) ch 8.

[21] See ibid, ch 12.

[22] See Paul H. Robinson, Michael T. Cahill, *Law Without Justice: Why Criminal Law Doesn't Give People What They Deserve, Parts I and II* (Oxford: OUP, 2005).

[23] Throughout, when using the term 'norm,' I mean 'moral norm'—a shared understanding of what is properly held to be wrongful, not a common pattern of conduct.

requirements allow young men's damaging insensitivities regarding consent to continue unabated.

With this view, you would be likely oppose not only use of the higher culpability levels of purpose and knowledge, but might also be tempted to oppose use of the lower culpability levels of recklessness and negligence. The problem is that, at least in jurisdictions like those that take the Model Penal Code approach, the definitions of recklessness and negligence incorporate existing community standards by judging the young man's risk-taking or inattentiveness by standards of 'reasonableness'. That standard has the effect of relying upon the existing norms that the reformer thinks are so troubling.

It is not hard to see why the concerned rape reformer might be attracted to a rule of strict liability as to consent. She could very well argue that giving a defence to young men who have intercourse without consent, albeit mistakenly, only perpetuates the unacceptable existing norm. If the law is to get serious about social reform, intercourse without consent ought to be punished in all cases, the reformer might argue. Once young men understand this, she can argue, they will have a strong incentive to become careful about consent.

IV. The Importance of Criminal Law's Moral Credibility to Social Reformers

Unfortunately, I don't think things are so simple for the reformers. The primary problem is this: it is social reformers, perhaps more than others, who very much need the criminal law to speak to the community with strong moral authority. If the criminal law is to have sufficient moral authority to prompt people to rethink their views on what to expect of young men, it must have earned that moral credibility with those it seeks to influence. Every deviation from desert perceived by the community incrementally undermines the law's moral credibility.

It is not that a criminal law must be perfect in tracking community views or lose all credibility. Some deviations from desert will be quickly and easily excused by the community because they are seen as unavoidable. The criminal law can do only so much in trying to accurately re-create the facts of a past event, especially in reference to culpable states of mind that may be difficult to be sure of even at the time. Also, as mentioned earlier, there are other important societal interests, such as fairness, that may call for deviating from desert. Doing justice, while it is an extremely important interest to most people, is not the only interest. What a sophisticated criminal law can do is take every opportunity to build its moral credibility—building up its store of 'credibility chips'—with an eye toward prudently spending those chips on those special occasions that it judges to be worth the expenditure in order to shift an existing societal norm. And if the effort is successful at shifting the norm, then the conflict with community views will fade away as community views change.

What guidance can one give the savvy social reformer about how to perform this balancing act of when to follow community views and when to deviate from existing views in order to lead them? First, it would seem appropriate to always try to avoid blatant and serious conflicts with the community's shared intuitions of justice, that is, to avoid ever producing cases that will be perceived as instances of the criminal law intentionally doing what will be seen as serious injustice. That may mean, for example, that strict liability as to consent is a bad idea for the ultimate success of rape reform. Such a rule would invite serious liability for a mistake that could not have been avoided *even by the most thoughtful and careful person*. It also risks creating defendant martyrs, which will muddy the offender-victim distinction in such cases, hurting rather than helping the shift in community norms.

Second, it seems likely that the system ought to, in all other instances, try to track community views of justice in order to build up its reserve of 'moral credibility chips'. That is, it ought to avoid frittering them away with deviations from desert that have little payoff, such as doing what current law frequently does today in deviating from desert to advance general deterrence even when the prerequisites for effective deterrence are not likely to exist.[24] The central point here is that no deviation from desert should be tolerated unless the benefits from it are clear. Hopefully, the recent empirical work has at least discredited what was the common wisdom of the past 50 years—that deviations from desert are cost-free.[25]

Finally, when reformers do decide to spend some of their credibility chips, they should do so carefully and thoughtfully. This means 'picking your fights'. Understand that one has limited and dearly earned chips to spend. Don't spend them now if one will regret not having them for a more important purpose later. In the context of rape reform, for example, this might mean adopting a culpability requirement as to lack of consent (that is, avoiding strict liability), but perhaps setting it lower than criminal law might

---

[24] See eg Paul H. Robinson and John M. Darley, 'Does Criminal Law Deter? A Behavioural Science Investigation' (2004) 24 *Oxford Journal of Legal Studies* 173; Paul H. Robinson and John M. Darley, 'The Role of Deterrence in the Formulation of Criminal Law Rules: At Its Worst When Doing Its Best' (2003) 91 *Georgetown Law Journal* 949; Distributive Principles (n 7) chs 3–4.

[25] See eg Disutility (n 7).

normally set it. A negligence requirement would avoid the perceived injustices likely to result from a strict liability standard, and would place at centre stage the issue of what society should reasonably expect of its young men with regard to assuring full and free consent. Thus, every case litigated in public would become not an opportunity for hand wringing about the injustice being done to young men who make honest mistakes, as strict liability would risk, but rather an opportunity to promote the public discussion about what should be considered 'reasonable' in this context.

This does not mean that a few cases will produce a dramatic shift in societal norms. Norms are glacial—enormously powerful but slow-moving. However, when norms are successfully shifted, conduct does change, and not just the conduct that is likely to be caught and prosecuted as a criminal offence. The power of social norms is one that will seep into the conduct of two people in an intimate setting, the facts of which neither would ever seriously think to make public, let alone to involve the criminal law. Yet, a changed internalized norm will change even that private conduct, which presumably is what the social reformer is seeking.

V. Limits on and Techniques for Changing Norms

An important caveat remains to be made: not every judgement about wrongdoing is open to easy modification by social reformers, at least not through techniques that would be permitted by liberal democracies. (A good deal of modification can be done through coercive indoctrination techniques that require serious intrusion into and control over a person's life.[26]) Our best guess of the intuitions of justice that, as a practical matter, cannot easily be modified are those on which there is an existing near unanimity as to their central aspects, part of the 'core' of agreement. This core includes aspects of physical aggression and theft.[27] Out from this core, however, change is possible, probably including judgements about coercion to intercourse.

Appreciating the difference between intuitions that can be changed and those that cannot is important for reformers. First, it can avoid a waste of resources in an effort toward an unreachable goal. (Those who seek to persuade people that they ought not to want to punish, for example, are on

---

[26] See eg Paul H. Robinson, *The Case of Richard R. Tenneson, Criminal Law Case Studies* 4th edn (St Paul, Minnesota: West, 2009) 158–9.

[27] See Robinson and Kurzban, Concordance (n 13); Robinson, Kurzban, and Jones, Origins (n 15).

a fool's mission.[28] Reformers who want real change, rather than just an excuse for fiery rhetoric, must focus on what is possible.)

Second, savvy reformers can use the unchangeable core for their own purposes, if they acknowledge it rather than fight it. For example, an effective technique aims toward building up (or tearing down) the strength of the analogy between the unchangeable core and the norm out from the core that the reformers seek to modify. One can see this lesson at work in recent advertising campaigns, such as that of the music industry seeking to reduce the amount of unlawful downloading of music. A recent television campaign shows a person sneaking money from the pocket of a pleasant and hard-working musician. The message: unlicensed downloading of music is just like stealing. The campaign seeks to build the strength of the analogy between the core wrong of physical taking without consent and the unlicensed down-loading of music.

For rape reformers, the approach may suggest focusing public discussion and education on the impropriety of coercive pressure for sex – building the analogy between psychological coercion and physical coercion—and on the harmful effects of intercourse without consent—building the analogy to assault.

VI. Conclusion

For our larger criminalization project, the argument here is, first, that serious moral condemnation ought to be a prerequisite for criminalization; second, that for instrumentalist (and perhaps deontological) reasons the moral con-demnation relied upon ought to be that reflected in community views, not moral philosophy; but that, finally, there can be legitimate reasons for deviating from community views. Indeed, the most important point here may be that the persons who ought to be most interested in criminal law normally tracking community views are those who want to use the moral credibility thereby earned to bring about important changes in societal norms.

[28] See Implications (n 7) 11–18.

10

Preparation Offences, Security Interests, Political Freedom

Peter Ramsay[1]

The relationship between security and liberty has been high on the political agenda in recent years, especially in the context of counter-terrorism. As Victor Tadros points out, the focus of this debate has been the criminal process rather than the substantive criminal law.[2] Yet the substantive criminal law has been expanded in a way that both protects security interests and narrows the scope of individual liberty.

A striking example of this contrast in public attention concerns the powers to intervene early against terrorist planning. There has been extensive debate in recent years on government attempts to lengthen the period that the police may hold terrorism suspects before charging them. The official case under New Labour for increasing the period from 14 days to 28 days and even longer, was based on security: that the longer detention period allows the police to make early intervention into terrorist operations. The suspect is incapacitated while evidence of conspiracy and other offences is gathered. The obvious intrusion into the suspect's liberty has been hotly debated and the Coalition government gave up 28 days and reverted to 14. However another statutory reform that increases the capacity of the police to intervene early in terrorist operations has passed with barely any discussion at all beyond the expert literature. Section 5 of the Terrorism Act 2006 makes it an offence to commit any act preparatory to an act of terrorism intending to commit an act of terrorism or to assist another to commit such an act (the maximum penalty is life imprisonment). The offence allows the police to

---

[1] I am particularly grateful to Alan Norrie and Lucia Zedner for their helpful comments on and criticisms of earlier drafts. The usual disclaimer applies.
[2] V. Tadros, 'Crime and Security' (2008) 71(6) *Modern Law Review* 940.

arrest and prosecute anyone for making intentional preparations well short of actually trying to carry out a terrorist attack.[3]

The lack of public debate about this offence suggests that it has considerable intuitive appeal. In this chapter I want to investigate the character of the security interests that the offence serves to protect and the political assumptions that are necessary to justifying punishment for this offence. Since these assumptions have attracted so little political interest, they would seem to constitute our contemporary common sense. At the same time, we shall see that they also have disturbing implications for the scope of legitimate state power and the relationship of the citizen to the state.

The first three parts of the chapter develop an account of the different security interests that may be protected by the offences of attempt and preparation. Part I offers an analysis of the interests of the law's subjects in objective and subjective security and the interrelation of these two. Part II considers how the criminal law in general can be thought of as protecting each of these different security interests. Part III analyzes and compares the English law of criminal attempt and the offence of preparation of terrorism, in terms of their possible contribution to the protection of these different security interests.[4] In this part I will be drawing out some implications of the objectivist theory of attempts by refocusing that theory on to the interests protected by different offence definitions and away from the accountability of the actor for violating them.[5]

The chapter then seeks to catalogue the illiberal assumptions entailed in seeking to protect security interests by holding an actor criminally

---

[3] There has not been an extensive discussion even in the expert literature, but see D. McKeever 'The Human Rights Act and Anti-Terrorism in the UK: One Great Leap Forward by Parliament, but are the Courts Able to Slow the Steady Retreat that has Followed?' (2010) *Public Law* 110–39; P. Mendelle and A. N. Bajwa, 'Human Rights and Terrorism' (2008) 172 *Justice of the Peace* 486, 3. That there has been so little discussion of this offence is all the more interesting given that the idea of enacting the offence appears to have arisen as a potential solution to the very controversial detention without trial of foreign terrorist suspects under the Anti-Terrorism, Crime and Security Act 2001. That power was eventually to be ruled a violation of art 14 ECHR (see *A and others v Secretary of State for the Home Department* [2004] UKHL 56). The government-appointed independent reviewer of terrorism legislation suggested that the problem of detaining terrorist suspects without trial might be solved by the introduction of a preparation offence, see Lord Carlile, *Anti-Terrorism Crime and Security Act 2001 Part IV Section 28 Review 2003* (London: Home Office, 2004) para [101]. In the event, it was the terrorism Control Order that the government substituted for the detention power, but the preparation offence was nevertheless enacted a little later.

[4] For the sake of simplicity I am going to focus entirely on the conduct element of these offences. Both attempts and preparation of terrorism in English law require intention to be proved. The discussion may have implications for discussion of offences of reckless endangerment but they are for another time.

[5] For an extensive exposition of the objectivist theory see R. A. Duff, *Criminal Attempts* (Oxford: OUP, 1996).

accountable for a preparation offence. To do this, the earlier analysis of the preparation offence is evaluated in Part IV in the terms of Andrew von Hirsch's doctrine of the fair imputation of remote harms. This analysis supplies decisive reasons against the enactment and enforcement of the offence.

In conclusion, Part V of the chapter will consider the wider context of the analysis. First, I will suggest that counter-terrorism offences are not a special case but only the most prominent recent example of the use of the substantive criminal law to protect security interests. Second, I will briefly consider the way that key elements of liberal criminal law theory do offer a rationale of security laws like the preparation offence and the underlying tension within liberalism that is implied by this. Finally I will suggest that political theories of democracy may offer some firmer ground for a critical account of such laws.

I. Security

Lucia Zedner describes security as a 'a slippery and contested term'.[6] That is because the word can mean many different things including a state of being, a means to the end of that state of being, and more generally a guarantee.[7] For our purposes, however, it is the state of being with which we are concerned because that state of being can be regarded as something in which subjects have an interest, an interest that can be protected by criminal law. As a state of being in which we may have an interest, security is comprised of two analytically distinct qualities that are entirely entwined in lived experience. On the one hand, security can be considered as an objective quality of social relations and, on the other, as a quality of the subjective experience of those relations.[8]

As an objective quality, security is a question of the actual threat of harm to what we value. The lower the likelihood of that harm, the more objectively secure we are and vice versa. In so far as we are threatened by other subjects, this objective security can also be thought of as 'intersubjective' security.[9] But there is clearly also a sense in which security is experienced subjectively as a

---

[6] L. Zedner, *Security* (London: Routledge, 2009) 10.

[7] L. Zedner, 'The Concept of Security: An Agenda for Comparative Analysis' (2003) 23 *Legal Studies* 153.

[8] Zedner (n 6 above) 14–19; I. Loader and N. Walker, *Civilizing Security* (Cambridge: CUP, 2007) 155–61.

[9] Loader and Walker, ibid 155.

feeling. The lower we *believe* the likelihood of harm to what we value, the more secure we feel. An added complexity of this subjective security is that it is an interest that concerns not only our current perceptions of risk, but also our perceptions of future events and the risks they bear.[10] Fear of some definite risk is one kind of insecurity, anxiety about less definite prospects is another.

There is no necessity that the objective and subjective aspects of security will be in proportion. In the context of the risk of crime, the group most at risk of victimization by violent crime, young men, is the group that on average feels itself most secure from it and vice versa.[11] Partly this discrepancy will be a consequence of the fact that the subjective estimation of security involves more than just likelihood of victimization. The degree of harm that the subject believes to be risked in any possible encounter will affect the way they read the 'objective' circumstances. But as the scare quotes indicate, the objective circumstances are themselves a consequence of the subject's estimate of the risks, since to some extent the degree of risk of victimization will be related to the risk-avoidance measures taken by the subject. The more insecure a subject feels the more effort they are likely to make to lower their 'objective' exposure. To some extent, at least, the most objectively insecure group is so insecure because they subjectively fear victimization the least.

The distinction between objective and subjective security is, therefore, an analytical one. In lived experience, it will be hard if not impossible to know the extent to which the objective and subjective aspects are independent of each other. As Ian Loader and Neil Walker put it, 'the socially inflected experience of feeling or not feeling secure is itself internal to and partially constitutive of what we mean by (in)security'.[12] There is nevertheless an analytical distinction here, and it is possible to understand criminal law in general and inchoate offences in particular in its terms.

II. Criminal Law and Security

In criminal law theory setbacks to security interests have been described as second-order harms.[13] First-order harms are setbacks to interests in life,

---

[10] Ibid 157.
[11] C. Hoyle and L. Zedner, 'Victims, Victimization and Criminal Justice' in M. Maguire, R. Morgan, and R. Reiner (eds), *Oxford Handbook of Criminology* (Oxford: OUP, 2007) 465–6.
[12] Loader and Walker (n 8 above) 157.
[13] H. Gross, *A Theory of Criminal Justice* (Oxford: OUP, 1979) 125.

bodily integrity, sexual autonomy, property, and so on. Security interests concern the prospect of such first-order harms. Hyman Gross observes that 'merely presenting a threat of harm violates that security interest'.[14] But the analysis of security interests above suggests that this second-order harm can be analyzed into two distinct types—setbacks to interests in objective security and in subjective security.

Criminal law protects an interest in *objective* security to the extent that it prevents the doing of harms to the protected interests of other people. We are more secure from premature death from non-natural causes to the extent that the law of homicide deters homicidal conduct; more secure from physical invasions in proportion to the deterrent effect of the law of violence and sexual offences; from the deprivation of or damaging to our property by the effect of property offences and so on. While the precise deterrent effect of the criminal law's threats is a matter of controversy,[15] there are good grounds for believing that their existence has at least some general deterrent effect.[16] In addition to the law's negative deterrent effect on offending behaviour, German theorists have argued that punishment can be justified on the grounds that enforcement of the criminal law has a positive general preventive effect in so far as it reinforces and stabilizes the norms it upholds in the minds of those subject to it, making them less likely to offend.[17] Whether or not this is normatively adequate as a justification of punishment,[18] criminal law will nevertheless protect objective security in so far as it does in fact have the positive general preventive effect.

Since objective security is nothing more than the degree to which our various interests are effectively protected, we can say that the criminal law, in censuring and threatening with hard treatment those who would commit harms to our various interests, protects our interests in objective security to the extent that the threat of conviction and punishment lowers the likelihood of those harms occurring.

Criminal law can contribute to *subjective* security in two different ways. Firstly to the extent of our belief in its effectiveness in lowering the objective risk of first-order harm, any law that prohibits the causing of those harms will make us feel more secure than we would if it did not exist. The mere existence

---

[14] Ibid.

[15] See A. von Hirsch, A. Bottoms, E. Burney, and P.-O. Wikstrom, *Criminal Deterrence and Sentence Severity: An Analysis of Recent Research* (Oxford: Hart, 1999) 47–8.

[16] A. von Hirsch, *Doing Justice: The Choice of Punishments* (New York: Hill & Wang, 1976) Ch 5.

[17] See M. Dubber, 'Theories of Crime and Punishment in German Criminal Law' (2005) 53 *American Journal of Comparative Law* 679, 699–703.

[18] For a critical account in German, see T. Hornle and A. von Hirsch, 'Positive Generalpravention und Tadel' (1995) *Golddammer's Archiv für Strafrecht* 261–82.b.

of the law of murder makes us believe that our interest in not being deliberately killed is more secure. The reason is that, with the law of murder in place, we can go about out lives *secure in the knowledge* that the state does condemn the deliberate taking of our lives (without a special justification or excuse), and that it can punish anyone who kills us in this way. The consequence is that 'in a given social situation, we know what behaviour to expect from others because we know that if they behave differently they will be punished'.[19] The communication of the criminal law's norms in the form of penal threats serves a general reassurance function in so far as subjects know that violations of their protected interests will be taken seriously by the state.

Of course the mere existence of the law may not provide much in the way of subjective security if a number of other conditions are not also fulfilled, including: widespread public knowledge of the law's existence and the consequences of violating it; energetic and rigorous enforcement with adequately high clear up rates; belief that the courts and the criminal process generally do justice and that the penalties for violation of the law are adequate; all in all a high degree of public political confidence in the law's effectiveness.

The second way in which the criminal law can seek to protect subjective security is by criminalizing conduct which causes people the second-order harm of feeling insecure. The causing of fear to others and the running of a risk of causing fear or anxiety to others have been criminalized in a number of offences. An example is the Public Order Act 1986, s 5. Its conduct element includes: using threatening, abusive, or insulting words or behaviour, or disorderly behaviour, within the hearing or sight of a person likely to be caused harassment, alarm, or distress thereby.[20] In so far as this offence contributes to the maintenance of public order, it may also serve to protect objective security interests by permitting intervention before other invasions of protected interests occur. But that is not its substantive rationale and the protection of such interests is not necessary to its enforcement. For liability to be incurred, it is enough that people were caused to be afraid or even that the conduct would more probably than not have caused others to be afraid.[21]

---

[19] R. Dahrendorf, *Law and Order* (London: Steven & Sons, 1985) 25.

[20] It has been ruled that for the purposes of POA 1986 s 5 there is no requirement that feelings of harassment alarm or distress amount to fear but plainly fear is included in those feelings, see *Chambers and Edwards v DPP* [1995] Crim LR 896.

[21] Arguably common assault before the leading case of *Ireland; Burstow* [1998] AC 161 was more closely tied to the protection of objective security interests, since the threat was thought then to be one of *immediate* unlawful force rather than merely *imminent*. The difference is that by making a threat of immediate unlawful force the defendant creates an objectively dangerous situation in a way that he does not necessarily do on the looser definition in *Ireland*, see the discussion of attempts below.

It is this expansion into the realm not only of actual causation of fear but probable causation of insecurity that is particularly relevant to the discussion of preparation offences.

III. Inchoate Offences and Security

Many acts that, in themselves, involve no first-order harm, but that are done with the intention of committing an offence that would involve first-order harm, fall within the scope of inchoate offences. The reason is that 'the conduct itself may usefully be regarded as a second-order harm: in itself it is the sort of conduct that normally presents a threat of harm'.[22] But, as we have seen, that threat can be to either or both of two analytically distinct security interests. Here we will consider whether the preparation offence can be thought of as protecting either or both of these two security interests. We can set this out most clearly if we compare the preparatory offence with the ordinary English offence of criminal attempt because the offence of attempt precisely requires the prosecution to prove that the defendant did an act that was *more than merely* preparatory to the first-order offence.[23]

More than merely preparatory has been interpreted by the courts to mean that the defendant has tried to commit the offence or 'embarked on the crime proper'.[24] The case law appears to interpret the threshold at which mere preparation becomes more than mere preparation (and therefore an attempt) as the point at which there is some confrontation between the defendant and the object of his offence.[25] Though this approach has resulted in some controversial decisions, it has the effect of requiring the prosecution to prove that the defendant violated objective security interests. The reason is that the requirement that there be some confrontation between the would-be criminal actor and the object of her offence is, in effect, a requirement that the actor make her criminal intentions manifest to public view in the form of an 'attack' on a legally protected interest.[26] By attacking legally protected interests, the actor commits a dangerous *act*, an act that is *objectively* dangerous in the sense that it creates an increased risk of harm to the public that is now *independent of the defendant's subjective intentions.*

---

[22] Gross (n 13 above).
[23] Criminal Attempts Act 1981 s1.
[24] *R v Gullefer* [1990] 3 All ER 882.
[25] C. M. V. Clarkson, 'Attempt: The Conduct Element' (2009) *Oxford Journal of Legal Studies* Vol 29, No 1 25–41, 26–8.
[26] Duff (n 5 above).

When the actor *attacks* another's protected interests, she has ceased to have complete control over the outcome of her culpable actions.[27] In complete attempts, in which the actor has done the last act, the occurrence of the complete offence is entirely out of her control. In both complete and incomplete attempts the actor cannot control how both intended victims or bystanders will respond. Even if she were now to change her mind she may not be able to control the outcome.[28] We know this because, on the occurrence of such an act, it would be normal and reasonably foreseeable that another person present will form a belief in the necessity of force to prevent a crime, and the use of at least some force against the defendant would normally be reasonable and lawful in these circumstances.[29] As R. A. Duff puts it of the person who does a more than merely preparatory act with the ulterior intent: 'by committing himself to crime, he makes himself liable to defensive violence'.[30]

The more than merely preparatory act makes the world more dangerous in a way that people may feel forced to respond to immediately. And this is true even if nobody is actually forced to respond. The actor has willed an act that has made the world a more dangerous place in a way that he can no longer control. The threat to security is constituted by his act, and not by his intentions alone. It is for this deliberate violation of the objective security interests of intended victims, and possibly of others, that the defendant may be punished.[31] The prosecution of criminal attempts may also contribute to subjective security, to the extent that the existence and enforcement of these offences reassures members of the public, making them feel that the risk of attacks on their protected interests is reduced thereby. But that is a by-product of their existence. It is not part of their substantive rationale because conviction for a criminal attempt can only be on the basis of objectively

---

[27] For Lawrence Alexander and Kimberley Ferzan the law can continue to influence the actor's reasoning 'until the point at which the actor engages in some conduct that (he believes) has unleashed a risk over which he no longer has complete control' (L. Alexander and K. Ferzan, *Crime and Culpability*, (Cambridge: CUP, 2009) 199).

[28] Duff (n 5 above) 389–91.

[29] Criminal Law Act 1967 s 3(1).

[30] Indeed it is this requirement to cause manifest danger to protected interests that makes even objectivists uneasy about the decision in *Geddes* [1996] Crim LR 894 CA. The defendant was discovered hiding in a school toilet equipped with materials needed to kidnap a child. This was held not to be an act more than merely preparatory to kidnapping. But by lying in wait in a place where he manifestly had no good reason to be, others coming across him would have been unnerved. In that sense Geddes seems to have lost control of the outcome, although it is not clear that force would have been justified to prevent a crime.

[31] See also Clarkson (n 25 above) 36–7.

dangerous acts and not of acts that have simply contributed to a perception of danger.[32]

Merely preparatory acts do not entail the same kind of dangerous act. Mere preparations are acts that may be necessary precursors of the commission of an attempt but do not constitute an attack in the sense required for a criminal attempt.[33] Duff explains that with such actions the criminal intentions of the would-be offender have 'so far only a shadowy existence in the public world'.[34] This 'shadowy existence' means that the actual preparatory acts (buying and preparing necessary materials and equipment, practising necessary procedures, gathering information, reconnoitering sites, and so on) are not *in themselves* dangerous acts. The actor retains control over the outcome of his culpable actions which do not amount to an attack in the sense that the more than merely preparatory act does. The merely preparatory act does not make the world dangerous such that people may feel forced to respond to it immediately. Of course, it is possible to imagine situations in which others discovering criminal preparations might be caused to be suspicious and to alert the authorities, but it would be exceptional rather than normal for another person to come across such preparatory acts and form a belief in the necessity of immediate force to prevent a crime.

Preparatory acts are not, therefore, dangerous *in themselves,* because they do not *in themselves* make eventual harms more likely. If the would-be terrorist's intentions should change, any danger associated with the preparatory act disappears.[35] Merely preparatory acts only make eventual first-order harms more likely in so far as the preparer's criminal intentions persist. Unlike more than merely preparatory acts, merely preparatory acts are only remotely connected to any eventual harm to objective security interests. The connection is remote in the sense that it involves certain contingencies that intervene between the act and the harm risked.[36] There are different types of contingencies in remote harm causation, and von Hirsch refers to the type

---

[32] This might be the basis of a wider objectivist theory of inchoate crime. Intentional encouragement of others to commit crimes is a dangerous act since even if the encourager should subsequently change his mind he may not be able to control the results of his earlier intervention. Seen as a species of encouragement, conspiracy too is an objectively dangerous act. Agreeing with others to commit a crime is to encourage others to commit crimes in a way that may be beyond one's subsequent control (see Duff (n 5 above) 391–2).

[33] For examples from the case law that come alarmingly close to the line see *R v Campbell* (1991) 93 Cr App R 350, *R v Geddes,* and n 30 above.

[34] Duff (n 5 above) 387.

[35] Unless for example it involves another wrong of objective endangerment such as (unsafe) possession of explosives.

[36] A. von Hirsch, 'Extending the Harm Principle: "Remote" Harms and Fair Imputation' in A. P. Simester and A. T. H. Smith, *Harm and Culpability* (Oxford: Clarendon Press, 1996) 263.

involved here as remoteness due to 'intervening choices'.[37] The preparatory acts are connected to the eventual harm of objective insecurity, of an attack, but only through the subsequent intervening choices of the actor. Critically these are choices *that have not yet been made.* Merely preparatory acts might represent a setback to objective security interests, but it is *impossible to be certain.* The would-be terrorist has not yet committed a dangerous act; rather he has demonstrated that he has a will to commit dangerous acts. It is not the act but the actor that is dangerous.[38] The actor is dangerous by virtue of his willingness to act on his criminal intentions.

The merely preparatory acts of the dangerous actor, acts that remotely threaten objective security interests, are also only remotely connected to harms to subjective security interests. But the character of the remoteness is different. The intrinsically innocuous preparatory acts of the dangerous person (who intends by these preparatory acts to further his criminal intentions) make the world more subjectively insecure in so far as the dangerous person causes others to feel less secure. It is not necessary that this insecurity take the form of outright fear of the particular dangerous actor. It will probably be the case that terrorist preparations will normally only be directly known to the preparer, any confederates, and possibly members of specialist police agencies. It might be that none of these people will be made afraid by their knowledge. In this sense it might appear that most terrorist preparations would cause little fear. But subjective insecurities caused by terrorist preparations arguably run wider than the fears of those who actually know about some particular preparations.

In so far as the population is aware that some people are preparing to commit criminal actions their interest in subjective security may be set back. They may feel less secure.[39] Of course, many or most members of the public may be more robust than that, but it is enough that some section of the population is caused the anxiety of knowing that future terrorist atrocities are being prepared for us to be able to say that anybody who is preparing such offences is making some contribution to this perception of an increased risk

---

[37] Ibid 264.

[38] Of course a particular individual with terrorist intentions may not in fact be feared because notwithstanding his terrorist intentions he is not dangerous as he is wholly incompetent.

[39] Concerning the absence of precise public knowledge about the threat of terrorism Matthias Borgers and Elies van Sliedregt comment that 'the lack of transparency does not affect the perception of a threat. On the contrary, it seems to contribute to the elusive nature of the risk, which strengthens rather than reduces the feeling of the threat', M. Borgers and E. van Sliedregt, 'The Meaning of the Precautionary Principle for the Assessment of Criminal Measures in the Fight Against Terrorism' (2009) *Erasmus Law Review* Vol 2 No 2, 171–95, 187.

of a first-order harm.[40] Those preparations are therefore contributing to the second-order harm done to subjective security interests. The existence and prosecution of these preparatory offences serves to protect subjective security interests in two ways: firstly, in so far as they either deter or incapacitate dangerous individuals in advance of any attack on first-order interests; and, secondly, in so far as the public is aware that such preparations can result in official intervention and incapacitation long before the would-be offender is 'about' to commit the attack on the first-order interest.[41]

The type of remote harm to subjective security involved in the preparation offence is called 'accumulative' or 'conjunctive' by von Hirsch.[42] Any particular instance of the prohibited conduct may not be directly identifiable as the cause of the particular harm, but it runs the risk of making a contribution to that harm:

the proscribed act is a token of the type of conduct that cumulatively does the harm: the actor cannot draw a moral distinction between his behaviour and that of the others who contribute to the injury.[43]

By virtue of this accumulative remote contribution, a wrongful risk of causing subjective insecurity is always an incident of terrorism preparations.[44]

We can summarize the formal protection given to security interests by criminalizing attempts, on the one hand, and preparations, on the other, in the following way. Criminalizing the intentional more than merely preparatory act will normally serve to protect objective *and* subjective security interests, although it is the violation of objective security interests that is the gravamen of the offence. The reverse is true of criminalizing the merely preparatory act. It is the contribution to harming subjective security that is the gravamen of the preparatory offence. It may on some occasions

---

[40] It may of course be the case that there are other and more significant causes of such anxiety—such as the publicity given to any particular level of threat by the authorities. Even if this is the case, that does not alter the contribution made by terrorist preparations, and from the point of view of the Standard Harm Analysis does not necessarily amount to an argument against criminalization (see text at n 46 and n 66 below). Rather it might suggest that the authorities should react more cautiously and less publicly with their threat assessments.

[41] Section 24(1) PACE 1984.

[42] Von Hirsch (n 36) 265. Accumulative is replaced by conjunctive in the account given in A. P. Simester and A. von Hirsch, *Crimes, Harms and Wrongs: On the Principles of Criminalisation* (Oxford: Hart, 2011).

[43] Ibid.

[44] In this respect the preparation offence can be compared with anti-pollution laws. There is no requirement to prove that any individual incident of pollution increased the risk of harm to anyone. But the offender is not able morally to differentiate his own behaviour from that which would if repeated on other occasions increase the risk of harm (see ibid). Of course, the penalty with respect to s5 is much more severe but the remote relation to the harm caused is not more remote.

contribute to the protection of objective security, although no tribunal could ever be certain beyond reasonable doubt that any particular conviction had made a contribution to that interest.[45]

Having set out the contrasting forms in which criminal attempt and preparation offences protect different interests in objective and subjective security, we now turn to the assumptions that must be made in order to justify punishing actors for acts which have a relationship to harm that is dependent either on the actor making subsequent intervening choices or on the act being of a type the cumulative effect of which is to do harm.

IV. Preparation as Public Wrong

If, as a society, we believe that it is right for the state to prosecute and punish people for preparing acts of terrorism, what assumptions are entailed? Are these assumptions any different from those that are necessary to support the criminalization of the more than merely preparatory act? One way to identify these assumptions is to consider each construction of the offence in terms of the doctrine of fair imputation of liability for remote harms proposed by von Hirsch.

As we have seen above both constructions of the offence, as a threat to objective or to subjective security, can be characterized as offences of remote harm causation. In so far as they are causally related to the eventual harm that relationship depends on some contingent factors. Von Hirsch argues that in thinking about criminalizing conduct on the grounds of remote harm causation, it is necessary to go beyond what he calls the 'Standard Harm Analysis'.[46] In other words, to decide whether criminalization might be justified, it is not enough simply to undertake the standard analysis and assess the gravity and probability of the harm risked, weigh that against the value of the risk-creating conduct and the degree of intrusion on the actor's autonomy, and consider the effect of any side constraints such as fundamental rights that might be violated. Given that the remoteness of the harm risked from the criminalized action is due to the occurrence of further contingencies, von Hirsch argues that in taking the decision to criminalize the preparatory act

---

[45] The objectivist theory of attempts protects objective security interests because the dangerousness of the act is its essence. The subjectivist theory of attempts protects subjective security interests because it is rational to expect people to fear or be caused anxiety by the dangerous actor.

[46] Von Hirsch (n 36 above).

we should also ask the question: '*how and why, can the supposed eventual harm fairly be imputed to the actor?*'[47]

It may be that von Hirsch's doctrine is ultimately only a reformulation of the Standard Harm Analysis. It might be possible to argue that balancing the harm risked against the social value of the action and the actor's autonomy and taking into consideration fundamental rights amounts to asking whether or not it is fair to impute the harm to the actor. But even if that is right, von Hirsch points out that a disadvantage of the formulation of the Standard Harm Analysis is that it 'yields insufficient arguments of principle'.[48] The focus of the Standard Harm Analysis tends to concern empirical assessments of risk, costs, and benefits. Given that some harm to others is a consequence of almost all human activity,[49] and that in legal and political practice few of the constraining fundamental rights are absolutely protected,[50] the political neutrality of the Standard Harm Analysis has been exposed as specious. The problem is which harm-causing or harm-risking activity should be criminalized and which not, and the harm principle as such has proved vulnerable to the charge that it provides no useful standard for deciding that issue.[51] By contrast, von Hirsch's reformulation directly raises questions of principle, and in particular, as he notes, principles of 'political obligation: for example, about the extent of duties of citizenship'.[52] His claim is quickly confirmed if we now ask the question he poses of the preparation of terrorism offence: how and why can the eventual harm to security interests fairly be imputed to the preparer of terrorist acts?

In thinking about the possible answers to this question we will assume for the moment that the harms of terrorism *and* the second-order harms of objective and subjective insecurity are of the highest gravity, and that this combined with the probability that the preparatory act will be causally related to an eventual harm is high enough to outweigh any social value in the preparatory conduct. There is good reason to doubt some of these assumptions,[53] but that is not our concern here. Our present purpose is to bring to light certain other assumptions about the subject of criminal law and the

---

[47] Ibid 268–9 (emphasis original).

[48] Ibid 274.

[49] J. Feinberg, *Harm to Others* (New York: OUP, 1984) 12.

[50] In the ECHR, for example, only Arts 3 and 4 ECHR are absolute, the others might be thought of as being thrown into the balancing procedure of the Standard Harm Analysis by the various qualifications to them that are allowed.

[51] B. Harcourt, 'The Collapse of the Harm Principle' (1999) 90(1) *Journal of Criminal Law and Criminology* 109.

[52] Von Hirsch (n 36 above) 276.

[53] The predominant reaction of the public to recent terrorist atrocities has been calm and resilient, see F. Furedi, *Invitation to Terror* (London: Continuum, 2007) 178–80.

limits of the private sphere that must be made if these harms are to be 'fairly imputed' to the would-be terrorist.

Of course, the simplest answer to the question of why the supposed eventual harm to security interests can fairly be imputed to the preparer of terrorist acts is to point to the actor's intention to achieve the eventual first-order harm.[54] But von Hirsch's point is that, in itself, this answer is not enough.[55] We must ask why intention is sufficient when the harm is remote and evaluate any reasons that we might come up with. Let's consider the setback to objective security interests first.

We have seen that as a setback to objective security interests, the remote connection between merely preparatory acts and the eventual harm is one mediated by the actor's intervening choices. As Duff has argued, this type of remoteness entails the existence of a '*locus poenitentiae*', or place to repent, between the preparatory act and the eventual attack.[56] We cannot know for sure that the actor's criminal intentions will persist because the existence of the criminal law's threats of punishment may lead the actor to decide prudentially not to risk it, or even to remind the actor of the moral significance of the error she is making.[57] To regard the attribution of liability as being fair when this space to repent remains requires one of three assumptions to be made. Either:

(a) It does not matter normatively that some convicted preparers of terrorism would not have gone on to attempt or commit the first-order harm intended at the point of preparation. The state is therefore not required to prove any connection to a first-order harm stronger than the possible. This amounts to a substantive abandonment of the burden of proof and the presumption of innocence without a formal abandonment of it. This problem does not attach to liability for the more than merely preparatory act which entails proof of an attack on a first-order interest.

---

[54] This is the standpoint of longstanding subjectivist theories of attempt (see text at n 87 below).

[55] Von Hirsch argues that culpability and imputation are separate questions, see n 36 above, 269.

[56] Duff (n 5 above) 37.

[57] The same cannot be said for more than merely preparatory acts that involve attacks that are dangerous and unnerving to the public. Here the offender's criminal intentions have come out of the shadows and into the public realm. In the normal course of events the actor's acts might cause victims or observers to believe that force will be necessary if a crime is to be prevented. Even if some narrow space to repent remains before the actor commits the last act and a complete attempt, the actor's repentance may not be sufficient to avoid some harm to legally protected interests resulting from his criminal intentions.

(b) A more nuanced version of the previous assumption might be that there ought to be an irrebuttable presumption of law that a person who prepares an act of terrorism will go on to attempt it. Such a doctrine would *entirely discount* Duff's place to repent which remains between the merely preparatory act and the first-order harm. As Duff argues, to ignore it when it is present is to fail to treat the law's subjects as rational moral agents who are able to adjust their conduct to the law and to assume that the law cannot successfully communicate its norms to its subjects.[58] By contrast, the person who commits the more than merely preparatory act has either given up the space to repent entirely (where she has done the last act and committed a complete attempt) or herself voluntarily discounted its significance by losing control of the outcome of her criminal intentions in the process of an incomplete but still dangerous attack on a first-order interest.

(c) The harm risked is of such a magnitude that the criterion of retributive justice, of restricting punishment only to those whom we are sure deserve it for culpable violations of legally protected interests, must be overridden in the interests of society as a whole.

The third assumption is an argument from necessity and emergency rather than fairness, so we will delay discussing it until later on.[59] For now we should note that the first two assumptions undermine the entire project of liberalism. The presumption of innocence is the bedrock of the individual subject's, and more especially citizen's, independence of the state. On the other hand, to presume that the harm will be carried out by the preparer is even more radical. If the law assumes that those who make preparations will inevitably go on to carry out an attack on first-order interests, and *that that eventual attack is the harm that justifies punishment*, then punishment occurs before the actual offence has been committed. As Saul Smilansky puts it:

To punish before an offence has been committed ... is to treat the person merely as an object. Respect for her moral personality and choice requires of us to give her a moral chance to remain innocent, and not treat her as guilty before she actually is. Whether she currently values this possibility or not is irrelevant.[60]

There is nothing unfair about incapacitating objects in advance of the harm that they might do. Objects do not need general laws that leave them free to adjust their own conduct in order to comply. Indeed they cannot enjoy any

---

[58] Duff (n 5 above) 387–9.
[59] See text at n 82 and n 83 below.
[60] S. Smilansky, 'The Time to Punish' (1994) 54 *Analysis* 50.

freedom at all, including any role in democratic deliberation. Here it is not only liberalism, but a wider humanism that is undermined, and, arguably, the entire project of 'law'.

The rather severe implications of treating the preparation offence as a setback to objective security interests seem, at first sight, to be mitigated if we consider the offence as a setback to subjective security. From this perspective the remote connection to harm is mediated by the accumulative effect of many such instances. Terrorist preparations might cause no direct fear to the public, rather the knowledge that they are occurring creates a climate of insecurity in which fear and anxiety about the possibility of atrocities is experienced, especially (the argument runs) if the police lack powers to intervene. It is this harm that is remotely risked by each and every act of preparation. Neither of the first two assumptions that are required to justify the punishment for the preparation offence on the grounds of objective security need to be made in order fairly to impute to the actor the harm done to subjective security, since it is the preparatory act itself that makes the *accumulative* contribution to the harm and this act must be proved before the actor will be liable. The law gives the actor warning of, and opportunity to adjust her own conduct to, the law's requirements in a way that seems to respect her moral agency. On the face of it, we might answer von Hirsch's question by saying that the harm may fairly be imputed to someone who knowingly defies the law's demand that its subjects not contribute to the harm of subjective insecurity that is caused by terrorist preparations.

Von Hirsch notes that fair imputation of accumulative harms to remote actors must be based on obligations of cooperation that all have to avoid the particular harm. But he suggests that 'such cooperative obligations . . . cannot be unlimited. . . . At some point, the actor—when confronted with the question "What if everyone did what you are doing?"—should be entitled to say that that is not and should not be made her business'.[61] At first sight this too might not seem to be too much of a moral problem when thinking about obligations to refrain from causing fear of terrorism. But when such a cooperative obligation to prevent insecurity is enforced by defining default as a public wrong another assumption with highly illiberal implications must be made.

Criminalizing the preparatory act as a remote harm to subjective security interests formally preserves a place to repent, but this place is reduced to a mental space entirely. As soon as an intention is acted upon it becomes the subject matter of potential prosecution and punishment by the state because

---

[61] Von Hirsch (n 36 above) 268.

that act is a public wrong. In this regime, the private sphere exists only in our heads. What is private sphere for the purposes of protecting objective security by means of attempts liability becomes, through preparatory liability, a public wrong against subjective security interests. In all our actions—however 'private'—we are required to consider others' feelings of (in)security before we act, and to act only in a way that will not contribute to others feeling insecure. This is what it means to have a public duty not to *be dangerous* as opposed to a duty not to perform dangerous acts.

In effect, the assumption being made is that the cooperative obligations in relation to causing insecurity extend as far as an obligation *not to be a dangerous person,* with the accompanying assumption that since it is dangerousness as such that comprises the public wrong, no sphere of action is therefore immune from the possible wrongful manifestations of dangerousness. The illiberal aspect of this construction is apparent. By treating preparation as a threat to subjective security, the non-public space for repentance is narrowed to a purely subjective mental space and *everything else* is the legitimate sphere of official intervention.

Considered as criminalizing a setback to *objective* security interests, the preparation of terrorism offence eliminates any need for a realm of private moral reflection; considered as criminalizing a setback to *subjective* security it narrows the realm of private morality to thoughts alone. But even this latter construction takes a sizeable step on the slippery slope to eliminating the private sphere entirely. We allow the authorities to invade the private sphere with surveillance, search, and arrest powers on grounds of reasonable suspicion that a public wrong may be committed. Making a public wrong of merely preparatory acts at the very least legitimates official surveillance of the *purely mental space,* since this is where we find out if a preparatory act is about to be committed. And, having gone this far, why not follow the logic further? If the actor's dangerousness is the wrong targeted and *any act* (providing it is done with the criminal intent) is enough to prove the dangerousness of the actor, then what price the act requirement? Why wait for an act if the actor's dangerousness is the public wrong and there are other ways of reliably assessing dangerousness (such as unrecanted opinions or association with known terrorists)?[62] To answer that the preparatory act is not *merely evidence* of the wrongful dangerousness, but rather constitutes it, merely begs the question.

---

[62] The Control Order arguably takes the next step down the slope; see P. Ramsay, 'Theory of Vulnerable Autonomy and the Legitimacy of the Civil Preventative Order' in B. McSherry, A. Norrie, and S. Bronitt (eds), *Regulating Deviance: Redirection of Criminalisation and the Futures of Criminal Law* (Oxford: Hart, 2009) 109.

At the bottom of this slope are thought crimes. 'By deciding to commit a crime and acting on the decision', the dangerous individual is one who, in George Fletcher's words, 'pits himself against the community' because his act 'represents a rejection of the legal order'.[63] As Fletcher goes on to observe, to make this a criminal offence amounts to a penal demand for attitudinal conformity, on the basis that 'those who display an attitude of hostility toward the norms of the system show themselves to be dangerous and therefore should be subject to imprisonment to protect the interests of others'.[64]

The public 'wrong' punished by the preparation offence is this hostile attitude towards the existing order. What this analysis suggests is that criminalizing mere preparation implies an obligation on citizens not to manifest disloyalty to the legal system.[65] To the extent to which this is internalized by citizens as a norm, a high degree of public and private conformity will be achieved.

V. Security, Liberalism, and Political Freedom

The conclusion drawn above about the nature of the preparation offence might seem abstract and extreme. It might be thought that the practical effect on liberty of criminalizing terrorist preparations is of almost no account, since we have no good reason to value those activities, while the benefit in terms of protecting our security may be considerable. Since the law prohibiting those preparations is addressed generally to all subjects, there is nothing unjust about enforcing it.[66] But this argument expresses exactly the weakness of the Standard Harm Analysis pointed out by von Hirsch. As a practical balance of interests, criminalization of terrorist preparations seems unarguable. But this apparently sensible law entails making a very radical assumption about either the agency of the law's subjects or the appropriate limits of the sphere of public surveillance. As we noted, these assumptions seem to have intuitive appeal since they have passed into law without much interest being shown. And these assumptions raise two questions of fundamental principle: is law a system of power that respects and is restrained by some

---

[63] G. Fletcher, *Basic Concepts of Criminal Law* (Oxford: OUP, 1998) 179.

[64] Ibid 180.

[65] One which extends to denizens and visitors as well.

[66] For the equivalent argument in relation to possession of automatic weapons see Tadros (n 2 above) 945.

degree of independence and capacity for self-determination in its subjects? is there any sphere of human life that ought not to be subject to the surveillance and intervention of the authorities?

We have at least three good reasons to think hard about the theoretical assumptions that the preparation offence requires us to make if we are to regard our punishments as justified, and about the issues of principle that this raises. Firstly, these questions of principle are urgent ones since assumptions like the ones discussed here are not restricted to the preparation of terrorism offence but increasingly prevalent in the criminal law. Secondly, this prevalence is able to exploit tensions in the liberal tradition of theorizing about criminal law, a tradition that appears to lack the resources to resist the expansion of the scope of the criminal law, and of its attendant powers of surveillance and intervention. Thirdly, these issues seem to emphasize the limitations of the moral philosophy that has predominated in criminal law theory and to draw attention to the need for theorists to turn to questions of political theory. Let's look at each of these questions in turn.

A. Security and the 'end of criminal law'

If we regard terrorism since 9/11 as an extraordinary threat then perhaps the official pressure on private activity that section 5 represents might be regarded as less objectionable.[67] Moreover, there seems to be at least an argument for believing that the political motivation of the terrorist is grounds for regarding their preparatory acts as increasing the objective risk of attacks on first-order interests in a way that ordinary criminality might not. Shlomit Wallerstein formulates the argument in respect of a category overlapping with terrorism that she calls 'anti-democratic' activity:

there is a hidden threat in such acts, a threat found in the anti-democratic beliefs of the agents. If the anti-democratic agent is caught . . . at the specific preparatory stages

---

[67] The extraordinariness of the threat of contemporary terrorism appears to arise from the perceived possibility of surrender to terrorism. For example, Borgers and van Sliedregt note that many terrorist attacks may cause little harm but insist that the threat of terrorism remains the threat of catastrophe: one must not lose sight of the fact that terrorist attacks are committed precisely with the intention 'to intimidate a population, or to compel a government or an international organization to do or to abstain from doing any act [citing Art 2 of the International Convention for the Suppression of the Financing of Terrorism (1999)]. When terrorist actions succeed in realising this intention, the consequences for the stability of democratic societies are far-reaching' (see n 39 above, 188). They do not consider the possibility that democratic societies might refuse to be intimidated by any amount of terrorist violence (for a critique of this assumption, see Furedi (n 53 above)).

and is not punished, then it is highly probable that, motivated by belief in the righteousness of his or her ideas, he or she would attempt other harmful acts.[68]

Notice that this line of argument confirms that it is motive and attitude that are at the core of the public wrong but, in so far as this motivational increase in risk can be imputed to the terrorist, then the presumption that preparation leads to attack might be justified.

There are two problems with this argument, however. Firstly it is not clear that contemporary terrorists are in fact more highly motivated than ordinary criminals. Secondly, the formal protection of security interests by substantive criminal offences is not restricted to counter-terrorism offences, and it would be a mistake to think of terrorism as a special case. There are simply too many laws on the books that either impose liability for risking remote harms in a way that reaches into the private sphere of action or that demands outward attitudinal conformity.

The great bulk of them lie in the regulatory law which restricts the way people may carry on their private activities often imposing severe burdens of risk avoidance. These may indeed amount to a special case in so far as they are restricted to particular activities that nobody has to engage in and are only really private in the sense that they are formally the activities of private businesses or corporations. But others are much more generally posed. Possession laws have been increasingly widespread over the course of the twentieth century. The case for possession offences depends on remote harm arguments,[69] and while these may have some purchase on offences of possession with ulterior intent or conceivably on possession of firearms or explosives, they are highly attenuated as a justification of drugs possession offences.[70]

More recently there has been a marked tendency to expand offences protecting security interests, and this both predates the war on terror and covers a scope much wider than terrorism. Measures that criminalize both the direct creating of subjective insecurity and remote accumulative contributions to insecurity have been taken against anti-social behaviour, sex offenders, football hooligans, organized crime, and so on.[71] Duties to inform the

---

[68] S. Wallerstein, 'Criminalizing Remote Harm and the Case of Anti-Democratic Activity' (2007) 28 *Cardozo Law Review* 2697, 2721. Wallerstein appears to be describing rather than proposing this argument.

[69] Von Hirsch (n 36 above).

[70] See D. Husak and P. De Marneffe, *The Legalization of Drugs: For and Against* (Cambridge: CUP, 2005) 36–7.

[71] See P. Ramsay, *The Insecurity State* (Oxford University Press, forthcoming).

authorities of suspected wrongdoing have expanded.[72] Attempts have been made to enforce official surveillance of everyday social relations through administrative schemes backed by criminal sanctions for non-compliance.[73] Criminal offences that serve to protect security interests have been introduced in public order law, the law of assaults, money-laundering, and fraud.[74] In sentencing law the power to detain 'dangerous' offenders indefinitely has been introduced.[75]

The existence of this wider process of 'securitizing' the criminal justice system is well recognized, and has been analyzed in terms of a number of different theoretical frameworks. Richard Ericson developed a formulation for these types of power from the work of Michel Foucault and called it 'counter law'.[76] Counter law comprises both 'law against law', in which '[n]ew laws are enacted . . . to erode or eliminate traditional principles, standards of criminal law that get in the way of preempting imagined sources of harm',[77] and the expansion of the 'disciplinary apparatus based on surveillance' that as we saw in relation to preparation is unleashed by the law's greater scope.[78] Another conception of these precautionary laws has been dubbed 'the new science of police'.[79] This concept draws on the eighteenth-century concept of police, which comprised all the state's powers to promote the public welfare.[80] A third security framework is Gunther Jakobs' 'enemy criminal law', in which legal powers protect a 'right to security' precisely by abandoning the requirement to prove harms committed or to extend procedural guarantees that is the norm in 'citizen criminal law'.[81]

---

[72] See eg Proceeds of Crime Act 2002 s 330 duty to report transactions which a reasonable person would suspect involve money laundering. Such duties also apply to terrorism: see eg the offences of failing to provide information about terrorism, Terrorism Act 2000 s 38B(2). For a discussion, see C. Walker, 'Conscripting the Public in Terrorism Policing: Towards Safer Communities or a Police State?' [2010] 6 *Criminal Law Review* 441.

[73] Although at the time of writing the most prominent of these—the identity card scheme and the Independent Vetting Authority for people working or volunteering with children—have been abandoned and subjected to review respectively.

[74] For a more detailed account see Ramsay (n 71 above).

[75] For an analysis of this power in terms of the protection of security, see P. Ramsay, 'A Political Theory of Imprisonment for Public Protection' in M. Tonry (ed), *Retributivism Has a Past: Does it Have a Future?* (Oxford University Press, forthcoming).

[76] R. Ericson, *Crime in an Insecure World* (Cambridge: Polity, 2007).

[77] Ibid 24.

[78] Ibid 27.

[79] M. Dubber and M. Valverde (eds), *The New Police Science: The Police Power in Domestic and International Governance* (Stanford: Stanford University Press, 2006).

[80] M. Dubber, *The Police Power: Patriarchy and the Foundations of American Government* (New York: Columbia University Press, 2005).

[81] See C. Gomez-Jara Diez, 'Enemy Combatants vs. Enemy Criminal Law' [2008] 11(4) *New Criminal Law Review* 529. See also D. Ohana, 'Trust, Distrust and Reassurance:

Each of these frameworks can offer an account of the preparation of terrorism offence. But each of these frameworks emphasizes the contrast between an ordinary law on the one side and a 'counter' or 'police' or 'enemy' law on the other. The preparation offence might be located as a counter law, a police power, or enemy criminal law, but as we have seen with the relation of the preparation offence to criminal attempt, the slide between law and counter law, law and police, or citizen law and enemy law is less clearly marked out in practice than these theoretical formulations imply. The preparation of terrorism offence, as we saw, retains key aspects of liberal legal doctrine—a conduct element, a fault element, and a burden of proof on the prosecution. One theoretical framework that may to some extent avoid this failure to take account of the overarching unity of these apparent opposites is the idea of the 'normalization of emergency' powers.[82]

We noted above that one possible assumption which might justify liability for terrorist preparations on grounds of the remote risk to objective security interests they pose is that of necessity. In the 'state of emergency' the possibility of very grave harms to the social order justifies the suspension of normal legal guarantees in the common interest. Such a process might account for the s 5 offence, except that the offence is contained in a normal statute, with no sunset clause or requirement for regular renewal. Moreover, as we have just seen, the protection of subjective security is not limited to counter-terrorism law. Rather, what we seem to be witnessing is the normalization of emergency power over a wide scope of social life. The theoretical material associated with this idea emphasizes the expanding scope and the tendency to permanence of explicit emergency powers over the course of the twentieth century.[83] Here we seem to see the obverse tendency, in which standards that are applicable to emergency insinuate themselves into 'ordinary' laws, and in circumstances that do not seem, on the face of it, to amount to an emergency.

Both processes of normalization draw our attention to one of the most interesting aspects of these laws: although they are a threat to liberal assumptions, these laws are a threat that comes from within. They are not

---

Diversion and Preventive Orders Through the Prism of Feindstrafrecht' (2010) 73(5) *Modern Law Review* 721.

[82] K. Scheppele, 'Law in a Time of Emergency: States of Exception and the Temptations of 9/11' (2004) 6 *Journal of Constitutional Law* 1001; G. Agamben, *State of Exception* (Chicago: University of Chicago Press, 2005); M. Neocleous, *Critique of Security* (Edinburgh: Edinburgh University Press, 2008) ch 2.

[83] Ibid.

particularly associated with any explicit authoritarian attack on the idea of liberal democracy.[84] There is much force to Ericson's argument that:

> While some requirements of *actus reus, mens rea* and due process remain formally in place in some areas of criminal law, they function primarily as a veil of administrative decency over preemptive counter-laws that . . . fundamentally undermine law as the democratic institution of liberal social imaginaries. We are witnessing the end of criminal law.[85]

But, even if he does not exaggerate the threat to what historically has been identified as criminal law, Ericson underestimates the extent to which the 'end of criminal law' is itself a legal process. The presence of *actus reus, mens rea* and due process is more than a mere 'veil of administrative decency': it gives expression to the ideological flexibility of legal categories and indicates that the path to the end of criminal law may be smoothed by the mobilization of liberal theoretical resources.

It is in this context of tensions internal to liberalism that we should reconsider the dominant approach of criminal law theory to the issue of the fairness and the limits of liability to state punishment.

B. Threats from within

Two of the main principles deployed by criminal law theorists when thinking about when it is appropriate to punish are the harm principle and the culpability principle. What is apparent is that neither seems to provide much restraint on the scope of preparatory liability. We have seen how the harm principle in its conventional form can countenance the preparation offence at least in respect of terrorism and possibly more widely. To provide any theoretical resistance to preparatory offences, the harm principle at the very least needs supplementing with something like von Hirsch's doctrine of fair imputation of remote harms. In searching for a principle that might make it unfair to impute liability for terrorist preparations, we found that once subjective security interests are taken into account, it is the protection of the private space for moral and political reflection that is menaced by the preparation offence. In other words, as suggested above, it is not really the harm principle that provides any limit on criminalization here, but rather a much more robust enforcement of the 'side constraint' provided by the protection of privacy.

---

[84] J. Simon, *Governing Through Crime* (New York: OUP, 2007) 15.
[85] Ericson (n 76 above) 213.

Equally the principle that individuals should only be punished to the extent that they are culpable for the wrongful choices they have made provides no point of resistance to protection of subjective security by means of the preparation offence. This is particularly striking since the proposition that liability should only arise for culpable acts is a cornerstone of liberal criminal law theory. This 'subjectivism' is the basis of a theory of excuses that seeks to ensure that the punishment is not arbitrarily imposed on those who are not at fault for any harms that they may have had a hand in causing. In one of the best-known formulations of the underlying rationale for this subjectivist approach to the criminal law, H.L.A. Hart argued that it ensured to individual subjects 'the satisfactions of a choosing system'.[86] While this theory had the effect of limiting whom could be punished for wrongful and harmful conduct, it has no limiting effect on what conduct might be regarded as wrong. Indeed subjectivism's focus on culpable choices in itself tends to expand the scope of the criminal law. The choice to make preparations with the purpose of carrying out an act of terrorism is a wrongful choice and subjectivism in itself has no objection to criminalizing such a choice.[87] But as we have seen, the effect of this offence is to eliminate the sphere of action in which the satisfactions of a choosing system can be enjoyed. Any action that manifests a culpable choice will ground liability to coercion and punishment.

Only criteria drawn from the rival objectivist theory of criminal culpability seem to limit this effect of subjectivism. The objectivist account recognizes that individuals should only be punished where they are subjectively culpable but adds a further constraint that only choices to undertake certain types of harmful act—attacks or violations of first-order interests—should count as *criminally* culpable.[88] Unlike the subjectivist culpability principle, the source of this objectivist limit in liberal theory is more obscure. Indeed George Fletcher identifies objectivism as a form of criminal liability inherited from the law of pre-liberal societies, a form that Fletcher refers to as the 'manifest pattern of criminality'.[89]

---

[86] H. L. A. Hart, *Punishment and Responsibility* (Oxford: OUP, 1968) 49.

[87] Of course, subjectivism does not necessarily lend support to life imprisonment as a penalty for mere preparation, but both the 'objectivist' Duff and the 'subjectivist' Andrew Ashworth agree, subjectivism itself contains no principled reason to prefer a more than merely preparatory threshold to any other including the first act in a series. See Duff (n 5 above) 168.

[88] Ibid 193.

[89] In the 'manifest pattern of criminality', questions about the actor's intentions are only relevant if their actions are objectively incriminating. Fletcher notes that the effect of this is to protect the privacy of the actor's mental world and to minimize the scope of the law. But he regards this effect as an 'incidental benefit of the court's carrying forward criteria of criminality that originated in the private slaying of manifest thieves'. These ancient criteria nevertheless 'gave full expression to the

It seems that both the harm principle and the culpability principle require external supplements if they are to avoid collapsing into illiberal results. Interestingly, the supplementing constraints identified here are not among those that Douglas Husak includes in addition to harm and culpability in his recent efforts to produce a liberal theory of criminalization.[90] It seems that in order to protect both the law's respect for individual autonomy as such, and the scope for the practical exercise of that autonomy, principles have to be sought from outside the resources of liberal criminal law theory.

This may be a problem intrinsic to liberalism itself. Mark Neocleous has observed that liberalism's project of liberty has always been 'wrapped in' the project of security.[91] He argues that the security of property was always the condition for the enjoyment of liberty in liberal thinking. For that reason he suggests liberalism has found it difficult to resist the siren calls of security and the normalization of emergency has been one result. Certainly the conceptual resources of liberal criminal law doctrine seem, to some extent at least, to bear him out.

It is significant that the issue of principle that did seem to be invoked by our analysis of the preparation offence in terms of the imputation of liability for remote harm is that of the proper limit of the state's power to intrude on the private sphere. This raises questions of political theory rather than of the moral philosophy that has been the mainstay of criminal law theory for several decades.

C. Towards a political theory of criminal law

I have elsewhere argued that the broad outlines of the history of subjective fault requirements in the criminal law can be explained in terms of the dominant concept of citizenship.[92] We saw above that von Hirsch, in raising the idea of fair imputation of remote harms, hoped to be able to apply principles of political obligation, of the appropriate scope of an individual

---

maxim that no one should be punished for thoughts alone'. It is interesting that it is the opposing subjective principle, which Fletcher identifies as emerging in the nineteenth century, that should be so closely identified with liberal thinking about criminal law. See G. Fletcher, *Rethinking Criminal Law* (Oxford: OUP, 2000) 88–90.

[90] See D. Husak, *Overcriminalization* (Oxford: OUP, 2008). For the application of Husak's theory to the preparation of terrorism offence, see P. Ramsay, 'Overcriminalization as Vulnerable Citizenship' (2010) 13(2) *New Criminal Law Review* 262.

[91] Neocleous (n 82 above) 22.

[92] P. Ramsay, 'The Responsible Subject as Citizen: Criminal Law Democracy and the Welfare State' (2006) 69(1) *Modern Law Review* 29.

citizen's duties to the state, to the problem of the limits of criminalization.[93] Where the moral philosophy of harm and culpability seem not to impose clear limits on the scope of the preparatory liability, political theory may provide a more secure contemporary foundation for the objectivist limit. In the different context of the appropriateness of force in mistaken self-defence, Alan Norrie has argued that the different duties appropriate to ordinary citizens, on the one hand, and state agents, on the other, can provide external criteria for resolving the problem of choosing between objective and subjective tests of liability.[94]

The unrestrained subjectivism of the preparation of terrorism offence poses the question of the appropriate relation of state and citizen. It is the capacity of the state to intrude into the private sphere of a citizen's activity and even of their thoughts that is expanded by the preparation offence. This increased capacity must be a concern for any theory of representative government. The less seriously the executive takes its citizens as autonomous moral agents, and the more that the executive is able to coerce the purely private activity and attitudes of individual citizens, the less meaningful is the claim of government to *represent* the citizenry (and the more the citizenry appears to be required to represent government). And, as we have seen, it is precisely the wrongful or 'dangerous' attitude of the violator of subjective security interests that is the target of the preparation offence.

---

[93] See von Hirsch (n 36 above).

[94] A. Norrie, 'The Problem of Mistaken Self-Defense: Citizenship, Chiasmus and Legal Form' (2010) 13(2) *New Criminal Law Review* 357.

Index